Art Wars

AMERICA IN THE NINETEENTH CENTURY

Series editors:
Brian DeLay, Steven Hahn, Amy Dru Stanley

America in the Nineteenth Century proposes a rigorous
rethinking of this most formative period in U.S. history.
Books in the series will be wide-ranging and eclectic, with
an interest in politics at all levels, culture and capitalism,
race and slavery, law, gender, and the environment, and
regional and transnational history. The series aims to
expand the scope of nineteenth-century historiography by
bringing classic questions into dialogue with innovative
perspectives, approaches, and methodologies.

ART WARS

The Politics of Taste in Nineteenth-Century New York

RACHEL N. KLEIN

PENN

UNIVERSITY OF PENNSYLVANIA PRESS

PHILADELPHIA

Published by
University of Pennsylvania Press
Philadelphia, Pennsylvania 19104-4112
www.upenn.edu/pennpress

Printed in the United States of America
on acid-free paper
1 3 5 7 9 10 8 6 4 2

Library of Congress Cataloging-in-Publication Data

Names: Klein, Rachel N., author.
Title: Art wars : the politics of taste in nineteenth-century New York / Rachel N.
   Klein.
Other titles: America in the nineteenth century.
Description: 1st edition. | Philadelphia : University of Pennsylvania Press, [2020] |
   Series: America in the nineteenth century | Includes bibliographical references
   and index.
Identifiers: LCCN 2019044998 | ISBN 9780812251944 (hardcover)
Subjects: LCSH: American Art-Union—History—19th century. | Metropolitan
   Museum of Art (New York, N.Y.)—History—19th century. | Art
   museums—Social aspects—New York (State)—New York—History—
   20th century. | Art and society—New York (State)—New York—History—
   20th century. | Aesthetics, Modern—Social aspects. | Aesthetics,
   Modern—19th century. | New York (N.Y.)—Civilization—19th century.
Classification: LCC N600 .K59 2020 | DDC 709.747/109034—dc23
LC record available at https://lccn.loc.gov/2019044998

For Robert Westman

CONTENTS

The Importance of Taste

Intellectual Roots

You will notice several pale-faced, white kidded
fashionables, with pretty accompaniments leaning languidly
on their arms; young clerks; school boys and girls; the
mechanic and his family; the cartman in his clean linen
frock; the portly merchant; the honest bronzed face of the
farmer; the poor seamstresses and sewing girls . . . *there* they
are all earnestly contemplating the works of art with which
the walls are covered. All social distinction is lost in
admiration of Art—all are happy.
> —*Oswego Commercial Times*, December 1, 1848

Fully two-thirds of the visitors are of foreign birth—
German, French, Spanish, Italian, and Russian their
physiognomy and their tongues proclaim them. I saw
several well-dressed attractive Japanese—men and
women—in American garb. Among the Americans chiefly
women are those who have no holiday but Sunday, and to
whom a sight of the art treasures will shed a halo of beauty
over the humdrum days of the week.
> —*Washington Post*, July 26, 1891

This book is about three protracted public battles that marked significant
transformations in the nineteenth-century American art world and in the
culture more broadly. The first battle began in 1849 and resulted in the
downfall of the American Art-Union, the most popular and influential art

institution in North America at midcentury. The second erupted in 1880 over the Metropolitan Museum's massive collection of Cypriot antiquities, which had been plundered from the island of Cyprus and sold to the trustees by the man who became the museum's first paid director, Luigi Palma di Cesnola. The third struggle escalated in the mid-1880s and forced the Metropolitan Museum to open its doors on Sunday—the only day when working people were able to attend. Each of these disputes allows us to glimpse cultural fissures that ran far deeper than the specific complaints that landed the directors of each institution in court.

Attacks on the Art-Union signaled tensions over the commercialization of culture and the scope of the tasteful public. Would the art world continue to be presided over by well-to-do, civic-spirited amateurs or would it become a part of the burgeoning world of commercially organized urban amusements? Was the taste for art an exclusive quality or was it freely available as a source of class and political cohesion? The battle over the Art-Union did not so much resolve these questions as bring them into the open. The enlistment of art for purposes of moral uplift outlived the Art-Union, but the utopian vision of aesthetic taste as a means to national unification could not survive the political upheavals of the mid-nineteenth century. Even within the realm of imagination, social and political tensions could no longer be contained within the walls of the art gallery.

The issue that galvanized critics of the Metropolitan Museum in the early 1880s was the allegation that workmen, under Cesnola's direction, had fraudulently altered sculptures not only by joining broken, unrelated pieces but also by camouflaging lines of attachment and creating wholly new parts. The episode sparked efforts to professionalize the museum and gained momentum amid the class resentments that divided the city and nation during the 1880s. Controversy surrounding the Cypriot antiquities also highlighted alternative visions of display and acquisition. Cesnola justified his collection by invoking historical and ethnographic narratives. He insisted that it revealed the prehistory of classical Greek art and civilization. Objects widely perceived as the ugly products of lesser people had a place in the museum because of their historical, ethnographic, and archaeological value. Cesnola's leading critics, concerned with the uplift of American character through the improvement of domestic taste and design, insisted that only objects of beauty—preferably the best exemplars—could serve the purpose of aesthetic education. They too were invested in the incorporation of foreign artworks, but they focused on form, color, workmanship, and decoration rather than raising inconvenient questions about the cultures from which the art came.

Following closely on the Cesnola controversy, the movement to open the Metropolitan on Sundays demonstrated the depth and breadth of popular engagement with the museum. It drew strength not only from New York reformers, liberal religious groups, and the popular press but also from working-class immigrants and labor activists. The first Sunday openings, which finally arrived in the spring of 1891, attracted tens of thousands of visitors and belied the trustees' effort to define the museum as a "private" institution.

The scope, persistence, and intensity of these conflicts—their extended, bitter engagement with a wide public—justifies use of the term "art *wars*" and points to their broader social and political meanings. The rise and fall of the Art-Union cannot be understood apart from deepening class tensions of the 1840s and escalating political struggles over slavery and abolitionism. In fact, the organization was, in part, a product and casualty of those conflicts. The Cesnola controversy also had a class dimension, but its particular intensity derived as well from late nineteenth-century racial anxieties associated with the global transfer of people and products. Cypriot antiquities raised a host of unnerving questions, not least by challenging notions of Greek—and hence European—racial distinction and cultural lineage. At a time when non-Protestant, working-class immigrants were transforming the culture and politics of the city, Cyprus—a polyglot entrepôt of the ancient world—assumed special significance.

The art wars of the 1850s and 1880s also illuminate the changing role of art exhibition in nineteenth-century American thought and society. The Art-Union embodied the particular vision of the merchants who predominated among New York City's antebellum elite. It came into being at a time when the public display of pictures still appeared as a potential counterweight to political disunity and class antagonism. The act of looking at pictures had widely acknowledged public implications. Yet by the time the Metropolitan opened at its permanent Central Park location fantasies of art-induced political unification no longer seemed plausible, particularly to the industrialists (and their retainers) who predominated on the museum's board of trustees. Other concerns and possibilities, related to domestic design and the incorporation of non-Western objects, roiled the museum in the 1880s. The aestheticizing turn, which made deep inroads into early twentieth-century art museums, marginalized unsettling questions about producers of artworks and linked the museum, albeit indirectly, to the new world of consumer culture. Far from challenging the educational mission of the art museum, leading proponents of decontextualized, aestheticized exhibitions framed the museum's educational purpose as the improvement of consumer taste and home decoration.

The epigraphs at the start of this introduction bespeak central themes of the book. Both of the quotations are taken from newspaper reports. The first celebrates the Free Gallery of New York's American Art-Union in 1848 near the height of its popularity. The second offers a description of the Metropolitan Museum on a Sunday in 1891, soon after the trustees finally capitulated to the open-Sunday movement. The commentaries affirm the persistence of popular interest in art exhibitions during the middle and later nineteenth century, and they testify to the reformist project that encouraged the establishment of art museums throughout Europe and the United States. By celebrating the diversity of people who flocked to the galleries, both writers proclaimed the educational value of art to working-class spectators. In the process, they evoked the connection between the galleries' objects and subjects. Spectators, in the act of looking, became parts of the display—evidence of art's uplifting potential. Throughout the nineteenth century, art promoters insisted that art held the power of moral improvement while offering a healthy diversion from dangerous pleasures. The full galleries seemed to confirm the claims and aspirations that linked New York's American Art-Union to its far more enduring successor.

And yet these passages also hint at significant changes. By 1891 the vision of a multiclass (if entirely white) audience had dissipated. Accounts of the Metropolitan Museum's earliest Sunday openings stressed the foreignness of working-class visitors—their social, racial, and cultural distance from more experienced museumgoers. The type of artwork deemed worthy of display had changed as well. Rather than focusing on American graphic art, the Metropolitan included casts of celebrated Greek and Roman sculptures as well as monumental stone antiquities excavated from the island of Cyprus. Ancient pottery, glass, and jewelry, antique European laces, and Chinese and Japanese ceramics were also on display. Painting played a significant role in the exhibitions, but most of the museum's graphic holdings were of European origin. The Art-Union reflected the founders' interest in using art to promote the political unification of citizens; by the time the Metropolitan opened on Sundays, many promoters as well as critics envisioned it primarily as a means to the self-cultivation of viewers and as an educator of domestic taste.

New York City is a particularly fitting place in which to explore these changes. As early as the 1820s it had eclipsed Philadelphia as the hub of the American art market and was becoming a magnet for aspiring artists. Art exhibitions of various sorts were already gaining popularity. New York was also the site of furious public controversies over art, audience, and exhibition, and those battles captured considerable national attention. Most important, the city gave rise to historically connected institutions that allow us to examine art-related cultural transformations in a focused way. The American Art-Union purchased paintings by living American artists, put them on exhibition in the centrally located "Free Gallery" and at the end of each year, distributed them by lottery to the subscribers. At its high point in 1849, subscribers, concentrated in the Northeast and Midwest, numbered close to 19,000. That year, when the population of New York City totaled about a half a million, managers claimed that 750,000 people visited the Free Gallery. Yet the Art-Union, which inspired imitators throughout the nation, provoked a group of angry critics who challenged its vision of public culture. The organization disbanded in 1852 after having been prosecuted as an illegal lottery.[1] Twenty years later, following several years of planning, the Metropolitan Museum opened at a temporary location, and in 1880 moved to its permanent building at Central Park. Like the earlier institution, New York's art museum was a project conceived by the city's elite, and its founders included several surviving members of the Art-Union's leadership. These continuities make those institutions particularly useful contexts for exploring changes in the cultural outlook of the men who conceived and managed them.[2]

But this book is not simply about the wealthy art enthusiasts who managed the Art-Union and sat on the Metropolitan's early board of trustees; it is equally concerned with audiences, broadly conceived. "Audience" here includes not only the people who visited the galleries of New York's various art institutions and who remain, to a great extent, shrouded behind veils of highly charged representations; it also encompasses people who wrote about sites of exhibition for a widespread readership. Both the Art-Union and the Metropolitan became the subjects of contentious, multifaceted, public conversations that have much to say about changing nineteenth-century notions of art and aesthetic taste.

Indeed, the history of New York's nineteenth-century art institutions was intertwined with the development of the press. The 1840s witnessed a proliferation of newspapers and periodicals that attended to the subject of culture in the process of serving and constructing their own readerships. The growth of the Art-Union was wholly dependent on the press, which also contributed mightily to the organization's demise. In 1851, according to the editor of New York's *Tribune*, the city's five cheap daily papers could claim a circulation of about 100,000.[3] These papers joined an array of more specialized city newspapers as well as a growing number of urban periodicals whose sales were national. The late nineteenth century saw a further explosion in the numbers and circulation of New York papers, led by the *New York World*, which in 1891 boasted an average daily circulation of 314,718. In addition, the 1870s and 1880s saw the marked expansion of periodicals that focused exclusively on art-related topics.[4] These publications, like their antebellum precursors, stoked controversy while making art, artists, and art-related institutions matters of popular concern.

To acknowledge the role of the press in nineteenth-century museum building is to revise one of the most compelling scholarly frameworks for thinking about art museums—namely, as ritualized spaces that help to legitimate power. Museums, from this perspective, invite visitors to enact hidden scripts embodied not only in the architecture of the buildings but also in the displays themselves. At the Metropolitan, according to one important line of argument, the script, embedded in donor memorials, period rooms, and lavish displays of decorative art, reifies the wealthy men and women who at one time lived among the objects on display.[5] And yet, to extend the metaphor, major exhibition spaces generally embody several, at times contradictory, scripts written by multiple authors. This study explores divergent narratives written into sites of exhibition not only by the men who controlled them but also by critics in the press. Occasionally, as in the case of the Metropolitan's earliest Sunday openings, it is also possible to glimpse visitors themselves reimagining the museum in unforeseen ways. One way of conceptualizing the art wars that exploded in the early 1850s and again thirty years later is that scripts written into highly charged exhibition spaces were impossible to control.

Studies of nineteenth-century American cultural transformation—particularly with respect to art institutions—generally focus on either the pre– or post–Civil War periods, with one particularly notable exception: The most influential account is still Lawrence Levine's *Highbrow/Lowbrow: The Emergence of Cultural Hierarchy in America*, first published in 1988. Levine built on work by the sociologist Paul DiMaggio and the historian Neil Harris, both of whom located the Art-Union among the popular, urban, and generally commercial institutions that proliferated in American cities before the Civil War. Levine argued that antebellum audiences made little distinction between education and entertainment, and he suggested that notable cultural institutions of that era did their best to draw in large numbers of people from a wide swath of the population. Only in the later nineteenth century did rigid distinctions between "high" and "low" culture appear in the realms of theater, music, and art. New institutions, organized on a noncommercial basis, restricted access, celebrated artistic uniqueness and originality, and imposed increasingly strict standards of aesthetic classification. By the century's end, cultural tastes, practices, and institutions increasingly mapped the growing class divide. According to Levine and DiMaggio, the educational mission that initially helped to animate late nineteenth-century art museums dissipated relatively quickly, replaced by a tendency to present artworks as ineffable, sacred exemplars of transcendent beauty—objects whose quality could be appreciated only by a select few.[6]

In effect, these scholars identified the later nineteenth and early twentieth centuries as decades in which leading American art museums came to embody the elitist tendencies that the sociologist Pierre Bourdieu analyzed in his studies of twentieth-century French museums and culture. Bourdieu described aesthetic taste as a form of "cultural capital" that may appear to be individual and personal but in fact represents the array of lessons learned from family, school, and other arenas shaped by privilege or lack thereof. The "sacralization" of art described by DiMaggio and Levine (or "religion of art" in Bourdieu's terms) effectively denied the hidden cultural capital that made aesthetic taste possible. Insofar as art museums presented objects as having transcendent spiritual meaning, they downplayed their role as educators of a broad public and positioned themselves as exclusive sites for the enactment of class distinction.[7]

Yet neither the Art-Union nor the Metropolitan fits this grand narrative. Founders of the earlier organization did their best to increase the number of subscribers and to draw people into the Art-Union's Gallery, but their motivation was class uplift and political unification rather than profit. They believed that graphic art had the ability to convey powerful moralizing national messages. As I show in the following chapters, promoters and officers of the organization insisted on its noncommercial structure and emphasized its distance from the various commercial entertainments of the day. Meanwhile historians have chipped away at the image of early twentieth-century museums as mausoleums of high art, willfully removed from popular and commercializing cultural tendencies. Late nineteenth-century and early twentieth-century museum builders were far from unified in their vision of the wider public. And while they drew clear distinctions between their own institutions and earlier commercial entertainment centers epitomized by P. T. Barnum's American Museum, the relationship between art museums and other engines of consumer culture (fairs and department stores) was varied and complex. Key figures on the Metropolitan's turn-of-the-century board of trustees and curatorial staff identified the museum's civic purpose as the uplift of national character through the improvement of American taste, architecture, and design. Rather than turning away from reformist projects, the Progressive Era Metropolitan became actively involved in an effort to educate consumers through the display of decorative art. In the 1910s the Metropolitan's workrooms were turning out replicas of furniture on display while members of the museum's curatorial staff also worked as store designers. By the following decade, the Metropolitan and other museums were borrowing display techniques from department stores.[8] The very period that Levine and DiMaggio identified as the culmination of high cultural distinction appears in more recent historiography as the period in which important American art museums adopted a new role as a standard bearer within consumer culture.

In fact, New York's major nineteenth-century art institutions were deeply engaged with a wide public and attracted far more popular controversy than scholars have generally recognized. They became lightning rods for conflict not only because Americans invested aesthetic taste with moral and civic consequences, but also because they were part and parcel of explosive processes associated with the rise of industrial capitalism. Elite New Yorkers spearheaded the creation of the Art-Union and the Metropolitan, but those institutions became enmeshed in popular struggles related to slavery, immigration, race, industrial production, and the rights of laboring people.

Intellectual Resources: The Language of Taste

New York's art-related culture wars had intellectual roots in eighteenth-century British commentaries that gave aesthetic taste both moral and public significance. Art was a fraught topic in Anglo-American discourse because republican and revolutionary thinkers linked it to the dangers of "luxury." Patronized by kings, aristocrats, and the Vatican, art (including architecture) carried connotations of corruption, degeneration, and the general loss of republican virtue.[9] But counterarguments gave the taste for art quite different implications. Sir Joshua Reynolds, as president of London's Royal Academy, presented a civic republican justification of art and artists that became common parlance for art promoters across the Atlantic. In his *Discourses* presented to students at the Royal Academy from 1769 to 1790, Reynolds used the language of civic humanism to argue for the link between fine art and public virtue. Above all, painting, as distinct from craft production, was for him an intellectual pursuit. Just as the artist abstracted from particularity to convey general truth, so the citizen rose above private interests and appetites to consider the public good:

> The art which we profess has beauty for its object; this it is our business to discover and to express; but the beauty of which we are in quest is general and intellectual; it is an idea that subsists only in the mind; the sight never beheld it, nor has the hand expressed it: it is an idea residing in the breast of the artist, which he is always laboring to impart, and which he dies at last without imparting; but which he is yet so far able to communicate, as to raise the thoughts, and extend the views of the spectator; and which, by a succession of art, may be so far diffused, that its effects may extend themselves imperceptibly into public benefits, and be among the means of bestowing on whole nations refinement of taste . . . and conducting the thoughts through successive stages of excellence, till that contemplation of universal rectitude and harmony which began by Taste, may, as it is exalted and refined, conclude in Virtue.[10]

For Reynolds, grand narrative painting that depicted historical and religious scenes constituted the highest form of art precisely because it was best able to convey abstract ideas conducive to public virtue. As John Barrell points out, Reynolds drew a direct analogy between the community of taste and the political community. His imagined "republic of taste" was an elite, exclusively male world, but one that extended beyond the ranks of aristocracy to include artists as well as wealthy men of trade. It did not include artisans or, for that matter, most of the "mixed multitude of people" who composed the audience for art. Refined ladies might attend exhibitions; they might also be versed in the elegant art of drawing, but the highest forms of production and appreciation were, in Reynolds's view, confined to prosperous, educated men.[11] Art could inspire the "contemplation of universal rectitude and harmony," but only among the select few who already held the qualifications of citizenship. The position of history painting atop the hierarchy of arts was consistent with Reynolds's vision of taste as a marker of public virtue in the traditional republican sense. It is not hard to see why this republican celebration of painting gained a following among American artists who were concerned about the status of art and artists in the United States.

Yet Reynolds himself assumed a place within a much wider discussion of aesthetic taste understood most broadly as a realm of refined pleasure associated with uplifted moral quality. Ian Pears observed that treatises on taste "poured from the presses" in England during the first half of the eighteenth century, motivated in part by concerns about the excesses of courtly culture but also by efforts to redefine political virtue beyond the perquisites of aristocratic birth. Taste offered access to social inclusion but it also provided new criteria for exclusion. It offered a critique of dissipated extravagance without demanding Spartan denial. Precisely what taste was and how standards might be determined remained the subject of extended debate, but it is important to recognize that eighteenth-century thinkers regarded aesthetic and moral standards as fixed. From their perspective, it was the human capacity for perception that varied among individuals and groups and over time. The seeds were present throughout humanity but only those with wide-ranging associations (available only to the most cosmopolitan and educated subjects) had the means of developing taste to its highest levels.[12]

Debates about taste extended throughout Europe, most notably into France and Germany, but it was the British and particularly the Scottish thinkers who had the most widespread impact within the post-Revolutionary United States. A lively transatlantic trade in books brought multiple British printings to America, and select works underwent republication in the United States. *Elements of Criticism* by Henry Home, Lord Kames, originally published in Edinburgh in 1762, underwent forty-six American printings in many editions between 1796 and 1860. Archibald Alison's *Essays on the Nature and Principles of Taste*, first published in Edinburgh in 1790, also gained great renown. As required reading not only at colleges but also at young women's academies, it underwent eleven American printings in several editions from 1812 to 1860.[13] These works, as well as the writings of David Hume, Francis Hutcheson, Alexander Gerard, and the Irish political philosopher Edmund Burke, set the terms of American engagement with art and artists into the 1840s.[14]

For purposes here it is significant that the Scottish thinkers reset the boundaries of the tasteful community beyond those created by Reynolds. They did so by linking aesthetic appreciation rather generally to morality, benevolence, commerce, and what they saw as the progress of civilization. Whatever their differences, the Scottish writers identified aesthetic appreciation as an emotional response—a form of pleasure—that signified moral sensitivity and facilitated uplifted social interaction. Lord Kames made the point quite clearly when he observed that "the venting [of] opulence upon the Fine Arts . . . instead of encouraging vice, will excite both public and private virtue." In other words, he allowed that fine art might inspire virtuous actions in the public realm, but he also identified taste with qualities that he considered private. The cultivation of taste, he believed, had the power to "invigorate the social affections" while moderating "those that are selfish." And to "the man who has acquired a taste so acute and accomplished, every action wrong or improper must be highly disgustful."[15]

The belief that aesthetic taste constituted a disinterested and therefore elevated form of pleasure derived in part from the conviction that it was distanced from mere bodily feeling. As Alison elaborated, the emotions of taste "afford an innocent and elegant amusement to private life, at the same time that they increase the Splendour of National Character; and in the progress of Nations, as well as of Individuals . . . they serve to exalt the human Mind, from corporeal to intellectual pursuits."[16] Alexander Gerard suggested that "a man of an improved taste puts very little value on sensual delights."[17] Writers linked taste to the senses of sight and sound (considered more elevated than those of taste [for food], smell, and touch) but they also went out of their way to insist that taste involved processes of thought. From their perspective, the senses could evoke taste only with the addition of imagination—the chain of thoughts or associations that gave meaning to sight and sound. It was this mental process that produced the intrinsically pleasurable "emotions of taste"—namely, the feelings of beauty and sublimity.

Writers described those feelings in various ways, but they generally linked the former to delicacy, calm, and cheerfulness, while they identified the latter with awe, grandeur, largeness of scale, solemnity, and even terror. Lord Kames observed that "all the various emotions of beauty have one

common character, that of sweetness and gaiety. The emotion of grandeur
has a different character: a large object that is agreeable, occupies the whole
attention, and swells the heart into a vivid emotion, which though
extremely pleasant, is rather serious than gay."[18] To this combination of
sensation and imagination, the additional feature of intellectual judgment
(or what Hume referred to as "practice") was necessary for those who
hoped to arrive at a true or discriminating taste. Edmund Burke made the
point by observing that "what is called Taste, in its most general accepta-
tion, is not a simple idea, but is partly made up of a perception of the
primary pleasures of sense, of the secondary pleasures of the imagination,
and of the conclusions of the reasoning faculty."[19]

Eighteenth-century theorists were in general agreement concerning the
objects of taste—namely, natural scenery and the fine arts. They identified
the latter with painting, poetry, and music, and they generally included
some combination of architecture, gardening, sculpture, and oratory. To
appreciate the lesser, necessary, or mechanic, arts (also referred to as the
"useful arts") might be an indication of polite or refined character, but they
linked moral elevation to higher forms of pleasure. Even David Hume, who
made the case that "innocent" luxuries were actually beneficial to the public
interest, placed the emotions of taste, associated with the fine arts, on a
higher plane than other forms of "refinement on the pleasures and conve-
niences of life." As he observed, "nothing is so improving to the temper as
the study of the beauties either of poetry, eloquence, music, or painting."
And when he wrote that such study "produce[s] an agreeable melancholy,
which, of all dispositions of the mind, is the best suited to love and friendship," he was referring to an elevated form of sociability that transcended
sensuality.[20]

The distinction between beauty and sublimity offered a way to preserve
the traditionally public or political connotations of taste even as the term
assumed more private meanings. At least Alexander Gerard made this move
by investing beauty and sublimity with gendered meanings. He associated
beauty with "tenderness and softness"—qualities that were distinct "from
the more elevated emotions of the soul." Sublimity, in his view, was "a still
higher and nobler pleasure." He linked it, among other things, to heroism,
patriotism, "greatness of power," and he invested it with military imagery.[21]

Notions of taste remained entwined with nationality. Insofar as imagination was based on associations, one's national circumstances came into
play. As Archibald Alison wrote, "national associations have a similar effect

in increasing the emotions of sublimity and beauty, as they very obviously increase the number of images presented to the mind." It followed that fine art would have a particularly strong impact on audiences who shared the national associations of the artist. Alison continued: "the fine lines which Virgil has dedicated in his *Georgics* to the praises of his native country, however beautiful to us, were yet undoubtedly read with a far superior emotion, by an ancient Roman."[22] And Hume, who believed that the most delicate taste could transcend the limitations of time and place, nonetheless observed that "we are more pleased, in the course of our reading, with pictures and characters that resemble objects which are found in our own age and country, than with those which describe a different set of customs."[23] That artists could evoke national feeling was also apparent to Adam Ferguson, who observed that "fine artists . . . are but few, compared to the numbers of a people; but there are none, whose apprehensions or thoughts communicate more effectually with the minds of their countrymen."[24]

If taste served as a way to conceptualize bonds of friendship, community, and national sentiment, it also provided a means of constructing differences of value among individuals and groups. Kames could hardly have been more straightforward when he wrote, "Those who depend for food on bodily labour, are totally void of taste; of such a taste at least as can be of use in the fine arts. This consideration bars the greater part of mankind."[25] And while the majority was excluded from the tasteful community by manual labor, others were denied entry based on extravagance. Kames was not alone in making the point that beauty and sublimity involved simplicity. That belief allowed him to "bring under trial the opulent who delight in expense," men whose "appetite for superiority and respect, inflamed by riches, is vented upon costly furniture, numerous attendants, a princely dwelling, sumptuous feasts, everything superb and gorgeous." Such extravagance, indicative of "self-love," was quite distinct from taste, which involved "simplicity, elegance, propriety, and things natural, sweet, or amiable." In short, "the exclusion of classes so many and numerous, reduces within a narrow compass those who are qualified to be judges in the fine arts."[26]

If Kames was invested in the establishment of clear boundaries between the possessors of taste and their moral inferiors, other writers saw taste as a matter of degree. Alison acknowledged that "even the peasant" might have imagination derived from associations to local scenes. However, he also suggested that "the greater the number of associations we connect with it [the object of taste], the stronger is the emotion of sublimity or beauty we receive from it."[27] In other words, he gave considerable advantage to cosmopolitan subjects. Similarly, Hume distinguished between men possessed of the most discriminating or "polite" taste and others who took pleasure in the various fine arts. (Hume used the term "liberal arts.") Only the former had the reason, knowledge, and discrimination to overcome the prejudices of time and place and to discern transcendent quality. He believed that such men, though "rare . . . are easily to be distinguished in society by the soundness of their understanding, and the superiority of their faculties above the rest of mankind."[28]

Women occupied a pivotal but ambiguous place in this imagined community of taste. They were nowhere to be found at the most rarefied levels of discrimination where reason and (in Reynolds's view) the ability to generalize, were defining attributes. It is telling that even Alison neglected to mention female subjects in his essay on taste. Yet we know that women played a prominent role in the polite society of eighteenth-century London and Edinburgh; they read poetry, attended exhibitions of painting, and studied drawing as well as music. Reynolds resolved the problem by distinguishing the tasteful minority from the audience at large, and to the extent that other theorists allowed for gradations of taste, they seemed to make room for women's engagement in what Joseph Addison famously called "the pleasures of the imagination."[29]

The fact that women were both the objects and subjects of taste complicated the question.[30] Hume could declare that "it is with books as with women, where a certain plainness of manner and of dress is more engaging, than the glare of paint and airs and apparel, which may dazzle the eye, but reaches not the affections."[31] He and others suggested that a woman who embodied the attributes of beauty—including simplicity and virtue—could have an uplifting impact on men.[32] Insofar as Scottish Enlightenment thinkers considered the progress of civilization, they made the treatment and elevation of women a critical benchmark. By this logic, refined women and fine art were almost precisely analogous. As objects of beauty, both had the capacity to elevate and inspire morally sensitive (tasteful) viewers; at the same time, respect for worthy women, like the appreciation of fine art, signaled virtue in men. For all its limitations and mixed messages, the discourse of taste would become a potent resource for educated women in nineteenth-century North America.

The community of taste eluded definition, particularly at the margins, but this very malleability helps to explain the power of the concept across the Atlantic. Political and cultural leaders of the Revolutionary generation hoped that taste might contain republican liberties and offset the danger of factionalism. Well into the antebellum decades, a rich patriotic visual culture testified to the broad popular investment in a national community, distinct from corrupting influences associated with Europe. At the same time, the theory of taste offered urban elites a way to claim both moral superiority and public authority. It gave aspiring middle classes a framework for group identity—a mark of moral distance from the laboring poor and luxury-loving rich. Insofar as the idea of taste conceptualized the progress of society from savagery to refinement, it helped to underwrite colonial projects across the continent. For women, notably women of the middle class, it offered a way to claim moral standing, and, as the notion of taste evolved in the antebellum era, it helped to justify domestic consumption against the constraints of Calvinist orthodoxy. Yet there remained an unresolved—and unresolvable—contradiction: As a mark of distinction, taste was intrinsically exclusionary; as an engine of public uplift, it was necessarily expansive. This tension remained in check until the 1840s when escalating social and political conflicts placed new pressures on both the theory and practice of taste.[33]

Even as discussions of taste evolved over the course of the nineteenth century, a fundamental tenet of Scottish thought remained in place among art promoters and museum builders—namely, that taste was a moral quality with public and private implications. The Art-Union sought to galvanize taste in the interest of civic uplift and national unity. The Metropolitan increasingly addressed its visitors as consumers of household objects. New York's art wars chart that evolution.

CHAPTER 1

Paintings in Public Life

The Rise of the American Art-Union

When an art enthusiast declared in 1845 that "*pictures* are more powerful than *speeches*," he invoked long-standing associations between paintings and public life. The Reverend Joel Tyler Headley delivered these words at a meeting of the American Art-Union (AAU), the most popular American art institution of the 1840s. As a man of letters, interested in the fine arts, and the author of a number of history books, he must have been familiar with the statement by Joshua Reynolds, first president of England's Royal Academy of Arts, that ideas expressed through painting "may extend themselves imperceptibly into public benefits." Like Reynolds, the Art-Union's managers focused attention on the graphic arts as the form most likely to create a "republic of taste," but in a decade characterized by escalating political turmoil at home and abroad, they looked to art not as a signifier of elite citizenship but rather as a stabilizing guarantor of democracy, an antidote not only to class tensions within the city but also to political tensions associated with slavery. Unlike Reynolds, they located cultural authority not with artists but with themselves.[1]

Painting and Public Life: Sites of Exhibition

The Art-Union had its roots in a world that associated the fine arts, notably painting, with public life. The Revolution had fostered suspicion of art as a dangerous luxury, an emblem of aristocratic dissipation, and a potential drain on taxpayers, but it also promoted the visual memorialization of Revolutionary heroes and patriotic events. Promoters of the fine arts insisted that America's distinctive political system and natural environment were particularly conducive to the production of morally uplifting pictures, and they argued that art had the power to foster public virtue along with the attendant qualities of moderation and self-restraint. It is no coincidence that New York's primary site for the display of American paintings immediately after the Revolution was City Hall, where portraits of Revolutionary leaders, commissioned by the Common Council of the City of New York, hung on the walls of the main chamber until 1812, when the collection was moved to the elegant Governor's Room of the newly constructed City Hall.[2]

In practice as in theory, republican visual and political cultures were intertwined. Public events in the early republic were suffused with visual symbolism and spectacle. Artisans marked patriotic occasions with parades in which they carried elaborately painted banners depicting the public value of their crafts. Such festivities, in which food and especially drink played a prominent part, generally culminated in a spectacular display of "rockets" (fireworks). The artist and naturalist Charles Willson Peale created pictures on transparencies for Fourth of July festivities in Philadelphia, and comparable pictures, lit from behind, accompanied patriotic events elsewhere. In 1800, New Yorkers who could afford the price of admission had the opportunity to celebrate the night of the Fourth of July by visiting Columbia Garden, where music accompanied the display of six transparencies. Among the glowing images was a portrait of George Washington "ornamented with Garlands of Flowers and supported by . . . the geniuses of Commerce, and the God of the sea on grouped Dolphins." Also on display was the picture of a "woman representing Piety covered with a veil holding the 'Cornucopia' in the right hand, and her left hand placed on the head of a child." An image of "Force" took the form of "Hercules, with a club and the skin of a Lion, a symbol of heroic virtue."[3]

Such displays were not unique to New York or the nation's other cities. When the Democratic-Republicans of Salem, Massachusetts, celebrated Independence Day in 1804, they all but converted their church into a patriotic gallery. Below the pulpit they placed "an elegant engraving of Jefferson." To Jefferson's right was a likeness of Washington and to the left was "a beautiful figure of Liberty." Images of other national dignitaries were on view as well, but to "give a presence" to the region's own "venerable ancestors," women of the town, likely with help from the minister, also assembled a display that included portraits of several Massachusetts governors as well as Salem's first minister and the town's "first merchant."[4]

The artisan background of most American artists helps to explain their general conviction that art should serve a useful public purpose. Well into the antebellum era, most New York (and American) artists remained closely connected to the world of the crafts, and those connections fostered rhetorical and practical associations between painting, sculpture, and the "useful arts." In 1801 there were no self-described "artists" listed in the city directory. Four men and one woman called themselves "portrait painters" and/ or "miniaturists." Among them was Caleb Boyle, who had also worked as a builder and painter of carriages. John and James Vanderpool listed themselves in the directory as sign painters, though they also painted portraits. The most successful New York portraitist of the early nineteenth century was the notoriously hard-drinking John Wesley Jarvis, who began his career as a sign painter and remained a lifelong friend of Thomas Paine. From 1808 to 1810, Joseph Jenkinson listed himself as a miniature and house painter. Joseph Wood, who listed himself as a portrait painter in the city directory of 1803, worked for a silversmith before learning the art of miniature painting. By 1802 he shared a studio and business with Jarvis. John Quidor, who was Jarvis's student, painted signs before he turned to figurative painting on canvas. The renowned painter William Sidney Mount followed a comparable route. Such connections extended to the men who emerged as prominent landscape painters of the antebellum era. Asher B. Durand began his career as an engraver. Even in 1830, only two men designated themselves as "artist" in the city directory and both were involved in the creation of theatrical scenery. In that year an additional 123 people—all male—identified themselves as portraitists and/or miniaturists. Insofar as the term "artist" signified a distinctive realm of activity superior to artisanal production, it was slow to take root.[5]

And yet, New York's first institution devoted to the fine arts of painting and sculpture was not the creation of artisans; rather it was the project of New York's merchants, professionals, and political leaders who assumed that the government, presided over by themselves, had a role to play in the promotion of culture. They created their organization not only to proclaim the importance of New York to America's national project but also to create a community of taste within the city comparable to the cultural centers of Paris and London. The New York Academy of Art, founded in 1803 and renamed the American Academy of Art in 1808, was the product of the closely knit community of politically influential men who presided over an array of cultural institutions through the first two decades of the nineteenth century. They saw the fine arts as an important emblem of civic progress and assumed that it was the role of enlightened government to lend support. The academy's founders were the brothers Robert and Edward Livingston, scions of New York's landed gentry. Robert was Jefferson's minister to France, and his purchase of casts from Europe became the foundation of the academy's permanent collection.[6] Edward, as mayor, presided over the establishment of the academy. From the passage of the Embargo Act of 1807 through the War of 1812, the organization languished, mostly in storage, but it reopened amid great fanfare in 1816 in rooms that would later be decorated with the improbable goal of simulating the Louvre.[7]

The site of the revived academy was a building behind City Hall that the common council had remodeled and renamed the New York Institution for the Promotion of the Arts and Sciences. Other tenants included the New-York Historical Society, the Literary and Philosophical Society, and Scudder's Museum. The common council acknowledged the public mission of these institutions by offering rooms rent-free at an annual rate of "one Pepper Corn if lawfully demanded."[8] Mayor DeWitt Clinton, who later presided over the creation of the New York Institution, was actively engaged with several organizations housed in the building, and he served as president of the American Academy of Art from 1813 until 1817, when he became New York's governor.[9]

For Clinton, who was the prime political mover behind the Erie Canal, commercial and cultural progress went hand in glove with republican principles. He envisioned New York as a new Athens and suggested that fine art would thrive in the context of commercial development and American political institutions. Speaking on the eve of the American Academy's 1816 opening, he famously declared that "a republican government, instead of being unfriendly to the growth of the fine arts, is the appropriate soil for their cultivation." He believed that American history offered "magnificent subjects" to painters, while portraitists and sculptors "may transmit to posterity the likenesses of those men who have acted and suffered in their country's cause." Clinton spoke the language of Scottish Enlightenment writers when he hailed the natural environment of the United States: "This wild, romantic and awful scenery, is calculated to . . . elevate all the faculties of the mind and to exalt all the feelings of the heart: but when cultivation has exerted its power—when the forest is converted to fertile fields, blooming with beauty and smiling with plenty, then the mind of the artist derives a correspondent colour from the scenes with which it is conversant; and the sublime, the wonderful, the ornamental and the beautiful, thus become, in turn, familiar to his imagination."[10]

Like other members of his group, Clinton was oriented to Europe, eager to prove the power of the new republic to equal and surpass European cultural, scientific, and philosophical accomplishments. That Robert Livingston invited Napoleon Bonaparte to become an honorary member of the academy was a savvy move, bringing with it donations in the form of books and engravings, not to mention loans of valuable paintings; it also testified to the founders' sense of their own preeminence—their leadership within a city and a nation that merited international recognition as a place of refinement and political virtue.[11] The academy testified to the tremendous optimism of its early promoters—their confidence that the creation of institutions would somehow bring their grand cultural vision into being.[12]

At the time the American Academy opened at the New York Institution, the city's overlapping political and cultural elites were more or less unchallenged in their assumption of cultural stewardship. Clinton's speech at the academy in 1816 acknowledged the city's artisan majority by pointing to the primacy of the "useful" over the "fine arts." But in the realm of fine art, Clinton assumed that merchants (art-loving "amateurs") would take charge. These men deemed artists, at least most of them, inherently "interested" parties insofar as they were subject to rivalries that might distort judgments of taste. The twenty-five-dollar annual membership fee excluded most artists (and artisans) with the result that members of the organization generally mapped the city's well-to-do cultural and political leadership.

Although John Trumbull, who took over the presidency of the American Academy in 1817, was an artist, his background and outlook linked him to the institution's elite membership. The Federalist son of a Connecticut governor, he was educated at Harvard and at London's Royal Academy of Arts. His historical paintings celebrated the American Revolution in the grand tradition of neoclassical, European academic painting. One of the first acts of his presidency was to insert the word "fine" into the name of the academy—American Academy of Fine Arts—thereby emphasizing the distinction between artists and artisans as between the fine and useful arts. For annual exhibitions, Trumbull made a concerted effort to include borrowed European works together with paintings by mostly senior American artists, including himself. Throughout the year he rented out space in the academy's rooms to artists, collectors, and auctioneers who charged the public (generally twenty-five cents) for admission. His goal was to incorporate European canonical traditions in ways that celebrated the United States. Insofar as the organization sought to educate American artists and artisans, it did so primarily by presenting elevated artworks for study and comparison.[13]

What audience did the American Academy address and what sort of people, besides artists, actually visited the exhibitions? From its reopening in 1816 through the 1830s, some shows drew crowds. Fifteen hundred guests attended the preview of the exhibition of 1816, and for several weeks thereafter an average of 150 people visited daily. In 1818 an exhibition of Trumbull's *Declaration of Independence* attracted more than six thousand visitors over a nearly five-week period. The usual twenty-five-cent admission fee would not have kept most artisans away, and the city's more prominent craftsmen were undoubtedly among the intended audience. Contemporaries identified the academy as a "fashionable resort"—a source of "elegant amusement"—and that, it seems, was the goal that the founders had in mind.[14]

It is possible to find among early nineteenth-century art promoters an inkling of the reformist goals that would emerge in the antebellum decades, but these references generally constructed taste as a counterweight to elite rather than lower-class dissipation. The merchant John Pintard, among the founding members of New York's American Academy, said as much in a letter to his daughter on the eve of the 1816 exhibition: "To afford innocent amusement to growing opulence is among the duties incumbent on all those who regard the morals of Society. Mankind cannot always be praying, nor working." In expressing the wish that the American Academy would "soon become a popular place of resort," he was referring to men of wealth and leisure for whom "opulence" posed a danger. Joseph Hopkinson, president of the Pennsylvania Academy of the Fine Arts, made much the same point in a speech that he delivered in 1810. He declared that the new institution would provide "an innocent, an interesting, and dignified source of pleasure" that would "not only draw the mind from gross and vulgar gratifications; but finally so entirely absorb and purify it; so quicken its sensibility and refine its taste that pleasures more gross lose their attractions and become disgusting." But Hopkinson, like Pintard, was referring primarily to men of leisure "whose inclination and fortune withdraw them from scenes of active and necessary business." Such men risked sinking "either into a distressing lethargy or low and corrupting vices," and it was primarily

for them that "the fascinating gardens of Taste" offered "refuge."[15] From
the perspective of leading art promoters, great cities required a layer of
polite society—a community of refined taste.

Early museums in New York and other cities offered another context
for the display of paintings and sculpture, one that grew out of a distinctly
artisan vision. Rather than identifying painting and sculpture as a distinctive realm of production, the museums, organized on a commercial basis,
brought together some combination of paintings, taxidermy, and other
objects of nature, as well as Native American artifacts, wax figures, and
curiosities from far-off places. The goal was to entertain visitors but also to
educate them with informational, patriotic, and morally uplifting displays.
Toward this end, proprietors devoted attention to classification and
arrangement, and it is telling that Scudder's American Museum in New
York identified objects with Latin as well as English labels.[16] To attract
customers, museums offered musical accompaniments. They also presented mechanical and electrical displays that highlighted the proprietors'
vision of painting as a useful art, inextricably connected to practical
knowledge and invention. Charles Willson Peale had referred to his Philadelphia Museum as a "temple," and his turn-of-the-century counterparts
evoked a similarly seamless link between God's plan in nature and its ful-
fillment in America's republican government. Within the space of the early
museums, Indian relics evoked the uniqueness of America's natural environment just as paintings of Revolutionary heroes celebrated the promise
of the new republic. And insofar as museums promoted close observation,
their proprietors claimed to promote critical qualities associated with
responsible citizenship.[17] A notice in 1801 for New York's Waldron's
Museum captured this sentiment. The advertisement informed readers
that "even a slender knowledge of nature removes a certain littleness of
mind, protects us from compositions which affected greatness too often
attempts on ignorance and credulity, and calls forth emotions of gratitude
to the great Parent of All."[18]

New York's first museum, called the "American Museum," was established in 1791 under the auspices of the Tammany Society, an organization
initially dedicated to the promotion of a unified patriotic, republican culture. Artisans were among the society's founding members, but so was the
merchant John Pintard, who spearheaded the museum project.[19] Within a
few years the museum had become a commercial enterprise, falling into the
hands of successive proprietors, including William I. Waldron and then

Edward Savage, a painter and engraver. At Savage's newly named Columbian Gallery and Museum visitors could find among the many paintings, engravings, and sculptures "originals of the Washington Family, the Goddess of America, Columbus's first landing in the new world, all the size of life." Savage also offered his own productions for sale. Among them were engravings of "The Washington Family, Liberty, Columbus, Etna, Vesuvius, a large whole length of Washington, Dr. Franklin, Dr. [David] Rittenhouse, Dr. [Benjamin] Rush" and other prints.[20] In 1810 John Scudder, a taxidermist, purchased the remains of the Tammany collection. His focus was on objects of natural history, but included pictures as well. Scudder, who supplemented his collection with gifts from around the world, invited not only "the friends of science and the arts to visit his museum" but also "those who are yet unacquainted with nature and its variety, and the wonders of creation, to come and view them." Where, he asked, "can they spend an hour more instructing—or with more amusement blended?"[21] It is significant that Scudder obtained a rent-free space in the New York Institution—a clear marker of the location of his museum within the lexicon of public culture envisioned by DeWitt Clinton.[22]

Like Scudder's American Museum, John Vanderlyn's Rotunda—created for the display of large panorama paintings—might be described as an early form of commercial entertainment, but it too was situated within the public culture envisioned by Clinton and embodied by the New York Institution for the Promotion of the Arts and Sciences. Born in 1775 in Kingston, New York, Vanderlyn studied in New York City with Archibald Robinson and later in Philadelphia with Gilbert Stuart. Under the patronage of Aaron Burr he spent five years studying in Paris and in 1803 returned to that city as an agent for Robert and Edward Livingston to make copies and purchase casts for the new American Academy. (Vanderlyn's Democratic-Republican political views would contribute to his alienation from John Trumbull and the American Academy.) Working in the French neoclassical tradition, he had a successful career as a portraitist of prominent national figures, and his reputation grew after 1808, when he won the Napoleon Gold Medal from the Academy of Artists in Paris for his painting *Caius Marius amid the Ruins of Carthage*. Perhaps because he was slow at portraiture—too slow to acquire a substantial income—he turned his attention to panoramas after returning to the United States in 1815. Through subscriptions from wealthy New Yorkers Vanderlyn raised money for the construction of his Rotunda right near the New York Institution on land owned by the city and

granted to the artist rent-free for a period of nine years. The accompanying
statement by the city council says a great deal about the public purpose
that Vanderlyn and others associated with the enterprise. According to the
councilmen, the artist deserved the "liberal grant of the public ground . . .
which besides ornamenting the City will encourage the Arts and Sciences,
chasten the public Taste and do honour to the Institutions of our City."[23]
For twenty-five cents, visitors would walk upstairs to a central viewing area
where, beneath skylights, they looked out upon the enormous circular
painting that surrounded them. The setting created the illusion of looking
out over an extensive vista. Best known among Vanderlyn's panoramas
were *The City of Paris* and *The Palace and Garden of Versailles*.[24]

Not surprisingly, given the social and political group that backed his
project and patronized his work, Vanderlyn geared his enterprise to prosperous visitors. In one of many anxious letters written to his nephew and
assistant, he inquired about attendance at the Rotunda and asked especially
about "casual visitors of distinction." He urged his nephew to "listen to
what they say & remark" and write it down on the receipts.[25] At the same
time he sought to align his enterprise with the public purpose by offering
an exhibition for the benefit of the Society for the Instruction of the Deaf
and Dumb, which was itself housed in the New York Institution. Vanderlyn
knew that the benefit would attract just the sort of visitors he aimed to
please. He hoped that the Rotunda would thereby "acquire more popularity
in consequence of many having seen it and [because they would recognize]
that it has done some good to the institution of the deaf &c."[26] The Rotunda
would eventually fail in part because receipts from the sale of tickets were
never sufficient to cover debts acquired in the course of constructing the
building, but also because the staid European subject matter of the paintings was increasingly out of step with the interests of New York audiences.[27]
For purposes here, it is significant that the Rotunda shared in the public
culture that characterized the New York Institution, and it thereby points
to changes and continuities that would be embodied by the Art-Union.

The vision of public culture articulated by Clinton took shape during
the first two decades of the nineteenth century when the hierarchies embedded within New York society were contained, and artisans still played a
central role in urban political culture. In 1820, the city's population was
concentrated in the southwestern part of Manhattan, between Battery Park
and Chambers Street, where laborers, servants, artisans, and well-to-do
merchants lived interspersed among the pigs and chickens that still roamed

the streets along with the occasional small herd of cattle. Merchants resided close to their places of business, the wealthiest clustering near City Hall and Bowling Green. However, poor neighborhoods bordered the wealthier streets. The area that would become Washington Square Park (see Figure 1.1) was still a burial ground for indigent people, and the further northward migration of wealthy families had only just begun. Not until the end of the decade would the wet, polluted area bounded on the east by the Bowery begin to assume its identity as the impoverished, crowded, Irish and African American neighborhood known as Five Points. New York's population was 123,706 in 1820, nearly double that of its closest rival, Philadelphia, but not until the following decade would the rate of population growth begin to explode.[28] In 1820 more than 500 of the city's nearly 10,368 African American residents were still enslaved, though the state's gradual emancipation acts of 1799 and 1817 would come to fruition in 1827.[29] Wealthy men could still identify themselves with the public at large because their cultural and even political preeminence was as yet unchallenged, at least relative to the upheavals of the antebellum decades. The 1820s and 1830s would see enormous social, political, and spatial transformations, but at the start of the decade they were barely underway.

Theatrical evenings at the Park Theater, the city's principal theatrical venue through the first quarter of the nineteenth century, say a great deal about class, race, and gender relations in early nineteenth-century New York. Differential pricing of tickets not only drew audiences that traversed class lines but also ensured that seating would replicate social hierarchy. A visitor to the Park in 1817 found that people seated in the pit "consisted of none in dress, manners, appearance, or habits above the order of our Irish bricklayers." Polite society occupied the boxes where seats cost a dollar. There the city's leading merchants and professionals could be seen in attendance, often without their wives. Meanwhile, according to the traveler, "a part of the gallery is allotted for negroes, they not being admitted into any other part of the house." They shared a separate entrance with prostitutes who mingled in the upper gallery with men of various means. Between the acts of the play "the house, in every part, was deserted, except by the ladies," because the men were stepping out for a drink. Theaters were male-oriented spaces.[30] Audiences could get rowdy. Indeed, artisans identified their participatory, often noisy engagement with performances as an extension of their rights as citizens. Occasional theater riots punctuated life in the city, but the structure of the theater generally contained the conflicts

Figure 1.1. This map of New York City, published in 1833, represents the north-ward expansion of building and settlement. Washington Square Park, located in the 15th Ward, had been in existence for barely five years. Lionel Pincus and Princess Firyal Map Division, New York Public Library.

much as the republican culture of the city contained the social divisions within it. It was no coincidence that New Yorkers referred to the theater audience as "the town."[31]

None of New York's genteel cultural amusements—pleasure gardens, museums, exhibitions—were welcoming to the city's substantial black population; theaters were unusual in practicing segregation rather than full-out exclusion. Black-owned oyster cellars and taverns attracted poor white as well as black customers, but the more elegant amusements (friendly to families and well-to-do women) were not available even to African Americans who could afford the price of entry. The 1820s were years of cultural and political activism among black New Yorkers, and for a brief period, a pleasure garden turned theater, founded by a former ship steward and free man of color named William Brown, offered an alternative to the humiliation of third-tier seating. The enterprise was successful in attracting black as well as white audiences, but it confronted almost constant harassment, instigated in part by the owner of the rival Park Theater. In 1823, after only two years, Brown's theater closed, though it proved a training ground for two black actors who achieved some success on the New York stage during the 1830s. Meanwhile, the legislative act of 1821 that enfranchised propertyless white men raised property requirements for New York's black voters. It thereby contributed to an increasingly hostile cultural as well as political environment for African Americans—one that worsened with the rise of virulent anti-abolitionism in the 1830s.[32]

Early nineteenth-century New York art institutions were more exclusive, genteel sites than theater—notably lacking in the traditions of popular participation that shaped theatrical audiences. They were also more attentive to women and likely more restrictive than theater with respect to color. Long before entrepreneurs of culture created matinees in order to attract middle-class women, proprietors of museums, galleries, and commercial sites of exhibition did their best to affiliate their enterprises with the qualities believed to inhere in refined womanhood. Peale's museum attracted female visitors and the same was likely true of Peale's imitators in other cities. Similarly, New York's Shakespeare Gallery, among the earliest spaces that offered pictures for public inspection, gave special attention to women. The owner of the gallery, which was open from 1801 to 1818 and located several doors down from the Park Theater, was the printer and publisher David Longworth. The gallery housed an exhibition space and a periodical reading room where, for twenty-five cents, visitors could see prints of

European paintings and other images emphasizing literary and patriotic themes. In 1802 the proprietor invited people to see "Full Length Portraits of their Excellencies G. Washington, T. Jefferson, & J. Jay, as large as Life." An advertisement recommended the gallery as providing "entertainment of a rational and innocent nature, calculated as well to gratify persons of literary acquirements, as to form the taste of those who have not enjoyed familiar advantages." Longworth made a special appeal to women, inviting them to see colored prints of the "the newest fashions with respect to female dresses" from London and also signaling the gentility of the gallery as a whole.[33]

The men who founded the academies in New York and other cities recognized women as necessary elements of uplifted sociability, and they tried to make middling and elite women welcome despite countervailing social pressures. Joseph Hopkinson, president of the Pennsylvania Academy in Philadelphia, articulated a view shared by others of his ilk when he declared, "in the present state of society, woman is inseparably connected with every thing [sic] that civilizes, refines, and sublimates man." He celebrated the presence of women in the galleries, while expressing regret that "the objects of the institution were so novel in this country, as well as its exhibitions, that it required no inconsiderable share of good sense and fortitude in a lady to countenance them."[34]

The "novel" objects referred to by Hopkinson were the nude casts that constituted permanent collections at both the New York and Philadelphia academies. Managers, in their effort to create decorous sites, suitable for upstanding women, sought to protect female visitors from potentially offending objects. Toward that end, they also struggled to suppress the popular misogyny evoked by the casts. One method was to segregate women from men in the presence of sculptures. At the founding of the American Academy, directors established that Saturdays would be "exclusively appropriated to the visits of such Ladies as may be disposed to view the collection." They also purchased "fig leaves" for statues, presumably in order to protect the modesty of women. But such precautions did nothing to prevent the appearance of graffiti. During the exhibition of 1817, the academy's Committee on Visitors reported not only that loose engravings had been torn and defiled, but that "the torso of Venus has been frequently most indecently disfigured." They recommended, "this beautiful bust should be removed beyond the reach of this profanation."[35] It is unclear whether Trumbull was correct in blaming disgruntled artists for the graffiti or whether the directors followed through on the committee's further recommendation to place the statue on a pedestal, surrounded by a rope barricade, but the introduction of a sign-in book in 1825 proved to be a relatively successful restraint.[36] A few years later, when the British traveler Frances Trollope visited the Pennsylvania Academy of the Fine Arts, she was surprised at being ushered behind a screen so that she could view the casts protected from the gaze of men. Upon entry she found "a written paper, deprecating the disgusting depravity which had led some of the visitors to mark and deface the casts in a most indecent and shameless manner." In her view, the difficulty arose from the "course-minded custom" of segregated viewing. As she observed, "I never felt my delicacy shocked at the Louvre."[37] Yet, Trollope's unpleasant experience says something about the outlook of early academicians who believed that a tasteful exhibition space required decorous behavior deemed appropriate for genteel women.

Linkages between art and genteel culture persisted with the founding of the National Academy of Design (NAD). By the early 1820s, younger painters were already pressing for the creation of an organization controlled by artists and oriented to their need for training, exhibition, and patronage. In 1826 thirty New York artists joined together to form the new institution. Samuel F. B. Morse, president of the NAD from its creation until 1845, helped to establish a structure whereby thirty full-fledged artist-academicians elected associate and honorary members, admitted students, and screened submissions to the annual exhibitions. Morse believed that national art would flourish only if professional artists, supported by educated elites, remained the locus of cultural authority.[38]

Yet in many ways, Morse shared the perspective of the men who had founded the American Academy. Born in 1791, the Yale-educated son of a prominent Massachusetts minister, Morse studied in Boston with the artist William Allston and at London's Royal Academy with the expatriate American painter Benjamin West. By the mid-1820s he was generally recognized as one of New York's leading artists, having won a one-thousand-dollar city commission to paint a portrait of the visiting Revolutionary hero the Marquis de Lafayette. Morse was committed to Reynolds's view of art as an intellectual profession, distinct from artisanal work, and worthy of high social status. "Never," he wrote in a letter to his parents, "will I degrade myself by making a trade of a profession. If I cannot live a gentleman, I will starve a gentleman." Morse's unabashed goal was to encourage art appreciation—and commitment to American artists—among New York's elite. Again, his model was England. "In America," he observed, art "was only thought to be an employment suited to a lower class of people." In England, by contrast, it was "the constant subject of conversation, and the exhibitions of the several painters are fashionable resorts. No person is esteemed accomplished or well educated unless he possesses almost an enthusiastic love for paintings. To possess a gallery of pictures is the pride of every nobleman."[39]

At a time when many painters and sculptors received early training as sign painters, limners, engravers, or ornamental carvers, the National Academy excluded from full membership those candidates who remained closely identified with the social world of the crafts. It offered honorary membership to patrician art enthusiasts and included portraits of prominent New Yorkers in its annual exhibitions.[40] Under Morse's leadership, the annual exhibitions of the National Academy were elegant occasions, widely reviewed in the press. Meanwhile, the academy did nothing to woo plebeian audiences. Morse believed that the moral and aesthetic improvement of American art would be furthered only if artists could be protected from debasing popular influences.[41]

By the time the Art-Union began to take shape, the marriage between city government and public culture had fractured. Indeed, the creation of the National Academy, entirely outside the auspices of the city government, signaled that process. The rise of Jacksonian politics, along with the rapid expansion of commercial amusements, made Clinton's vision of a publicly sponsored and controlled culture politically untenable. In 1828, the city council announced an end to public support for the New York Institution, and in 1830 it converted the building into city offices. The council also refused to renew Vanderlyn's rent-free agreement for use of the Rotunda on the grounds that it was "impolitic at present." Vanderlyn remained in the building until 1829, when the city finally took it over. The American Academy moved to much smaller quarters but managed to survive for twelve more years primarily as a rental space for traveling exhibitions. Clinton's cultural vision had become the object of ridicule among a younger generation of intellectual and political leaders, notably a young and energetic Jacksonian state representative named Guilian Verplanck, who noted the distance between the grandiose rhetoric and the reality of the fledgling cultural organizations supported by the former governor. Of these, only the New-York Historical Society would survive—and thrive—beyond the 1840s.[42]

The Expansion of Commercial Culture: Art and Exhibition

The 1830s and especially the 1840s were years of explosive growth and transformation in the city's commercial amusements. Fueled in part by the swelling population, new sites of entertainment also benefited from the proliferation of cheap penny papers that depended on advertisements rather than subscription fees. Not only did papers publish notices for shows; they also made cultural sites the subject of commentary. No one made better use of publicity than P. T. Barnum, whose American Museum opened in 1841 with the remnants of Scudder's old establishment. Like his predecessors, Barnum displayed historical portraits, wax figures, Native American objects, and mechanical pictures along with taxidermy and other objects of natural history. But he abandoned taxonomic displays and drew crowds by focusing on oddities of nature—often manufactured—and other curiosities. In the 1840s he attracted visitors with the "Feegee Mermaid," and later he would create a bigger sensation with the "dwarf" Tom Thumb. The art gallery, along with didactic performances in the museum's expansive theater, or "Lecture Room," functioned as markers of respectability and assisted Barnum in his successful effort to attract middle-class women and children.[43] As in other theatrical venues, appeals to women and children accompanied the exclusion of African Americans. Barnum was more liberal than others in making the following appeal to black New Yorkers in 1849: "In order to afford respectable colored persons an opportunity to witness the extraordinary attractions at present exhibited at the Museum, the Manager has determined to admit this class of people on Thursday morning next, March 1, from 8 A.M. till 1 P.M."[44]

Meanwhile, New York theaters grew in size and number as audiences and dramatic tastes began slowly to diverge along class lines. According to Peter George Buckley's count, the city had seven theaters operating at some point during the 1820s, twelve during the 1830s, and thirteen during the 1840s. Buckley estimates that between 1820 and 1850 New York City saw at least a sixfold increase the number of theater seats.[45] By 1840, the character of theater audiences was changing as well. The uptown Astor Place Opera House (opened in 1847) kept ticket prices high along with its identity as a markedly elite cultural site, but other theaters, even the Park, brought prices down. The Bowery and Chatham oriented productions to distinctly working-class audiences, while others, beginning in the 1840s, made a point of wooing middle-class women and families with matinees. Prostitutes continued to occupy the upper tier of most antebellum theaters, but protest against their presence grew.[46] Buckley notes that contemporary observers "whatever their cultural persuasion . . . mapped the changes according to a simple rule of New York's social geography: that the 'low' forms of amusement and social life could be found in the Bowery 'and its dependencies,' Chatham Square and the Five Points, and that 'high' culture had followed 'uppertendom' to the further reaches of Broadway and the Fifteenth Ward."[47]

Paintings and painters took their place within this growing world of commercial entertainment. Artists situated their work almost wholly within the realm of respectable amusements rather than among the "low" entertainment associated with the Bowery, but they also cast their appeal beyond the confines of elite New York to the growing urban and provincial middle class. Traveling exhibition pictures gained currency during the early and mid-nineteenth century and they engaged audiences in ways that differed from the neoclassical style embodied in the work of John Trumbull and advocated by art promoters of the early national period.[48] William Dunlap, among the pioneers of the traveling exhibition in the United States, provides a case in point. Born in 1776, he worked in New York alternatively as a playwright, a painter of stage sets, a theater manager, a portraitist, and eventually a historian of American theater and art. He was also among the founding members of New York's Academy of Fine Arts and the National Academy of Design. From 1822 through 1828 he painted and exhibited four large religious paintings (*Christ Rejected*, *The Bearing of the Cross*, *Calvary*, and *Death on the Pale Horse*) and hired an agent to help him exhibit the pictures up and down the East Coast, from Boston to Richmond, Virginia. (The first and last of these paintings were modeled on works by Benjamin West.) During the winter of 1827–1828, the paintings tracked the revival circuit in western New York where audiences alternatively lionized the exhibits or vilified them. "At one place," observed Dunlap, "a picture would be put up in a church, and a sermon preached in recommendation of it; in another, the people would be told from the pulpit to avoid it, as blasphemous. . . . Here the agent of a picture would be encouraged by the first people of the place, and treated as a saint; and there received as a mountebank, and insulted by a mob." This sort of emotional response was not the effect that early national art promoters sought to evoke. And yet, as Dunlap noted, when Trumbull exhibited his own painting at the American Academy in 1824 receipts were insufficient to cover the rent. By contrast, *Christ Rejected*, which showed in the same venue, made a profit.[49]

The appeal of Dunlap's pictures resided not only in their religious subjects, but also in their melodramatic theatricality, spectacular size, and narrative accompaniment. The artist's rendition of *Death on a Pale Horse* was twenty by ten feet, and *Calvary* was eighteen by fourteen feet. In 1832, when Dunlap exhibited all four pictures together in the gallery of the NAD, the *New-York Mirror* claimed that the series occupied "nearly one thousand square feet of canvas, displaying seven or eight hundred figures." Dunlap, who lectured on the paintings in the evenings with the canvases illuminated by gas lighting, created an emotionally charged narrative for spectators in which suffering women played key roles. Speaking on the subject of *Christ Rejected* before an audience that included several of the city's clergymen, he described the "principal characters who are actors or sufferers in the awful scene," and he gave special attention to female figures. The wife of the "indifferent" centurion, draped over her husband, looks "with sympathy on the man of many sorrows" who bleeds from the crown of thorns and "evinces, by his attitude and countenance, his superiority to his clamorous enemies, and resignation to the death he had chosen." Meanwhile, "Caiaphas, in all the pomp of his once high office, with violent action, cries— 'Away with him! Crucify him!'" Watching the scene, "the beautiful Mary Magdalen, whose locks disheveled with which she had wiped the feet of her benefactor, looks to him in an agony of unmitigated sorrow; while the mother, in the majesty of woe, subdued by knowledge of the future, stands erect, with her eyes turned to heaven. . . . Others of the daughters of Jerusalem are overwhelmed with grief and consternation, while friends and enemies await the decision of the man on whose words life and death seem to hang."[50] Dunlap drew audiences with religious narratives and images that featured female subjects and apparently appealed to women as well as men.

Even before Barnum opened his American Museum, entrepreneurs were looking for other ways to turn paintings—dioramas and especially panoramas—into moneymaking spectacles. Far more popular than the static circular panoramas that continued to be shown in New York through the 1830s were large moving pictures. These long canvases were lit from behind and slowly turned on large rollers before seated viewers. As early as 1828 Dunlap wrote a play titled *A Trip to Niagara; or, Travelers in America; A Farce* for the purpose of accompanying a moving panorama created by Bowery Theater's scene painter.[51] In the 1839–1840 season, New Yorkers who could afford twenty-five-cent tickets had the opportunity to attend two new moving panoramas and the numbers grew over the course of the following decade.[52] Showings could last as long as two hours and were accompanied by lectures and often music. Among the things that distanced these spectacles from Vanderlyn's displays was the theatricality of the presentation, the focus on the American continent or religious subjects, and the ability to depict change over time. Advertisements for panoramas identified the shows as educational entertainment, appropriate for women and children, but rather than positioning them as elevated exemplars of high art, entrepreneurs emphasized their verisimilitude—their ability to transport viewers without the inconvenience, expense, or danger of actual travel. The most popular moving picture of the 1840s was John Banvard's *Panorama of the Mississippi River*, shown in New York in 1847–1848. Advertisements proclaimed that it covered three thousand feet of canvas, though it was probably about two-thirds that size. Among the testimonials printed in the accompanying pamphlet was one from "officers of steamboats continually plying on the Mississippi river" who proclaimed the painting's "fidelity and truthfulness to nature."[53] Art historians have noted the ways in which panorama theater influenced landscape painting of the era while attracting attention and collaboration from landscape artists.[54]

Mechanics fairs, organized first by the General Society of Mechanics and Tradesmen and subsequently by the American Institute (founded in 1828) and the Mechanics Institute (founded in 1831), offered another distinctly popular venue for the exhibition of painting. By the 1830s, these organizations, initially designed to foster artisan education, were becoming identified with the interest and outlook of wealthy artisans and, increasingly, manufacturers. In fact the American Institute was aligned with pro-tariff, manufacturing interests from its inception. The American and Mechanics Institutes, seeking to improve the quality of commercial products, fostered artisan education in the fine arts and toward that end collaborated with the National Academy of Design in several educational ventures during the 1830s and early 1840s. At the fairs, artists from the National Academy served as judges in the fine art category. But unlike the National Academy of Design or the American Academy of Fine Arts, the mechanics fairs presented paintings and sculpture as "useful arts" on a par with the vast array of goods celebrated for the ingenuity and skill that went into their production.[55] At fairs of the 1830s, judges offered prizes not only to artists but also to the producers of "machines and models," "carriages and sleighs," "glass and earthenware," "carving and gilding," "mathematical and philosophical instruments," and "mammoth vegetables," as well as furniture, silver work, and clothing, among many other things.[56]

At mechanics fairs, young artists and amateurs had an opportunity to show their work, but the fairs extended the category of fine art well beyond painting and sculpture. In 1830 William Sidney Mount received the first prize for his painting *Rustic Dance* under the category of "Pictures, Sculpture, &c." Another prizewinner in the same category was the creator of "ingenious and beautiful specimens of fancy, transparent weather proof sign cuttings."[57] Later fairs linked paintings to ornamental household objects under the shared rubric of "The Fine Arts." At the American Institute's fair in 1833 one of the winners in the fine art category was Joseph Hemphill for "splendid specimens of porcelain vases, tea sets, fruit baskets, &c, painted, enameled, gilt, of tasteful proportions and shapes."[58] Three years later the winners in the fine arts included the artist and former coach painter Bass Otis for his portrait of General William Henry Harrison, Thomas W. Hope for "a moonlight scene" painted in oil, and George Heisher for "a beautiful oil painting." James H. Farrand also received notice for his "beautiful specimen of transparent blinds" and Richard Sealy for "a fine specimen of window curtains." The gold medal in fine art went to Thomas Thomas for "a most beautiful specimen of stained glass."[59]

The mechanics fairs welcomed women as consumers and displayed an array of goods produced by women. In fact, the very layout of fairs could invite visitors to imagine paintings as a form of domestic decoration oriented to female consumption.[60] A report on the Mechanics Fair of 1823, the second in the history of the city, noted the wide array of products, including "paintings, hearth rugs, lace veils, American wove and printed silk." An announcement for the event gave special invitation to "the Ladies, who are generally good judges of these articles."[61] The fairs also located the paintings with ornamental work produced by female labor. By 1837, when the fair was held at Niblo's Garden, the fashionable theater and pleasure garden on the city's primary commercial thoroughfare, a reporter noted that "about one hundred omnibuses were running up and down Broadway, literally filled with beautiful young women, elegantly dressed all hastening to the Fair."[62] Among the goods on view were "two beautiful pictures—by a young lady—chaste and classic designs and excellent in execution" as well as "six bed quilts, exhibiting much beauty and skill in the workmanship made by six young ladies of 30,000 pieces of patchwork." Also on display was a "needle work portrait of Washington."[63] Perhaps the most telling indication of the cultural distance between the fair of 1837 and earlier sites of exhibition was the featured display of a "most *magnificently worked Petticoat* valued at $700 intended as a present to the queen Victoria," produced by "seven young ladies of this city." The petticoat, in its magnificence and royal destination, signaled a marked departure from the male-oriented republican vision that shaped New York's earliest exhibition sites and much of the city's visual culture.[64]

The Art-Union Vision

The Art-Union created a new context for the promotion and display of painting that was quite distinct from any that already existed in the city. Its wealthy managers evoked (and doubtless remembered) the model of cultural stewardship embodied in the New York Institution, but they also tried to situate their organization within the burgeoning world of popular commercial amusements. Initially called the Apollo Association, it came into being in 1838—the second year of a severe economic depression that would last until 1844. The founder, James Herring, was a portrait painter and the proprietor of a lending library. He was also affiliated with the American Academy of Fine Arts, serving as its secretary from 1831 to 1834. Herring sought to create an organization that would help the city's artists exhibit and sell their work. His plan was for a committee of managers, consisting of art-loving amateurs, to collect five-dollar annual subscriptions and then use the funds to purchase paintings by American artists. The works would be distributed by lottery to subscribers at the end of each year or housed in what Herring initially envisioned as a permanent gallery. Subscribers would receive a yearly engraving in addition to the lottery ticket. By 1844 the organization was incorporated by the New York State Legislature as the American Art-Union. The gallery, which initially charged twenty-five cents for admission (or fifty cents for a year's subscription), became the "Free Gallery" in 1842. In 1847, following several moves to rented spaces, the Art-Union opened a new gallery in a building that it purchased at 497 Broadway. From 1848 until the downfall of the organization in 1852, the managers provided subscribers with an increasingly elaborate magazine that appeared monthly from April through December.[65]

The American Art-Union and its various American imitators represented a distinctive manifestation of a much broader transatlantic phenomenon. The sheer number of art unions, and their geographical and temporal
spread, suggests that the system was capable of accommodating varied
groups with somewhat different specific goals, but in general the organizations can be linked to the nationalist movements that swept Europe during
the first half of the nineteenth century. They represented an effort to liber-
ate national art from dependence on aristocratic patronage and, in some
contexts (notably Scotland and the United States), to foster national culture
in the absence of aristocratic and princely support. The American organization was modeled on the Edinburgh Art Union, which in turn, followed in
the footsteps of the German and Swiss *Kunstvereine*, founded during the
period from 1788 to 1839 by civil servants and professionals. By 1839, twenty-
nine art unions were operating throughout Germany. Between 1829 and
1860 comparable organizations appeared in Milan, Florence, and Turin.
During the 1820s and 1830s elites in French provincial cities began forming
their own *sociétés des amis des arts*, which were also modeled on the art-
union plan. London's Art Union, which was in existence longer than any
of the others, came into being in 1837 and survived until 1914. Comparable
organizations appeared in Birmingham, Manchester, and Dublin.[66] The relative absence of state sponsorship for the arts in the United States enhanced
the role of the American Art-Union relative to its European counterparts,
as did the absence of large aristocratic collections. Nonetheless, it is useful
to remember that the rise and demise of the American Art-Union points
not only to the particular cultural politics of antebellum New York City but
to a more general moment in the history of transatlantic art institutions.
When the managers renamed the Apollo Association in 1844, they were
knowingly linking their organization to European precedents and much
that they signified.

By the late 1830s, the promise of a democratic, distinctly American art
and literature was galvanizing a younger generation of New York artists,
writers, editors, and politicians. Affiliated with the Democratic Party, they
identified their group as "Young America." According to Edward L.
Widmer, the movement "involved taking control of American culture from
Boston, from the Whigs, and from old conservatives everywhere. At the
heart of this regional, political, and generational argument were basic ideas
we now take for granted; namely, that a creative artist does not have to be
educated or wealthy to be taken seriously as an intellectual; . . . that a

successful work ought to speak clearly to the mass of the American people, not just to intellectuals." This outlook was shared by the painters William Sidney Mount and Francis Edmonds, among others, as well as literary figures Nathaniel Hawthorne and Herman Melville (before their later disillusionment) and Walt Whitman. John L. O'Sullivan, editor of the *Democratic Review*, who coined the term "manifest destiny" in 1845, emerged as the central figure in the movement. At their heyday in the early and mid-1840s, O'Sullivan and other members of Young America envisioned continental expansion as a peaceful, inevitable process, aligned with democratic institutions. They spoke of democracy in religious, millennial terms and identified its spread in the United States with the liberal, nationalist revolutions that swept Europe during the 1840s. Aligned with Martin Van Buren's "Barnburners," the group was generally unfriendly to slavery, but to varying degrees their focus on the white working class and efforts to bridge the sectional divide inclined them to leave the slavery question in the background through the early 1840s.[67]

The Young America movement energized and shaped the Art-Union and, as Widmer points out, a number of its leading figures became involved in the organization. Evert Duyckinck, a prominent member of the group, is best known today as a friend of Herman Melville. From 1840 to 1842 he edited a journal called *Arcturus* with Cornelius Mathews, also a literary proponent of Young America, who coined the term in 1845. Duyckinck was on the Art-Union's board of managers from 1848 through 1851. By that time he was also editor of the *Literary World*. Charles F. Briggs, an Art-Union manager, was founder and editor of the *Broadway Journal* (1844–1845) and, according to Widmer, leaned toward Young America. The merchant and poet Prosper Wetmore, who served as a manager of the organization throughout its twelve-year existence and as its president from 1847 through 1850, was closely identified with the group. His friend Townsend Harris, a merchant with trading experience in China and the East Indies, was on the Committee of Management in 1847. Harris would later become the first U.S. consul in Japan. Other prominent Art-Union Democrats included James W. Beekman (AAU, 1848–1851), who served as a Democratic representative to the state legislature; the artist and banker Francis W. Edmonds (AAU, 1842–1847); and the prominent judge Charles P. Daly (AAU, 1849–1851). Cornelius W. Lawrence (AAU, 1848–1849) was a banker and Democratic mayor of New York from 1834 to 1837. The best known and most widely respected of the Art-Union Democrats was the poet William Cullen

Bryant, who was also the editor of the *New York Evening Post*. He served as president of the organization from 1844 to 1846, resigning when he moved from New York to his country home in Great Barrington, Massachusetts.[68]

And yet, it would be a mistake to read the Art-Union simply as an extension of Young America and radical democracy. The active presence of powerful Whigs among the eighty-three men who served as managers and/or officers of the organization greatly complicates the picture. Like the Young America contingent, they represented a distinctive wing of their party—established merchants and professionals, rather than manufacturers—men who were tied to earlier notions of cultural steward-ship and widely involved in an array of cultural and benevolent organiza-tions.[69] Most notable was Philip Hone, the former mayor of New York, who retired early after having made a fortune in the auction business. He was involved in the initial establishment of the organization and served on its Committee of Management from 1848 through 1851. Born in 1780, he was horrified by the rise of partisan politics and the transformation of class relations in the city. Hone tended to conflate "democracy" with urban vio-lence, the penny press, and what he saw as the broader problem of popular taste. In April of 1843, he reflected sadly on the radical "Loco Foco" triumph in the city elections and declared himself "thoroughly convinced that it is impossible for the country to sustain itself against the desolating effect of universal suffrage." Public virtue, observed Hone, "is the only foundation of a republican form of government, and that is entirely swept away." Some months later he vented his wrath on the penny press and its readership, observing that "licentiousness, no matter how disgusting, lies, however glaring, personal abuse without a shadow of foundation, must be served up to gratify the taste of the people or the papers will not sell."[70] For Hone and his group the Art-Union plan was attractive precisely because it promised to restore morality to politics and class relations by reshaping the "taste of the people."

There were other Whig managers, several of whom served longer in the Art-Union than Hone himself. Erastus C. Benedict, an Art-Union manager from 1842 through 1851, was an attorney and Whig political figure. He won election to the New York State Assembly in 1848 and later to the New York State Senate. Marshall O. Roberts, an Art-Union manager from 1846 through 1851, ran unsuccessfully for Congress in 1852 as a Whig. The anti-slavery Whig editor Henry J. Raymond, served on the Committee of Man-agement from 1847 through 1850. In 1851 he would found the *New York*

Daily Times. James Watson Webb was an AAU manager for only one year in 1839, but it is notable that he was editor of the Whig newspaper *Courier and Enquirer.*

Other Art-Union managers were members of the Whig-leaning social club that bore Hone's name. This small group met for convivial dinners twice a month. David C. Colden, a wealthy lawyer, belonged to the group, as did the merchants Moses Grinnell and Charles Handy Russell. The physician John Wakefield Francis, president of the Apollo Association and then the Art-Union from 1839 through 1841, was an honorary guest. Born in 1789, Francis had been actively engaged in the early history of the American Academy and the New-York Historical Society. Like his friend Philip Hone he embodied connections between the Art-Union and the upper-crust social world of the earlier era. In his memoir, initially published in 1858, Francis steered clear of political disputes that divided antebellum America, but it would be difficult not to read his critical commentary on the French Revolution, Thomas Paine, and the Democratic-Republicans of the early national period as a critique of subsequent democratizing currents.[71]

If we step back and look at the roster of managers as a group, independent of their political affiliations, commonalities emerge that help to account for the cross-party connections. Most Art-Union managers were successful merchants. Others were involved in banking. Only four—George F. Allen, owner of an ironworks; George Bruce, a typefounder; William H. Brown, a shipbuilder; and William Kemble, owner of a foundry—could be described as manufacturers, and none of them were among the most active contingent of the Art-Union leadership. The merchant majority represented various branches of the business; they were factors, shippers, grocers, wholesalers, and dry goods merchants. In addition to Hone, several of them were auctioneers. During the 1820s, Hone and David Austen (father of the brothers and AAU managers John H. and George W. Austen) owned the two largest auction houses in New York. Marshall O. Roberts was perhaps most notable as an owner of the U.S. Mail Steamship Company, which carried mail and passengers to New Orleans and to Panama for subsequent transport to California and Oregon. Like others of the group, he was an avid art collector and would later be involved in the railroad business.[72]

Charles H. Russell, whose daughter married Philip Hone's son in 1842, served as an Art-Union manager from 1848 through 1851. He exemplified the business and social connections that characterized a number of Art-Union leaders and linked the organization's Whigs and Democrats. Born in Newport, Rhode Island, in 1796, he was working in the wholesale foreign dry goods business before the age of twenty. By the mid-1820s he was in business with his brother and living in New York. In 1845 he retired, but like Hone remained very active, not only in an array of voluntary organizations but also as a director of the Pacific Mail Steamship Company. Like several other Art-Union leaders—Democrat and Whig—Russell served on the board of directors of several early railroad companies. Russell was a committed Whig (later Republican) but his identity as a merchant linked him to the Democrats on at least one important political question: He was a staunch advocate of free trade, firmly opposed to tariffs. He died in 1884 without having moderated his position on that issue.[73]

Whether Democrat or Whig, Art-Union managers tended to be well-to-do. Seventeen of them appear in Edward Pessen's account of New York City's "wealthiest one thousand" in 1845, and Pessen's list probably underestimates the extent of wealth among the Art-Union's leadership. A number of Art-Union managers were also conspicuous as the offspring of "old money" families. Notable among these were Evert Duyckinck, James Beekman, David C. Colden, William Kemble, Cornelius Lawrence, and the dentist Eleazer Parmly. The Austen brothers were not on Pessen's list, but their father was among the wealthiest men in the city. Philip Hone was not born to wealth, but he made his fortune before he became mayor of New York in 1826. By 1828 he was already among the wealthiest two hundred men in the city.[74] Marshall O. Roberts, born thirty-three years after Hone, was exceptional insofar as his wealth was recently acquired.

Given their wealth it is not surprising that by 1849 at least twenty of the eighty-three men who served at one time or another as Apollo or Art-Union managers and officials were living in New York's Fifteenth Ward—the wealthiest ward in the city. This was the neighborhood north of Houston Street that encompassed the newly constructed Washington Square Park and most of the current Greenwich Village. (Several other Art-Union leaders had already moved farther north to the fashionable, recently developed areas of Union Place and Gramercy Park, while others lived just south or west of the Fifteenth Ward, within close walking distance.) Philip Hone, whose prime address was on Great Jones Street on the corner of Broadway, had promoted the development of the Washington Square area when he was mayor. During the 1840s Erastus Benedict was the Fifteenth Ward's representative on the city council. Charles H. Russell was Hone's neighbor at Great Jones Street and Broadway. Although it was known as the "Empire

Ward" for its concentration of wealthy Whigs, the neighborhood also housed several Art-Union Democrats, notably Prosper Wetmore, Evert Duyckinck, Charles Leupp, and Townsend Harris. Francis Edmonds lived on West Sixteenth Street, just north of the Fifteenth Ward and a few doors up from the merchant and Art-Union manager Robert Kelly. These neighborhood connections both signify and help to explain the social ties among Art-Union leaders.

Art-Union Whigs and Democrats also shared in a distinctly uppercrust, nonevangelical style of elite male sociability. The managers appear to have eschewed evangelical churches, and it is telling that the wealthy liquor merchant Abraham Bininger was likely a member of the group. The largest identifiable contingent, including Evert Duyckinck, was Episcopalian.[75] Philip Hone, who lived his life far from the teetotal wing of his own party, appears to have taken great pleasure in the food and drink that accompanied his seemingly endless round of mostly all-male dinners. John Francis recalled that the fortnightly "festivals were of the highest order of gustatory enjoyment,—the appetite could ask no more."[76]

Similarly, Bryant, whose long life was punctuated by lengthy trips abroad in the company of male friends, was an active participant in the all-male dinners and clubs that organized elite social life in the antebellum city. He was a founding member of the Democratic-leaning Sketch Club that brought together literary men (including Duyckinck) and artists (including Samuel F. B. Morse, Thomas Cole, William Dunlap, and Asher Durand) and eventually merchant-collectors (including Jonathan Sturges and John Gourlie) at weekly dinners in which food and drink contributed to the conviviality. Minutes for one of the get-togethers in the winter of 1829 noted that there was "no Drawing but of corks."[77] Eighteen years later, Bryant invited Francis William Edmonds to join several other members of the club for a visit to his Massachusetts residence. He took the opportunity to note, "The only female at my place now is my wife, without whom I fear we should have to go without our dinner."[78]

Above all, the men who ran the Art-Union were temperamentally and ideologically united on the increasingly divisive issues of slavery and abolitionism. Their overarching concern was the maintenance of civic and national unity. Bryant was an outspoken opponent of slavery. Along with Duyckinck and other Young Americans, he was disturbed by Southern influence in the Democratic Party, troubled by Texas annexation, and opposed to the Mexican War. By 1848 he had moved to the Free Soil camp.

Later he would join the Republicans. Yet he was friendly with the South Carolina poet and slaveholder William Gilmore Simms, and he regarded the Boston abolitionists as "narrow minded and fanatical."[79] By contrast, Hone was never an outspoken antislavery advocate, but he was alarmed by the escalation of anti-abolitionist violence in the mid-1830s and expressed concern for the plight of black victims. Like Bryant, he had little sympathy for the abolitionists. In 1834 he was outraged when a mob, "after exhausting their rage at the Bowery Theater," proceeded to destroy the home of the wealthy abolitionist Lewis Tappan as well as the Episcopal African Church, and a number of African American residences. Earlier in the day Lewis and his brother Arthur had participated in a meeting at which black abolitionists addressed the audience. Hone directed his wrath not only at the mob but also at the "fanatical" abolitionist Tappan brothers, whom he accused of provoking the conflict.[80] In 1837, his great concern was that "the terrible abolition question" would "destroy the union of the States"—that both parties were "getting more and more confirmed in their obstinacy, and more intolerant in their prejudices."[81] This was a position consistent with the interest and outlook of New York merchants who feared that antislavery agitation might disrupt interregional trade and business connections.

Members of Hone's group, like their Democratic counterparts, hoped that national feelings, transmitted through culture, would have the power to assuage political differences. John Francis, reminiscing about the Hone Club, cut to the heart of this sensibility. He remembered never having "heard a breath in this Club of South or North: it had broader views and more congenial topics." When Daniel Webster attended one of the dinners as an honorary guest, he "talked of the whole country—its seas, its lakes, its rivers; its native products, its forests."[82] It was this transcendent national feeling that the Art-Union sought to promote. As James Herring observed in 1840, while serving as the traveling agent for the fledgling organization, it was the "*only institution* in the country which has ever been devised to unite the people of the whole land in Brotherly community free from sectional, party or sectarian strifes or jealousies."[83]

It is no coincidence that these transpartisan aspirations took shape during the 1830s. The escalation of violent public confrontations, documented in Hone's diary, was more than the product of the author's conservative imagination. From 1833 through 1837, the *Commercial Advertiser* commented on no fewer than fifty-two riots. That was more than double the number reported during the preceding ten years. The most violent of these upheavals arose from election disputes between the more or less equally divided Whigs and Democrats, labor struggles, and, above all, racial strife and virulent anti-abolitionism.[84]

The Art-Union brought Whigs together with Democrats in an effort to foster social, political, and moral unity through the creation of an American school of art. Managers believed that art held the power to raise the moral character of viewers and to promote an uplifted, unified polity. From this perspective, American art, by depicting familiar national themes and images, was most likely to spark the interest of American viewers and best able to evoke unifying sentiments. Managers sought to increase the numbers of American artists (and improve the quality of their work) by purchasing paintings from artists at various levels of training and experience. At the same time, they hoped to spark a taste for art among the populace as a whole. The engravings chosen for distribution and the paintings distributed through the lottery would be "sent forth, as so many missionaries to preach perpetual sermons of beauty and taste."[85] Meanwhile, the gallery that housed Art-Union acquisitions prior to the December lottery would exert its own uplifting influence within the city.

The Art-Union has been described as a "democratic" institution, but that term demands closer scrutiny. Insofar as managers assumed that "the love of art is a universal feeling," they were, in fact, democratizing the notion of taste. That assumption was the foundation of their utopian faith that taste would spread spontaneously if only people had an opportunity to encounter artworks of sufficient quality. In 1846, at the close of his successful presidency, Bryant suggested that the very success of the Art-Union demonstrated that it was "precisely what the people of this country want, that it commends itself to their good sense, that when you offer them a method of encouraging the Fine Arts, suited to their means, and to the equal condition of society among us, they adopt it readily, support it zealously."[86] The following year, Prosper Wetmore voiced comparable associations between political and cultural democracy when he declared, "We need not go beyond the limits of our own city to find the evidence that the freest institutions ever formed, have a tendency to expand the mind to its greatest limits and most national action. It would indeed be strange if this were not so, for Art must flourish most when its wings are widest spread and its ascent unchecked by the shackles of any master"[87] John Gourlie drew similar connections in a private letter to his friend Francis Edmonds when he observed that "the best thing to promote the interests of artists is to diffuse a taste for pictures *among the people* generally—the democracy—and when this is done artists will flourish."[88]

The Young America wing of the Art-Union's management apparently saw the market in culture as a vehicle for the democratization of taste. Duyckinck drew those connections when, in 1840, he declared that his journal *Arcturus* "would have its pages spread in the market place; would scatter its leaves, if they could, far and wide . . . gliding through the throng with a benignant recognition of all that is good, noble and pure."[89] Of course, Duyckinck and other literary men on the Committee of Management were directly involved in the explosion of print media that helped to drive commercial culture as a whole. It is not surprising that they celebrated the arena in which they were engaged.

Yet, from the outset, managers and promoters of the Art-Union assumed that the spreading of taste required stewardship from men such as themselves. It is notable that they turned to art (and the art gallery) rather than to theater as the most appropriate mechanism of popular uplift and unification. Theater, by far the more popular medium, carried with it a long tradition of rowdy, plebeian audience behavior. By contrast, art exhibitions had distinctly genteel connotations. As theater riots multiplied and escalated during the 1830s and 1840s, the sort of men who promoted the Art-Union sought assistance in an alternative cultural arena.[90] In any case, their sense of the people at large carried more than a small dose of judgment. Wetmore revealed this condescension when he expressed hope that "the silent yet eloquent teachings of the pencil and the burin, may contribute as extensively to elevate, instruct and refine the minds and the tastes of the people."[91] He carried the theme of instruction further when he spoke of pictures as "silent missionaries of the atelier and the studio" that would "elevate and purify" public taste.[92]

The Art-Union embodied a particular adaptation of eighteenth-century republican assumptions. To the men who managed and supported it, class antagonism and partisan politics appeared as expressions of "selfish" or "interested" motives. Notwithstanding Duyckinck's hopes for his own publications, the expansion of the market in communication and entertainment aroused suspicion because that process opened new arenas to plebeian voices, created additional opportunities for challenges to upperclass hegemony, and on occasion stimulated dangerous sensual appetites. Art, protected from the popular market in culture, seemed to offer the promise of a countervailing influence. Thus the Unitarian clergyman Henry Whitney Bellows, who addressed the Art-Union's annual meeting of 1844, declared that "if there ever was a people, or a community, that needed the softening, harmonizing and soothing influences of that which admits not of passionate and selfish devotion, it is we. . . . We want some interests that are larger than purse or party, on which men cannot take sides, or breed strifes, or become selfish. Such an interest is Art. And no nation needs its exalting, purifying, calming influences, more than ours."[93] In short, art, itself, would be a purveyor of public virtue and national unity.

In their effort to extend the influence of the organization, managers employed a variety of commercial strategies. Indeed, the Art-Union's successes during the late forties derived not only from the general improvement of economic conditions after 1844 but also from this purposeful popularizing project. To increase its list of subscribers, the Art-Union employed a growing army of local honorary secretaries who received a 10 percent commission on each membership fee that they collected. They were also responsible for distributing prizes and publications of the organization. Drawn from professional and business circles, the honorary secretaries expanded membership beyond New York City, through the ranks of provincial elites and middle classes. (Managers boasted that subscribers extended throughout the nation, but over 50 percent came from the state of New York.).[94] Numbers of honorary secretaries increased from three in 1839 to one thousand in 1851. Subscriptions increased as well from 816 in 1839 to a high of 18,960 in 1849.[95]

Managers had no qualms about making fantasies of acquisition part of the Art-Union's allure. When, in 1848, the organization featured Thomas Cole's series *The Voyage of Life*, the *Bulletin* forthrightly noted that "so valuable a prize as this has never before been offered in this or any other similar institution, and it is not to be wondered at that the hope of gaining it, should induce thousands to enroll their names in the subscription books of the Art-Union."[96] Not coincidentally, subscriptions increased from 9,666 in 1847 to 16,475 in 1848. Also in 1848, the Art-Union offered hundreds of prizes in addition to its collection of 454 paintings. Subscribers could hope to win a limited edition engraving or etching set, or a medal depicting a famous artist. The following year, the Art-Union included twenty statuettes among its list of prizes. Throughout the period of the Art-Union's greatest notoriety, managers complained that most subscribers waited until the eve of the widely publicized lottery distribution to sign up—a further indication that the fantasy of winning this or that painting or prize contributed to the organization's aura of excitement.[97]

When it came to the presentation of their collections, Art-Union officials were more than willing to appropriate elements of commercial culture.
Their purpose was to make the gallery sufficiently attractive to draw audiences away from popular amusements "of a bad or questionable character."[98] Concerned about thin attendance, they created an appealing setting
designed to lure people in. In effect, the Art-Union followed in the footsteps
of Barnum's museum by tempting spectators with a lavish display that
extended out to the street. One laudatory account for the *Literary World*
described the new gallery as the key to its success: "When the Art-Union
planted itself in the middle of Broadway; expended a little judicious capital
in the embellishment of its externals and appliances . . . invited all the
world into its parlor, and provided ottomans, gas lights, and fine pictures
for its entertainment, we foresaw the brilliant consummation."[99]

Through repeated renovations, the creation of an enticing facade, and
interior setting, the Art-Union located itself among the commercial amusements that attracted throngs of spectators. By all accounts, these strategies
succeeded in making the Free Gallery an enormously attractive urban
site—a popular meeting place that permitted casual sociability, freed from
the rituals of domesticity. For the wealthy lawyer George Templeton Strong,
the gallery offered an opportunity to "talk pictures" with a friend; it was
also a magnet for tourists. Commentators—even those sympathetic to the
organization—also suggested that it opened a door to illicit assignations. In
this regard, the journalist George G. Foster likened the gallery to the ice-
cream saloons where "cautious libertines" encountered "women whose
licentiousness has not yet been discovered and who pass for virtuous and
respectable wives, mothers, and daughters."[100] The Art-Union reported that
half a million people visited the Free Gallery in 1848, and the following year
it claimed that attendance was up to three-quarters of a million. This is a
remarkable figure, even allowing for exaggeration, because the city's entire
population in 1850 was just over 500,000.[101]

From the point of view of Art-Union promoters, this adaptation of
commercial culture was consistent with the broader mission of the organization. Only by drawing large numbers of spectators could the Free Gallery
perform its role as a public space, serving the needs of diverse groups rather
than partial interests. In this sense, the publicity of the gallery derived from
its inclusivity or supposed ability to evoke a transcendent unity among
classes. According to the *Literary World*, an evening visitor to the gallery
could "find every section of the social system. Here they all are, from the

GALLERY OF THE ART-UNION.

Figure 1.2. Gallery of the Art-Union. This image represents the managers' view of the popularity of the gallery. Figures depict divergent levels of sophistication. The studious, possibly working-class figure seated on the middle bench uses his bulletin as a guide, while the elegant figures standing by the left wall exude knowledge and confidence. The two standing female figures present the gallery as a suitable place for respectable women—even in the absence of male companions. Many of the visitors appear in conversation, reinforcing the managers' claim that the taste for art uplifted social relationships. From the *Bulletin of the American Art-Union*, May 1849, 6. New-York Historical Society.

millionaire of 5th Avenue, to the B'hoy of 3d, from the disdainful beauty of Fourteenth Street . . . to the belle of the Bowery."[102] The editor of the upstate *Oswego Commercial Times* evoked his own experience of the gallery by observing, "You will notice several pale-faced, white kidded fashionables, with pretty accompaniments leaning languidly on their arms; young clerks; school boys and girls; the mechanic and his family; the cartman in his clean linen frock; the portly merchant; the honest bronzed face of the farmer; the poor seamstresses and sewing girls . . . *there* they are all earnestly contemplating the works of art with which the walls are covered. All social distinction is lost in admiration of Art—all are happy."[103] Yet another writer believed that the Free Gallery had "grown to be a kind of municipal Institution, visited by the whole people."[104]

Envisioning National Unity

By designating themselves as disinterested stewards of culture, the Art-Union managers laid claim to aesthetic authority. Rotating subcommittees, selected from among the Committee of Management, examined artwork submitted to the organization and recommended paintings and prices to the committee as a whole. In purchasing pictures for exhibition and distribution, managers sought works that would woo audiences to art, raise the level of taste, and encourage promising but untrained painters. Artists, they insisted, would not be able to balance these concerns. Nor were artists capable of determining the monetary value of their own work. "Genius," observed the Art-Union's annual report of 1845, "is far from being the best Judge of its own productions." Artists, noted the managers two years later, were often "biased by their own peculiar methods, and inclined to praise or blame another, according as he may have followed or rejected some favorite theory."[105] This sense of prerogative informed the organization's correspondence with artists. "Your misfortune," observed the Art-Union's corresponding secretary to one rejected painter, "consists in not being competent to judge the merit of your own productions and in having friends who are not [honest?] enough to tell you the truth."[106]

Managers assumed for themselves the right and ability to arbitrate matters of artistic value, but they were also self-consciously eclectic in selecting pictures for the annual collections. Their purpose was to create a unified, uplifted culture by enlarging the audience for art, but to win the audience in the first place required a broad appeal. "We must,' declared the annual report of 1845, "minister to a various taste in making our gallery attractive."[107] Through the life of the Art-Union, managers purchased 2,481 artworks from over three hundred artists.[108] They generally preferred American scenes and they looked for paintings that would appeal to viewers at various levels of taste. Unlike the National Academicians, they refused to exhibit portraiture because they deemed it too narrow in appeal. They made extensive purchases of landscape paintings and sought to encourage aspiring artists by urging them to begin with simple still lifes. Officials believed that scenes of everyday life and pictures that told familiar or entertaining stories would win audiences to art, and they assumed that such images would be most successful in stimulating viewers to contemplate the moral message embedded in the artwork. Whereas the National Academy exhibited virtually no western genre scenes, the Art-Union purchased a number of paintings by Charles Deas, William Ranney, Arthur F. Tait, and George Caleb Bingham. Such scenes evoked popular interest in western expansion, western land, and the West as the site of unfettered, independent manhood. Native Americans figured in a number of Art-Union paintings. As emblems of American distinctiveness, they could appear either as subdued, noble subjects or as savage obstacles to national destiny. The art historian Patricia Hills points to ways in which these western scenes represented the outlook of the merchants who ran the organization.[109] In addition, the Art-Union acquired and celebrated examples of "ideal art," which were, in the words of the artist Daniel Huntington, "confined to no age or country, and depend upon no temporary excitement for their interest—but appeal to those feelings which belong to the human race."[110]

The Art-Union's distinctive republican perspective found visual expression in the choice of pictures engraved for distribution. Each year, managers selected at least one work of art to be reproduced as an engraving and sent out to the membership as a whole. The selection, production, and distribution of these images was, from the outset, central to the mission of the organization and represented a more considered judgment than the purchase of this or that painting for the annual collection. A striking feature of Art-Union engravings, considered as a group, was their tendency to locate significant moral action in a masculine sphere of public virtue rather than in the domestic sphere that was claimed and largely constructed by women. Managers turned, for the most part, to images of manly virtue or male bonding. Among the chosen paintings were John Blake White's *General Marion in His Swamp Encampment Inviting a British Officer to Dinner* (see Figure 1.3), Vanderlyn's *Caius Marius amid the Ruins of Carthage* (see Figure 1.4), and Asher Brown Durand's *The Capture of Major Andre*. In addition, such genre scenes as William Sidney Mount's *Farmers Nooning* (see Figure 1.5), George Caleb Bingham's *Jolly Flatboatmen*, and Richard Caton Woodville's *War News from Mexico* (see Figure 1.6), engraved in 1843, 1847, and 1851 respectively, were, among other things, evocations of male camaraderie.[111]

Figure 1.3. John Sartain, after John Blake White, *General Marion in His Swamp Encampment Inviting a British Officer to Dinner*, 1840. Apollo Association engraving. New-York Historical Society.

The Apollo Association's first distribution picture, an engraving of White's *General Marion in His Swamp Encampment Inviting a British Officer to Dinner*, embodied the goals and vision of the organization. It was significant not only that the artist was a South Carolinian, but also that the scene was simultaneously southern and national. The image was a visual reminder of the shared history that managers' saw as an antidote to sectional conflict.[112] At the same time, the picture can be read as a visual representation of precisely the sort of republican vision that helped to shape the organization. It depicts the manly dignity of Marion, who offers food from his humble table to the British officer. The equality of the two protagonists is in sharp contrast

Figure 1.4. Vanderlyn's painting depicts the Roman general Caius Marius, exiled in Carthage. It represents traditional concerns about the fragility of republics. By contrast, the great majority of Apollo Association and American Art-Union engravings portrayed distinctly American scenes. S. A. Schoff after John Vanderlyn, *Caius Marius on the Ruins of Carthage*, 1842. Apollo Association engraving. New-York Historical Society.

to the marked inequality of other members of the group. On the left, the slave kneels on the ground, tending to the fire, the only one of eight fore-grounded figures who isn't standing. Marion's militiamen stand resolutely, but politely, to the side. The artist may have placed the Indian to the right of the scene in order to highlight the notable civility of the two soldiers. White's painting represents an exclusively male public world characterized by defer-ential class and race relations and presided over by natural leaders whose gentility and masculinity transcends political difference.

There is no reason to think that African Americans were any more welcome at the Art-Union's gallery than in any of the other antebellum amusements enjoyed by middle-class white New Yorkers, but they were present as subjects on the walls of the gallery and prominently featured as in several Art-Union engravings. Mount's *Farmers Nooning*, painted for Jonathan Sturges in 1836, was the basis of a popular engraving distributed by the Apollo Association in 1843 (see Figure 1.5). In the picture, a young black man relaxes on a haystack in the company of four white males. One of the white boys studiously reads under a tree in marked contrast to the African American lounger; another man rests on his stomach; a third looks on, as the youngest member of the group uses a piece of straw to tickle the black man's ear. The black man in Mount's painting smiles only slightly and conveys a sense of dignity if only through the beauty of his form. He may be the butt of the joke, but the picture also appears to affirm the joys of restful leisure. Mount, who was steeped in the popular New York musical culture created by black New Yorkers, had a lifelong interest in black sub-jects and created representations that transcended the rabid racist imagery of his times. Yet there is nothing in *Farmers Nooning* that could have been construed as an endorsement of abolitionism—a position far afield from the artist's own Democratic Party affiliation.[113]

The Art-Union's 1851 engraving *Mexican News* (based on Richard Caton Woodville's painting *War News from Mexico*) represented the organization's increasingly futile effort to find a position of cultural unity capable of tran-scending the divide between proslavery and abolitionism (see Figure 1.6). The painting had been purchased by George W. Austen and hung on the walls of the Free Gallery in 1849. Woodville was a young Baltimore native studying in Düsseldorf during the late 1840s. He would die at thirty while living in London, having left little documentation to help guide future stu-dents of his work. *War News from Mexico* depicts an array of male charac-ters standing on the threshold of the "American Hotel" and listening as the

Figure 1.5. Alfred Jones, after William Sidney Mount, *Farmers Nooning*, 1843.
Apollo Association engraving. Courtesy RISD Museum, Providence, RI.

central figure reads excitedly from a newspaper. A black man sits on a step
to the side along with a raggedly dressed girl, while the sorrowful and shad-
owy figure of a woman gazes out of a side window. Scholars have seen both
pro-war and antiwar messages in the image. The figure of a young man
raising his arms with enthusiasm may suggest a readiness to sign up for
military service. Yet the other well-dressed young men, positioned near a
sign encouraging "Volunteers for Mexico," can be read as an ironic commentary. As was typical of antebellum American paintings, the African
American figures are placed in a marginal position, but a subversive message can also be seen in the sympathetically drawn images of the man and
the girl, probably his daughter. Was the artist reflecting on the war's impact on slaves and slavery? Were the figures intended as references to the

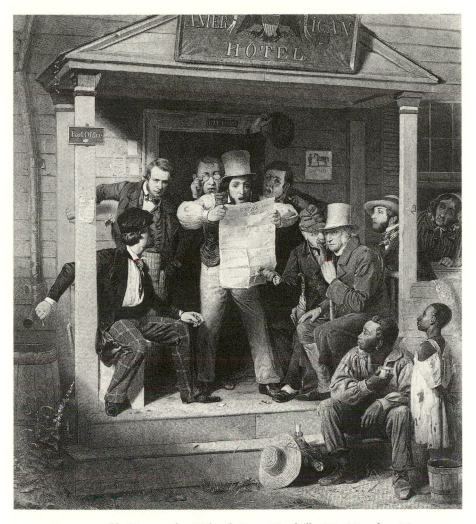

Figure 1.6. Alfred Jones, after Richard Caton Woodville, *War News from Mexico*, 1851. American Art-Union engraving. New-York Historical Society.

looming slavery question? And is the sorrowful face of the middle-aged white woman commenting on the young man's naive enthusiasm?[114]

The Art-Union did not take a position on these questions, though, as we shall see, some northern subscribers were angered by what *they* saw as the picture's unambiguous pro-war and pro-southern message. In fact, the organization's commentary on the *War News from Mexico* is notable for sidestepping controversial issues. In May 1849 the *Bulletin* carried the following curious description of the painting that hung in the gallery. It needs to be quoted in full:

> Woodville's style does not seem as yet to be entirely settled. It is different in the picture before us from that which distinguished the "*Cavalier's Return,*" of last year, while that work was quite unlike the "*Card Players*" of 1847. In tone and general effect, the "*Mexican News*" is less pleasing than the other two paintings. There is also something painful in the truth with which the squalor and rags of the poor negro girl are rendered. But as an exhibition of character and feeling, how admirable is the whole group! How much unity and completeness it possesses! How well the individual peculiarities of each person represented are shown beneath the momentary feeling of common interest which animates them all! The slouching bar-keeper, whom nothing but the recital of something astounding could have drawn from his bottles, is an entirely different sort of person in character and manners, from the free-and-easy, shabby genteel rowdy, who has just taken his cigar from his mouth in order to listen with more intentness. The vacant, unexcited aspect of the aged deaf man, into whose ear a friend is shouting the account of the battle, gives significance to the noisy exultation of the boy who is swinging his cap in the back-ground, and who evidently will be one of the first to volunteer for the war. The old negro sitting upon the step is life itself and deserves a place besides Mount's admirable representation of a kindred character in the "*Power of Music.*"[115]

This commentary has several peculiar features: The author uses the word "painful" in regard to the girl's ragged condition, truthfully rendered by the artist. But "painful" also refers to the aesthetic limits of the artwork, suggesting that the figure of the girl detracts from the "tone and general effect" of the picture as a whole. Especially striking is the reference to the "feeling of common interest" that momentarily transcends the "individual peculiarities of each person represented," even the distinction between the white figures and black slaves. This was precisely the fantasy of unity in diversity that animated the Art-Union. The writer proceeds to make an apt comparison between Woodville's image of the black man and a similarly effective

Figure 1.7. Joseph Ives Pease, after Richard Caton Woodville, *Old '76 and Young '48*, 1851. American Art-Union engraving. New-York Historical Society.

figure in Mount's *The Power of Music*, but in reading the image as a sympathetic racial archetype ("The old Negro sitting upon the stoop is life itself") the author effaced any antislavery meaning it may have had.

In 1851 the Art-Union distributed a second engraving based on another Woodville painting, *Old '76 and Young '48* (see Figure 1.7). It too addressed the subjects of slavery and the war with Mexico, but the Art-Union *Bulletin* interpreted it as a visual representation of unifying national sentiment. The scene takes place in the interior of a house. A young man returned from the Mexican War is talking to his grandfather, clearly a veteran of the Revolution. Other family members listen along with a group of slaves huddled in the doorway. For understandable reasons, some art historians have seen subversive implications in the image. Was Woodville pointing to tensions between the old man and his grandson, thereby raising questions about the

Mexican War? We know that enslaved people kept up with political news by surreptitiously listening to conversations. Was Woodville sensitive to that dynamic? Might he have intended the picture as an image of looming conflict?[116]

Whatever the artist's intent, the Art-Union's presentation of the image suggests that managers held to a different interpretation. A notice that appeared in the *Bulletin* said that the old man was "one of the most attentive listeners" to his grandson's account of the war. Meanwhile, "the other characters are the father, mother, and sisters, and several black servants, whose lively curiosity has gathered them in a group at the door." The young man turns away from the refreshment "and with the most animated air and earnest gestures, describes the perils he has encountered. The others listen with expressions of affectionate interest. The whole subject is presented in the most touching manner, while at the same time the details are painted with great precision and delicacy."[117] A later entry declared simply that the picture had "rarely been equaled by any American artist, in the fidelity with which it represents the kind of emotions which it seeks to express."[118] That managers favored the artist and commissioned the engraving is itself evidence that they saw it as an evocation of emotional affinities capable of binding national across regional lines. In this way the image could acknowledge the troubling subject of slavery while simultaneously marginalizing it.

In 1851, on the heels of the nation's first secession crisis and amid rising northern opposition to the toughened Fugitive Slave Act, Art-Union managers engaged in their own effort to forge a compromise. That year, they offered subscribers six engravings, all of which, according to the *Bulletin*, were "national in their character." But the selection also represented a careful regional balance. In addition to the prints based on Woodville's paintings, subscribers received two northern landscapes based on *Harvesting* by Jasper Cropsey and John Frederick Kensett's *Mount Washington.* Mount's *Bargaining for a Horse*—"a bit of Yankee nature that will be admired by everybody who sees it"—was the basis of a fourth engraving. The sixth print was based on William Ranney's *Marion Crossing the Pedee* (see Figure 1.8). It evoked many of the same themes as the earlier engraving based on White's painting of the South Carolina militia general. As the *Bulletin* observed, it showed "in a most lively manner some of the peculiarities of military life at the South during the Revolutionary War." It was also thematically similar to other Art-Union favorites insofar as it depicted a range of American male types. In this case, as in White's picture, unity and hierarchy coexisted. General Marion

Figure 1.8. Charles Burt, after William Tylee Ranney, *Marion Crossing the Pedee*, 1851. American Art-Union engraving. New-York Historical Society.

and other uniformed officers sit on horses, while the slave who rows the boat appears to be the only character engaged in hard physical labor.[119] *Marion Crossing the Pedee* deployed the image of an African American not to question slavery (much less racial hierarchy) but to naturalize it. In fact, the Art-Union's managers remained remarkably consistent on the slavery question. In 1850, they declared once again that the Art-Union "presents a field of work in which all may unite like brethren. It belongs to the *whole* people. It disregards all sectional differences. It is attached to no party. It addresses the South as well as the North—the poor as well as the rich—the followers of every occupation and believers in every creed. It was established to promote the rational enjoyment—to contribute to the refinement—to elevate the taste of all." What managers referred to as "this season of political agitation" only strengthened their determination to forge unity through culture.[120]

Figure 1.9. Alfred Jones, after Francis W. Edmonds, *The New Scholar*, 1850. American Art-Union engraving. New-York Historical Society.

While African Americans appeared as significant subjects in several Art-Union engravings, the popular theme of maternal influence did not find a place even among those engravings that focused on female figures. Managers consistently avoided the sort of domestic imagery that abounded in publications geared toward women. Even interior scenes (Alfred Jones's engraving of Edmonds's *The New Scholar* (see Figure 1.9) is an apt example) focus attention on male subjects.[121] In scenes devoted to women, managers favored depictions of female vulnerability and submission. A notable example was Huntington's *The Signing of the Death Warrant of Lady Jane Grey*, engraved for distribution in 1848 (see Figure 1.10), which linked contemporary anti-Catholic preoccupations to traditional republican notions of female malleability and weakness. The painting shows the seated Queen

Figure 1.10. Charles Burt, after Daniel Huntington, *The Signing of the Death Warrant of Lady Jane Grey*, 1848. American Art-Union engraving. New-York Historical Society.

Mary being instructed by the forceful Spanish ambassador as she signs the document. The note in the Art-Union's exhibition catalog pointed out that Queen Mary "was persuaded to sign the death warrant of her hapless kinswoman."[122]

Nor did Art-Union spokesmen emphasize connections between painting and household ornamentation. In this regard, the organization was out of step with *Godey's* and other periodicals that were beginning to present home decoration as a significant artistic endeavor.[123] Similarly, the Art-Union distanced itself from the mechanics' societies (and fairs), which simultaneously situated painting and sculpture near goods produced for the comfort and ornamentation of the home. The Art-Union's annual report of 1844 was explicit in distinguishing the arts of painting and sculpture from household decorations or objects of use. "It would," declared the writer, "be a sorry labor were we moved by no higher motives than to provide elegant ornaments for the parlors and halls of our citizens: if such were the case we might as well extend our purchases to the shops of the upholsterer and cabinet maker, as to the studios of our artists." The institution focused on paintings, and to a lesser extent, sculptures as "the palpable expressions of thinking minds; they lead us to something better than themselves, or they are of little worth."[124] For this author and the Art-Union in general, graphic art and sculpture were uniquely capable of delivering messages that had public implications. Not until 1849 did any speaker at any annual meeting suggest that lessons offered by the Art-Union referenced the potential impact of taste on "all the objects and appliances that a refined society needs for comfort and gratification."[125] Such distinctions were subtle, more a matter of emphasis than institutional dogma; yet they point to the managers' central preoccupation—namely, the use of graphic art as a means to national unity among male citizens.

As a staunch preserve of male control, the Art-Union's structure embodied the managers' gendered vision of public virtue. Although women were conspicuously present at the annual distributions, only men attended a well-publicized dinner celebrating the opening of the new gallery in 1849.[126] Honorary secretaries, who were responsible for soliciting new subscribers throughout the country, were all men. Through the mid-1840s fewer than 2 percent of all subscribers were women and from 1848 to 1850, as membership soared, female subscribers never exceeded 15 percent of the whole.[127]

Yet, over the course of the 1840s, the Art-Union's promoters emphasized the Free Gallery's suitability for women and children as a way of distancing it from other, presumably questionable urban amusements. Managers also responded as women became more interested in the enterprise—and in the visual arts more generally. There is some evidence that wives pressured their husbands to join the organization, suggesting that the names of women on the subscription lists understates their actual numbers as engaged participants in the Art-Union project. When John Adams Dix, serving as U.S. senator from New York, wrote to Francis W. Edmonds, requesting a ticket for the upcoming distribution of pictures, he did so on behalf of his wife: "You will much oblige her & myself by putting down my name and she specifically requests that you will choose a *lucky* number."[128] In 1849 the editor of *Godey's Lady's Book* recognized women's interest in the organization by placing a full-page advertisement in the *Bulletin*. That year, in the town of Norfolk, Connecticut, all eight of the Art-Union subscribers were women. The following year Philip Hone attended the drawing of prizes with all of his "lady folks." He noted that the "capacious hall was filled to its utmost capacity, with an audience of whom a large proportion were females." One can only wonder whether the gender composition of the event shaped Hone's perception of it as "dull, monotonous and of interminable length." It may have been in response to female attention that the managers, from 1848 to 1851, purchased eight paintings from Lilly Martin Spencer—an artist who concentrated on images of women, including domestic scenes.[129] Yet it is also telling that the Art-Union never had a Spencer painting engraved for distribution.

The inclusive public culture envisioned by Art-Union promoters had distinctive social, political, and ideological connotations. First, although managers found creative ways to attract subscribers and audiences, those popularizing practices were always grounded in an assertion of aesthetic authority and assumption of cultural stewardship. Second, while most Art-Union managers would eventually join the Republican Party and strongly support the Union's cause, their primary concern in the 1840s was to prevent the slavery question from fracturing the nation. Through images chosen for engraving (and statements that accompanied those images), they affirmed racial hierarchy, sidestepped the subject of slavery, and celebrated the shared Americanism of diverse male types. Third, despite growing interest in the organization among middle-class and elite women, managers were more interested in the creation of cultural unity among white male citizens.

Yet rather than assuaging the slavery question, establishing cultural stewardship, and promoting cross-class commonality, the Art-Union fell victim to the explosive social and political struggles of the 1840s and early 1850s. Only by recognizing the distinctive cultural space occupied by the organization can we comprehend the storm of opposition that eventually brought it down.

CHAPTER 2

The Limits of Cultural Stewardship

The Fall of the American Art-Union

In 1849, at the height of its popularity, the Art-Union became enmeshed in a contentious multifaceted argument played out in the New York press. While some papers challenged the organization for being too popular, others complained of its elitism. And, as the slavery question escalated as a national issue, the Art-Union became entwined with that conflict as well. Opposition came from three quarters, each articulating a distinctive vision of patronage, exhibition, and, above all, cultural authority. The first outspoken critic was the writer and editor Nathaniel Parker Willis, who expressed concerns that emerged more generally in the pages of the genteel, female-oriented press. Whereas the Art-Union promoted the idea of a unified national culture and sought to develop the taste of the broader populace, Willis embraced European culture and championed refined taste as the ultimate mark of social distinction. A second impassioned assault issued from the ranks of artists who charged that the Art-Union threatened to lower the quality of artistic production. Finally, James Gordon Bennett, editor of the city's most widely distributed penny paper, the *Herald*, dealt the third and most devastating blow. He charged the Art-Union with arrogance and repudiated the notion that it benefited the population as a whole. It was Bennett who provoked the court case that effectively terminated the Art-Union by ruling that it was an illegal lottery. Willis and Bennett approached the Art-Union from widely different perspectives, but both of them challenged the managers' claims to disinterested cultural stewardship. In the process, they offered up alternative perspectives on the role of taste within a democratic polity.

Missionaries of Art and the Decline of the Art-Union

Structural weaknesses made the Art-Union vulnerable to the attacks that eventually destroyed it. While the organization was growing during the 1840s as a powerful and controversial cultural site within New York City, it was also making its presence known in towns and cities across the nation. Provincial subscribers were central to the ideological rationale of the organization, and they provided the economic foundation upon which the whole enterprise rested. Letters from agents and honorary secretaries allow us to glimpse the impact of the organization beyond the city as well as its limitations.

The lottery eventually proved to be the Art-Union's foremost vulnerability, but the system was also the engine that drove subscriptions. Prizes won by subscribers could spark considerable excitement in local communities, particularly after 1846 when the managers began requiring honorary secretaries to organize weeklong exhibitions of artworks before conveying them to the lucky winners (see Figure 2.1). As the Art-Union grew, the system worked as planned. In 1845 an honorary secretary from Columbus, Ohio, hoped that he would be able to increase the number of subscriptions over the preceding year because one of his local subscribers had won a picture. He considered it "fortunate that so good a picture came to this place where persons from all parts of the state can see it and become acquainted with the object and design of the society."[1] Another honorary secretary, writing from Gettysburg, Pennsylvania, indicated that the possibility of winning a prize picture was driving subscriptions in his neighborhood: "We are in good hopes that one or more paintings may be our lot—It would give a great impetus to the success of the Union here."[2] Thomas B. White, honorary secretary from New Bedford, Massachusetts, had "no doubt but what the interest of the Art Union will be very much promoted by the exhibition of the Picture drawn by Mr. Clifford—provided it is a first rate painting as I presume it is."[3] Homer Foot, writing from Springfield, Massachusetts, wrote of his town's "great *luck* that two fine paintings should be drawn out of such a moderate list of subscribers, and by two individuals, both in the hardware trade and doing business on opposite [sides] of the street." Foot noted that the "public exhibition" was "thronged" with visitors and "greatly admired by all."[4] In January, following the December drawings, honorary secretaries were overwhelmed with

Figure 2.1. Francis Davignon, after Tompkins H. Matteson, *Distribution of the American Art-Union Prizes at the Tabernacle-Broadway, New York; 24th Dec. 1847*, 1848. American Art-Union engraving. New-York Historical Society.

inquiries from eager subscribers. The secretary from a town in the upper-most reaches of northern New York State complained in January 1848 that he was "besieg'd at every stand to know the fortunes of some 32 members of the A.U. for the distribution of the paintings & medals."[5] By the late 1840s it was not uncommon for subscribers to enhance their odds of winning by purchasing more than one ticket.

Correspondents provided relatively little information concerning the social position of local art enthusiasts, but we know that honorary secretar-ies tended to be merchants and professionals whose social connections would have tracked the middling and elite families who could afford the five-dollar membership fee. The situation in Bristol, Rhode Island, was not unusual. There, an applicant for the position of honorary secretary recommended himself by noting that he was an apothecary and owner of a drugstore and had "every advantage for engaging subscribers being acquainted with the first families in town." A recommendation for another prospective honorary secretary described the candidate as "a gentleman well qualified for this office, and by his position as a member of the bar of this state necessarily brought in contact with many who would not be likely otherwise to subscribe."[6] A letter from Pittsfield, Massachusetts, suggests how enthusiasm for art—and support for the Art-Union—could confirm distinctions that were already in place. In that town, the public exhibition became a festive occasion for the more prosperous residents. The winner of a landscape was George W. Campbell, "a rich bachelor of little more than forty." He invited more than 150 people to the public exhibit of his picture, "where a *splendid* entertainment was provided and the evening spent very agreeably—the 'elite' of our village being present."[7] Thomas B. White of New Bedford seemed pleased to report that "all the Pictures drawn by subscribers have fallen into hands of gentlemen, and men of wealth."[8]

And yet when communities failed to produce a winner, subscriptions could quickly dwindle, particularly as the economy faltered. An honorary secretary from rural New York observed that "in small places . . . if they [subscribers] are not fortunate enough to get a prize . . . the number always decreases; and then new places have to be sought out to make it up."[9] J. C. Partridge, writing from Watertown, New York, was "very sorry not to find any of our subscribers" among the prizewinners at the December 1846 drawing. He feared that "many will be disposed to say that the 'distribution was made unfair' & that it is a 'thieving operation' to fleece the country subscribers for the benefit of those in the city."[10] Hard times accentuated this problem. In 1851 the honorary secretary from Wallingford, Connecticut, expressed disappointment that he had been unable to generate many new subscriptions or to obtain renewals. By way of explanation he pointed not only to a "desolating Epidemic" coupled with "pecuniary pressure" but also to the feeling that "receipts from the A.A.U. had not been commensurate with their expectations (which doubtless were raised too high especially with regard to chances for drawing a prize)."[11] Likewise, William Baldwin of Bridgeport, Connecticut, complained, "Our people look more to the prizes than the support of the Fine Arts and the fact of our not getting a

prize last year rather dampened their ardor."[12] Also in December 1851 the
secretary from Jackson, Michigan, acknowledged that his efforts to add to
the subscription list had failed. Part of the explanation lay with "the
extreme *tightness of the money market*." The impact fell heavily on the
town's "business men" who had formerly subscribed to the organization.
But the writer also pointed out that "many who subscribe do so with the
expectation of drawing a 'prize painting' and as our place has not been so
highly favored they lose their interest."[13]

Dependence on subscribers proved to be a structural problem in part
because they often waited until the month of the distribution to purchase
their memberships. Officials never knew precisely how much money they
would have until the end of the year. As a result, they incurred resentment
by postponing purchases and delaying payment to artists. In 1851, as the
economy weakened, subscriptions dropped dramatically during the autumn
months, forcing managers to postpone the annual distribution. That situation not only angered people who had already joined the organization but
also became grist for critics in the press.[14]

Engravings played a critical role in wooing subscribers, but they could
also become a source of contention. Late arrivals sparked anger that provoked urgent pleas from honorary secretaries. The year 1846 saw many
delays. As one exasperated subscriber explained, "some of us begin to
think we have been duped." Meanwhile the Art-Union's agent, writing
from Columbus, Ohio, complained that a delay of six months in the
arrival of engravings had placed him "in an unpleasant situation and has
done the society no good."[15] "If we only had the *engravings* here now,
while the *excitement* is at the highest pitch," wrote Boston's honorary
secretary in January of 1848, "the subscriptions could be *collected* and
remitted at once." He promised his subscribers that the delivery would
come before April 1 but feared he might be proven wrong. A month later
an exasperated Boston subscriber wrote directly to the Art-Union, com-
plaining that after an entire year as a member he had not received his
engraving, despite the organization's claim that it would arrive in August.
"If explained satisfactorily," he wrote, he would continue his subscription. Otherwise he would "find other institutions to assist with what little
money I have to give."[16]

Although the number of selections grew over the life of the Art-Union,
the choice of engravings was not always sufficient. The honorary secretary
from Kennebunk, Maine, pointed to a dynamic that may well have worked

against the organization, particularly in difficult economic times. Unable to increase his list of subscribers, he observed that "in a village like this, any considerable number of members bring the same series of Engravings into too many families in the same visiting circle, &c."[17] The very familiarity of engravings diminished their value among the sort of people who could afford the subscription fee. Reproductions had their limits when the goal was social distinction.

By the 1850s, sectional conflict was also having a direct impact on subscriptions. Although managers expected engravings to elevate viewers above political conflict, one of the images had the opposite effect. John Hooker, the honorary secretary from Farmington, Connecticut, wrote in December 1851 of having generated only two subscriptions. He believed that one problem was competition from Boston's New England Art Union but the other was the engraving, *Mexican News*, based on Woodville's painting. The Mexican War, widely identified with southern, proslavery interests, was "held in such universal abhorrence" in Farmington "that the principle of the engraving is not very [illegible] attractive."[18] Meanwhile, escalating political tension was creating problems for at least one honorary secretary in the South. From Beaufort, South Carolina, A. McNair Cunningham wrote, "There has been so much bitter feeling in the political struggle in which our state has been engaged for the past season that it has reduced our list rather, together with our universally unsuccessful attempts at obtaining any of the tempting prizes held out to our admiring expectation."[19]

Competition between the American Art-Union and other art organizations created additional problems. The Art-Union's very success in generating imitators probably diminished its own subscription lists. In 1843 some Philadelphians supported their city's new art union in lieu of the original. Several years later the honorary secretary from Geneva, Ohio, expressed his regret at not having drummed up more subscriptions. He believed that competition from Cincinnati's Western Art Union was partially to blame.[20] A correspondent from Albany, New York, explained that "gentlemen" there were interested in the art association of their own town and gave that as "a reason for not renewing their subscriptions to the American Art Union."[21] At the same time the Art-Union provoked resentment among provincial elites by allegedly sapping funds from local projects. Such concerns may well have fueled assaults on the organization in local newspapers. A patron of the Albany Gallery of the Fine Arts wrote Asher Brown Durand that his institution was doing "very well until the Art Unions got agents here, they offer such *apparent* advantages to the people, that they received an income in this city last year of over $2800 when we could get but $1200."[22]

By 1851, some honorary secretaries were losing confidence in the very premise of the organization—namely, that the taste for art could be universally cultivated. In December of that year the managers received a discouraging report. An honorary secretary, writing from an unidentified manufacturing town that he described as "heterogeneous," despaired that the populace showed little interest in art or in "any other subject requiring education or taste to appreciate." Those who subscribed the preceding year were disappointed in their engravings. "In one house," he found "Cole's 'Dream of Arcadia' pasted over [a] hole in the chimney where a stove had been taken down." He noted "similar instances of appreciation" in other households."[23]

Given the Art-Union's dependence on subscribers, the *Herald*'s attacks were particularly damaging. From the outset, Art-Union officials had recognized their dependence on the goodwill of newspaper editors, especially for publicity outside of New York City. As early as 1840 James Herring noted the particular power of the *Herald* even in Richmond, Virginia, where it was "the only paper from N.Y. I meet *everywhere*." He urged the superintendent of the Apollo Association for the Promotion of the Fine Arts in the United States (officially renamed the American Art-Union in 1844) to patronize the paper and keep its editor "in good humor."[24] When the *Herald* went on the attack, it had an impact on subscriptions. In November 1850, James O. Brayman, honorary secretary from Buffalo, informed the organization that "in most instances when I apply to a person to subscribe, they object having read the New York papers which are . . . in opposition."[25] Another correspondent believed that there was "a prejudice against the Art Union growing out of the attacks upon the institution by a part of [the] New York Press."[26]

The Art-Union and the Astor Place Riot

To understand the varied critiques that ultimately undermined the Art-Union, it is useful to place the story in the broader context of antebellum New York City—a context of growing political polarization and class division. Those tensions exploded in the Astor Place Riot of May 10, 1849, when an angry working-class crowd assembled outside the elegant Astor Place

Opera House to protest a performance of *Macbeth* by the British actor William Macready. The violence and controversy associated with the episode provide a useful perspective on the related storm that engulfed the Art-Union. The events at Astor Place also laid bare the intense passions that infused questions of taste and cultural authority during the 1840s.

From the mid-1820s, newspapers had been tracking the rivalry between Macready and the American actor Edwin Forrest, a committed Jacksonian Democrat and hero to white male working-class audiences. The competition escalated in ominous ways during the 1840s as the personal relationship between the actors grew more embittered. Macready, who eschewed the melodramatic style favored by Forrest and the rowdy behavior that popular audiences still claimed as their right, won a following among elite northeastern theatergoers. In fact, prior to the riot, he had made plans to retire to Cambridge, Massachusetts, where the scholarly and literary communities welcomed him. By the 1840s, Forrest was also a wealthy man, the owner of several properties, including a Kentucky vineyard, but he identified with the Irish and native-born workingmen who loved him. Through the mid and later 1840s, the actors shadowed each other as they toured in England and the United States, sometimes performing the same play on the same night in different venues. Reflecting on the escalating rivalry, Philip Hone wrote that there seemed to be no other cause "except that one [Macready] is a gentleman, and the other [Forrest] is a vulgar, arrogant loafer, with a pack of kindred rowdies at his heels."[27]

"Forrest's B'hoys" were itching for a fight when Macready arrived in New York in the spring of 1849. On May 7, they overtook the Astor Place theater where Macready was performing and created such a disturbance that the actor decided to leave the city without completing his scheduled performances. Forty-seven prominent New Yorkers promptly signed a card that they published in leading newspapers, urging Macready to stay. They also called upon the mayor to provide armed protection at the next performance, which was scheduled for May 10. Macready agreed to proceed on that date, but the authorities failed miserably in their effort to control the enraged protesters who tried to storm the theater. Militiamen, who arrived to help the police, opened fire and killed twenty-two people, several of whom were innocent bystanders. In the melee, hundreds more were wounded, including some police and militiamen. Newspapers proclaimed the city to be in a state of "civil war," and some wealthy families temporarily fled.[28] Over subsequent months, reports on the trial of seventeen accused rioters dominated the New York press. The riot exemplified the widening chasm that separated working-class and elite New Yorkers. It also demonstrated that matters of taste could become the arena in which those divisions played out.

There were several direct connections between the Art-Union and the Astor Place protagonists. Forrest and his wife—the British-born actress Catherine Sinclair—subscribed to the organization in 1847 and 1848. They were lionized by the Young America Democrats who formed a significant contingent within the organization. William Cullen Bryant considered the couple to be personal friends, and, in the fall of 1846, when Forrest returned from a tour of England (where he had an angry encounter with Macready), Bryant wrote a note inviting him to a "public dinner" honoring the actor's "professional excellence and private worth." At the time Bryant was serving as president of the Art-Union. Among the forty-three men who signed the invitation to the dinner were several other Art-Union Democrats—Charles P. Daly, Evert Duyckinck, Charles M. Leupp, Jonathan Sturges, and Prosper Wetmore, a longtime friend and admirer of the actor.[29]

Yet, a year and a half later key Art-Union Democrats had soured on Forrest. Seven current or former managers of the Art-Union signed the card urging Macready, Forrest's arch antagonist, to proceed with scheduled performances under the guarantee of armed protection. That the Whigs John Francis, Moses Grinnell, and David Colden were among this group might have been expected, but the appearance of Duyckinck's name is noteworthy. By signing the card, Duyckinck signaled his shifting allegiance from Forrest to Macready and his rejection of Forrest's most ardent working-class supporters. Charles P. Daly was one of the judges who presided over the trial of the accused rioters. Despite his attendance at the 1846 dinner honoring Forrest, he proved to be markedly unsympathetic to the defendants when they faced him in court.[30] Bryant himself did not sign the card, though he appears to have been in New York at the time. But his friendship with the Forrests ended in 1850 when he unsuccessfully attempted to negotiate an amicable settlement to their divorce. Bryant's daughter and son-in-law, the Democratic journalist Parke Godwin, eventually broke with Forrest as well. They sided with Catherine in the divorce.[31] By 1850 Edwin Forrest's ties to the Art-Union Democrats had been severed.

The riot raised difficult questions for the Art-Union's wealthy supporters. Even before the outbreak of violence, Duyckinck had become friendly with Macready and disenchanted with Forrest, whose behavior and followers he increasingly regarded as rude. The riot simply crystallized the dilemma that he and others confronted. An article that appeared in the *Literary World* in August 1849 simultaneously raised and sidestepped the key issue: Could culture, as conceived by the likes of Duyckinck, overcome the deepening social chasm? The editors noted the publication of "a bulky pamphlet on the Astor Place Riot" that contained mostly prepublished articles and documents, but also a commentary. They were troubled that the commentary was "violent in its denunciations of an alleged aristocracy" and expressed regret that one writer, who signed his article "an American Citizen," had sought "to disseminate the absurd and criminal notion of an hostility of castes in this country."[32] One can understand why the editors were horrified by the intimation that Macready's supporters, with whom they were now fully identified, constituted an "aristocracy." Duyckinck and his group, both Democrats and Whigs, still claimed to speak for the whole people, but the democracy, as they had understood it, was rejecting them.

Several months later, an article in the *Literary World* offered a rebuttal to the class (or "caste") perspective that the editors rejected. Entitled "The Progress of Brutality," it linked the events at Astor Place to the "advances of a reckless, lawless spirit, destructive alike to all true progress." The author identified a litany of abuse from violence on the floor of the Senate ("attempts at assassination not only on the floor of the dram shops and in the haunts of vice, but under the dome of the capitol") to urban graffiti ("gross placards, which cover the dead walls and fences of the city, renewed every week with fresh reinforcements of filth"). The author laid considerable blame at the feet of the press, which fueled "this turbulent, unsettled, irresponsible order of things," but also suggested that "movements of benevolence" were no more effective than the police "at Five Points and along the wharves and quays of the city." By way of conclusion, the author reiterated the importance of "that portion of the press which aims to elevate the standard of public character and national reputation." The article, the journal, and, presumably, its editor were still claiming a disinterested or "elevated" position above the fray, but people and processes that they might once have interpreted as flowerings of democracy—the popular press, Forrest's American enthusiasts, debates within "the dome of the capitol"—now seemed to be poisoned by "the progress of brutality."[33]

Despite direct involvement by several Art-Union managers in the events surrounding the riot, the organization's own publications steered clear of the subject. Ebullient claims for the power of art continued to appear in the *Bulletin*, though the emphasis shifted slightly from the public impact of elevated taste to its beneficial impact at home. The Free Gallery opened in September 1849 in the midst of the trial of the Astor Place rioters and, according to the *Evening Mirror*, was "welcomed on all sides, and has been quite an event in the week; a topic of conversation in spite of the trial."[34] That the number of subscribers and visitors to the gallery reached record levels in 1849 apparently kept the managers' hopes high. Yet the social and cultural divisions that exploded at Astor Place would fuel challenges that eventually overtook the Art-Union.

Conflicting Visions of "Public" Culture

Precipitating the Art-Union controversy was the emergence of the International Art Union, an extension of a Paris-based company that made and sold prints. Goupil, Vibert & Co., founded in 1848, was modeled on the American Art-Union. It established a gallery, took subscriptions, provided subscribers with engravings, and distributed artworks through a lottery. Unlike its American counterpart, Goupil, Vibert & Co. purchased European as well as American paintings. Instead of providing exclusive support to American artists, the firm promised to pay the cost of sending one promising American artist to Europe each year for study. It also contracted with artists, including William Sidney Mount, for the right to produce engravings of paintings for sale.

Proponents of the American Art-Union initially welcomed the new institution but soon became enraged. The problem was not simply that Goupil, Vibert & Co. was competing for subscribers. In fact, the American Art-Union officially embraced competition from Cincinnati's Western Art Union and it politely tolerated the expansion to New York of the Düsseldorf Art Union and gallery. The problem was that the French firm was a profit-seeking venture posing as a public institution. "All works imported by these gentlemen," observed a writer for the *Bulletin*, "must be considered as objects of merchandise. They are imported to be sold, however that purpose may be disguised."[35] Another opponent of the French firm noted that "the system of the Art Union is public and voluntary in its character, and not a private enterprise for the advantage of any particular person or class."[36] That the new organization, during its first year in operation, attracted 5,600 subscribers and endorsements by prominent citizens made it particularly ominous in the eyes of its rival.[37]

Moreover, according to the Art-Union's advocates, Goupil, Vibert & Co. threatened to debase the national character by pandering to popular taste. Critics were particularly concerned about the French connection because they associated French art with a dangerous lack of inhibition. They feared that the new generation of French artists was preoccupied with naturalistic representation or "sensual" effect at the expense of moral and spiritual meaning. Although promoters of the American Art-Union heralded the historic and religious scenes celebrated by the Orléanist regime, they recognized that French art "developed since the late Revolution" was moving in new directions. A writer for the *Bulletin* observed that "the day of Vernet, of Delaroche, of Scheffer, is on the decline.[38] That attention to Form and Expression which distinguished these artists has given place now to the study of Color and Effect—of the sensual rather than the spiritual elements of Art." Especially disturbing was the unabashed sensuality in the representation of women. "In a great number of French paintings and statues," noted the author, "the *lascivious* is openly aimed at by the artists." Promoters of the American Art-Union offered as an example a picture of a woman entitled *Erigone*, engraved by Goupil, Vibert & Co., that sold "extensively" in the United States at "$3.50 per copy."[39]

In challenging their new rival, promoters of the Art-Union articulated a distinctive conception of public culture. They celebrated the "public" character of their own organization, by which they meant that it was not a profit-seeking venture, and insisted that art could exert its moralizing power only if selection and distribution were somehow removed from the vagaries of the popular market. The organization, noted one writer, "is simply and exclusively a *public* institution—incorporated by the State Legislature." It was "managed by gentlemen chosen annually by the subscribers themselves, and who receive for their services no compensation in any shape."[40] A defense of the Art-Union, originally published in the *Evening Mirror*, probed the underlying premise of this position by observing that "when pictures are bought to sell again, no other motive need influence the dealer than the desire to make a safe bargain; and if he ever should allow his taste or humanity to interfere in judging the mercantile value of a work of art, he would be constantly purchasing articles above the level of the public taste, and consequently unsalable."[41] "Private enterprise," declared another supporter of the Art-Union, "never did anything for the Fine Arts in this country," because that system "is particularly careful never to under-take what the public does not care for."[42]

Art-Union officials initiated the controversy by planting their challenge to Goupil, Vibert & Co. in a number of sympathetic newspapers. Angered by the favorable response accorded to the French firm, they embarked on a campaign to unmask its alleged deceptions. The response was disappoint-ing to the Art-Union leadership because the New York press divided sharply on the matter, with several prominent newspapers taking the opportunity to suggest that expanding markets and open competition would benefit American art.[43]

Nathaniel Parker Willis, editor of the *Home Journal*, placed himself at the eye of the storm; he moved from a defense of the French firm to an outright attack on the American Art-Union. Born in 1806, Willis grew up in Massachusetts, the son of a successful evangelical newspaper editor. By the time he was twenty-three he had been excommunicated by his father's church, apparently for attending theater. As he turned away from the rigors of his religious upbringing, he made room for more worldly pleasures by elevating the notion of beauty and investing it with religious meaning. He published his first volume of poetry while still a student at Yale, and by the time he was thirty, he was well known not only as a poet but also as a writer for the *New York Mirror*, a journal oriented to female readers that published short stories and articles on cultural topics. In 1846 he founded the *Home Journal* with his friend George Pope Morris. Willis also wrote for Bryant's *Evening Post*, though he was not affiliated with the Democrats. He is per-haps best known today as the model for the unappealing character of Hya-cinth in the popular sentimental novel *Ruth Hall*. The author, Fanny Fern (pen name of Sara Payson Willis), was his sister. As the employer of the fugitive slave Harriet Jacobs, Willis received brief and unflattering treat-ment as "Mr. Bruce" in her *Incidents in the Life of a Slave Girl*. He also played a role in Edwin Forrest's highly publicized divorce trial. When Cath-erine Forrest left her husband in 1849, she sought refuge in the home of Willis and his second wife. Mrs. Willis sat with her to give support through-out the divorce trial. Meanwhile, Forrest named Willis as his wife's seducer and physically assaulted him in Washington Square Park. Philip Hone, who was far from being friends with Willis, declared the accusation to be "an unqualified falsehood" and a further indication of Forrest's low character.[44]

Willis was closely linked to the Art-Union set but also emphatically outside of it. By the late 1840s, he was living in the elegant Fifteenth Ward not far from a number of current and former Art-Union managers. In fact, his second wife, Cornelia Grinnell, was the niece of the Art-Union manager Moses Grinnell. Yet he was conspicuously absent from the various membership lists that helped to define New York's male upper crust. The well-to-do and socially prominent lawyer George Templeton Strong referred to Willis as "the author of the Blidgims story and (according to common report) of other things only not quite so flagitious." Hone was more generous, referring to Willis's depiction of Daniel Webster as "graphic and amusing," despite being "flowery and Willis-like."[45] The novelist William Makepeace Thackeray wrote of Willis's "wit and smartness, his brilliant descriptions," but also expressed "amusement at the immensity of N.P.'s blunders, amusement at the prodigiousness of his self-esteem; amusement always . . . with or at Willis the poet, Willis the man, Willis the dandy, Willis the lover."[46] References to Willis as "the dandy" and "the lover" speak to a key component of the author's marginalization—his seductive success with women and his unabashed interest in matters of taste, including dress.

Willis's flamboyance, affiliation with women, and immersion in sentimental literary culture help to explain his distance from the Art-Union's leaders. His biographer observes that Willis "positioned himself, both personally and commercially, as a connoisseur of feeling and beauty" and noted that "he was unsurpassed among literary men of his day at ministering to . . . volcanoes of sentimental desire."[47] The *Home Journal*, like the *Mirror*, was addressed in large part to women, and the latter employed several female writers, including Willis's sister.[48] That Willis contributed to *Godey's Lady's Book* did not, in itself, set him apart from the Art-Union crowd. (Bryant also contributed to *Godey's* during the 1840s.)[49] What distinguished Willis was the fact that his professional life was wholly intertwined with female readers, and the private life that he publicized centered on friendships with women. In casting himself as the teacher of taste and refinement to the American middle classes, he was careful to acknowledge the critical role played by women in marking the social position of their households. Thus, the *Home Journal* could note that the "elevation and purity of the moral tone of a nation may be pretty exactly estimated from the social position and influence enjoyed by women."[50] By the 1840s, Willis was a celebrity writer and editor, catapulted to fame by an adoring female audience.

If respect for the influence of womanhood signaled one component of what the *Home Journal* termed the "free masonry of good-breeding," appreciation of European culture and tradition represented another critical element of social quality. From 1833 through 1835 Willis sent weekly "Pencil-lings" from Europe to the *Mirror*, and as editor of the *Home Journal* he featured such items as "Parisian Gossip" and "Paris Fashions for the New Yorker." Although he rejected "that nobility which is an accident of birth," he was fascinated by European aristocracy and sprinkled his writings with witty references to aristocratic British acquaintances.[51] Prosper Wetmore, as president of the Art-Union's Committee of Management, described Willis contemptuously as "de-nationalized."[52]

The message that Willis delivered through much of his voluminous writing was that taste—a mark of innate human value—was or should be the true measure of social distinction and power. Unlike the Art-Union's leadership, which looked to the democratization of taste as a source of social stability, Willis pinned his hopes on what he called the "inner repub-lic" by which he meant an exclusive social group with the power to subdue and influence others through the sheer force of its superior taste and charis-matic presence. He laid out his argument in the "Lecture on Fashion" deliv-ered at the New York Lyceum in 1844. Willis began by distinguishing between two ways of understanding the word "fashion." The first, more common usage connoted ephemeral, sometimes "ludicrous" trends in dress. The second meaning was social authority, a synonym for the "inner republic." It signified "a position in society—attained by different avenues in different countries—but, however arrived at, giving its possessor conse-quence in common report, value in private life, authority in all matters of taste, and influence in everything." In New York, Willis conceded, the "inner republic" had yet to coalesce, but the potential was present in the form of "nature's nobility—men of such spirit and bearing, and women of such talent and beauty, as would draw homage alike from the Indian on the Prairie, or the exclusives at Almack's."[53]

Willis saw danger lurking in urban popular culture and argued that the greatest threat to New York's social order was public opinion, which in turn gave voice to "the ignorant and vicious classes." "In our great cities," he observed, "more especially in our greatest city—the proportion of evil in the population gives danger to its sovereign impulse." The people, repre-sented by the popular press, exerted undue power over the laws of the land while also debasing "the arts and all the interests of taste and elegance." It was, declared Willis, "in this monster that envy and ill-will, and the natural hatred of the low and vicious for those above them, find a ready weapon for their malice." Against this hovering menace, the "inner republic" could serve as a counterweight. Whereas ostentatious displays of wealth provoked dangerous eruptions of lower-class envy, "taste," Willis argued, "is instinctive, and homage is paid irresistibly, by all human beings, to supremacy in elegance." It was at once the key to social harmony and the route to social status.[54]

Challenging the cultural authority of Art-Union officers, Willis imbued "taste" with connotations of femininity and European sophistication. While Art-Union promoters sought the creation of a unified national culture, Willis deployed his considerable energy to demarcate cultural hierarchies. Such preoccupations made him vulnerable to the charge of snobbery and dandyism. Yet he remains an interesting figure in part because he cast himself as a proponent of meritocracy. He constructed taste as a form of capital that was complementary to wealth but ultimately superior to it. For Willis, the very purpose of taste was to signify meritorious claims to social distinction.

Willis's break with the Art-Union erupted over the issue of Goupil, Vibert & Co. Interested in creating a lofty position for artists and other professional arbiters of taste, Willis challenged the cultural authority of the "merchant amateurs" who directed the Art-Union. He portrayed Goupil and Vibert as informed professionals and contrasted them to the "mere tradesmen" who demoralized America's best artists by bidding down the price of good pictures. Here, Willis evoked repeated complaints by artists who charged managers with consistently offering less than the price requested for paintings. Artists, observed Willis, were at a special disadvantage in the bargaining process because they were, like poets, inherently incompetent when it came to negotiating market matters. As the *Home Journal* noted, "men of genius are constitutionally improvident, and are so impatient of bargaining that they can be vexed out of half of their proper demands by delay and chaffering." Willis thus linked taste, class, and respect for womanhood by looking forward to a time when "the same feeling that makes it a shame to *strike a woman*, will make it a shame for a gentleman to do what the American Art-Union does whenever it buys anything of merit—*cheapen a work of art below its true value*."[55] Here Willis invoked a web of connections that extended back to the eighteenth century between civilization, respect for virtuous women, and taste.

From Willis's point of view, the problem was not simply the Art-Union's management, but its very system. The logic of the organization, which demanded a growing number of "prizes" for distribution, impelled the purchasing committee to acquire many paintings at the lowest possible cost. The Art-Union had become "guano to mediocrity," encouraging bad painters and discouraging better ones. Willis insisted that "when pictures which would never otherwise sell, and which cost no labor, are openly exhibited as 'Art-Union prizes,' how strong becomes the temptation to good Artists to paint no better, and to sign-painters and coach-painters to leave their mechanical branches of trade, and paint 'as well as that' for the Art-Union."[56] Willis could accept the value of the organization as a "charity," but insisted that a "more reverent and more careful vigil should be kept over the more timid interests of genius."[57]

The point was not lost on Art-Union promoters who did what they could to defend their own more inclusive aesthetic perspective. A writer for the *Knickerbocker* acknowledged that "one overhears constantly in the gallery the most annihilating criticisms" but then went on to ridicule a prototype that may well have been a stand-in for Willis—the man "fresh from Europe" and sporting a mustache who disdained the art of his native land and assumed European airs:

> Every opinion which comes from him is oracular. He has walked through the Louvre, the Pitti Palace, and the Vatican; . . . he has twisted his neck in the Rospigliosi, and bumped his head in the Golden House of Nero. . . . Of course nothing here pleases Kids-and-Moustaches. Not that he sees the pictures particularly; he pretends to be looking at them, to be sure, but all the while is thinking of himself, and trying to remember the big words of his Italian ciceroni, so that he may astonish the bystanders with the learning and pungency of his criticism.

The author believed that "the safest and happiest plan is to encourage a habit of *wide-liking*; to hunt for all the beauties and excellencies in any work which may be submitted to us." Managers acknowledged that some work exhibited in the Free Gallery was "deficient in some points of technical excellence," but they insisted that those very "inequalities attract attention and develop critical talent."[58] Likewise, a writer for the *Bulletin* questioned the opposition's underlying motive by challenging those "pretended connoisseurs" who assumed "that to admire the same picture which pleases an uncultivated mechanic is necessarily a sort of admission of their own want of taste and critical experience."[59]

Willis continued to push for stricter standards of classification while articulating a more rarefied vision of audience. Whereas Art-Union promoters celebrated the diversity of the people who visited the Free Gallery, Willis suggested that the emphasis on prizes and the low level of art on exhibit (notably a bronze statuette of a "naked Indian") promoted a lack of decorum and attracted the wrong sort of viewers. The gallery, he sniffed, had "furnished more than one kind of evidence that vulgarity there finds itself at home." On two occasions paintings had been destroyed by cuts with a knife, and "the scenes which compelled the Committee at one time to remove the sofas from the hall" had impelled many parents to "forbid their daughters to enter the place at all."[60] Another paper that was staunchly supportive of the *Home Journal* evoked similar anxieties about the protection of upstanding woman who frequented the gallery. The writer asked whether the managers were "so innocent and unsuspecting, as not to be able to distinguish a virtuous and respectable lady, from a common harlot of the town." The article concluded by warning that managers should be more careful and discerning, lest the Art-Union "be shunned because of the indecorous conduct of some of its visitors."[61]

Art-Union promoters represented the popularity of the gallery in markedly different terms. They took great pains to note the "decorous" behavior of spectators, and the subduing impact of paintings, but they did not equate decorum with silent reverence.[62] A picture published in the *Bulletin* depicted spectators in conversation, and directors apparently regarded conversation as part of the process by which viewers learned the meaning and experienced the power of paintings. While wryly acknowledging that "noisy school-boys" might disturb one's "meditations," they defended "the multitudes of working men and their wives and children . . . uttering their criticisms in uncourtly phrases." For the art exhibition to do its work, it had to address all classes. An essay, published in the *Bulletin,* lauded the gallery as "one of the city shows, and free to all the world," while ridiculing genteel critics by noting, "It has nothing of the curtained gloom, the subdued whispers, the nicely adjusted toilettes, and the perfume of bouquets which one is accustomed to associate with the exhibition of true 'gems'—veritable 'bijoux' of Art."[63]

As Willis and his supporters frowned upon the Art-Union's inclusivity, they also urged the organization to alter its mechanism of patronage. They pointed to the Art Union of London, which gave lottery winners awards in the form of ballots with cash value that could be exchanged for a painting or statue, sold in preapproved galleries and priced at an amount no more than that of the prize. The London plan promised to open the market in such a way as to answer three of Willis's complaints. It virtually eliminated the aesthetic authority of the organization's managers by putting an end to its annual collection. It allowed artists to set prices for their own work, and it made the necessary accommodation to divergent levels of taste. The winner, suggested Willis, could order "a work to his taste, and whether it be his own portrait or that of his dog, a Storm on the Hudson, or a Yankee Horse Trade, it will be just what he wants. The painter will then receive a fair price for his labor and the cause of art will not be trammeled by the jealousies and favoritism of a committee."[64]

As an alternative to the Art-Union's Free Gallery—effectively eliminated by the London plan—the *Home Journal* advocated the establishment of state-sponsored galleries on the European model and the periodic opening of private collections to the public. Through the contemplation of art, one writer observed that "the pride of worldly differences is abated on the one hand, and the jealousy of them is quenched on the other." But the writer warned that "exclusive displays of native talent" would not achieve the desired result. It was, rather, "the instruction of native talent and taste, by familiarity with a higher order of genius and beauty that is now called for." London's National Gallery offered a model as an institution financed in part by "gifts of opulent amateurs" and in part by the state.[65]

Willis's *Home Journal* openly identified itself with the artist-run National Academy of Design and to some extent it echoed concerns that had been brewing among the city's most established artists. The National Academy had an uneasy relationship with the Art-Union from the outset. First, the very existence of the Art-Union challenged the National Academicians' claims to professional expertise and represented a threatening alternative model of aesthetic authority. Second, at the height of the Art-Union's popularity, National Academicians blamed the Free Gallery for dwindling attendance at their own exhibitions. This was a serious charge because the National Academy depended upon admission fees for its survival. National Academicians not only charged that the Free Gallery drew viewers away from their own institution, but also complained that artists were choosing to sell to the Art-Union and thereby depriving the National Academy of pictures. Finally, National Academicians, like Willis, challenged the Art-Union's system of patronage. They accused managers of degrading the standard of art by creating "a demand for works of Art beyond the power of Art, as circumstanced, to supply." In other words, the Art-Union, in its effort to acquire large numbers of paintings at a relatively low cost, encouraged the spread of mediocrity and actually depressed demand for higher-priced work.[66]

The landscape painter John F. Kensett gave voice to this complaint in a private letter to his uncle. Writing in 1849, he acknowledged that over the preceding four years "the considerable impulse given to the fine arts" might be "in some measure . . . attributed to the Art Union." But he feared that the organization had "induced a number of young aspirants to embark in the pursuit of art who have not the ability to reach mediocrity." That Kensett had recently received $300 from the Art-Union for one of his landscapes—the highest price yet paid for any of his pictures—points to the conflicted experience of many artists. Throughout the 1840s the artists generally sympathized with the NAD, but, as Kensett noted, they looked to the other organization "for something more substantial than mere honorary distinction."[67]

The focal point of institutional competition between the National Academy and the Art-Union was the latter's gallery, an issue that ignited periodic conflicts through the 1840s. Initially, the Apollo Association refused to purchase works from any artists who did not exhibit in the Apollo's rooms at its own annual exhibition. Officials of the National Academy worried that the plan would drain pictures from their own gallery. In response the Apollo modified its rules in 1840 by agreeing to purchase pictures from other New York exhibitions. In other words, artists could exhibit their works either at the National Academy or the Apollo prior to purchase. Still, leading members of the National Academy objected, demanding that the Apollo leave to the NAD "the exclusive exhibition of the works of living artists never before exhibited in the City of New York." This the Apollo refused to do.[68] In a private letter, the Apollo manager John Gourlie expressed his frustration with the National Academy even as he revealed the arrogance that angered many artists. "The artists," wrote Gourlie, "don't know their own interest. If they did they would tell every body to join us [the Apollo Association]."[69]

Managers of the Apollo refused to abandon their central mandate—the purchase and distribution of works by living American artists—but they did temporarily abandon their gallery. The manager Francis W. Edmonds, who was also an artist-academician, mediated an agreement between the organizations whereby the Apollo agreed to give up its annual exhibition.

For the season of 1843, managers not only closed the gallery; they also made more than half of their purchases from current or soon-to-be-members of the National Academy. That year only three of the Apollo's acquisitions came from artists who had never exhibited at the National Academy. Had this practice continued, the two institutions would likely have merged, with aesthetic authority vested in the city's most established artists.[70]

But sparks flew again after 1844, the year in which the Art-Union rented new rooms and reconstituted its gallery as a perpetually free exhibition space that displayed pictures prior to the December distribution. As the popularity of the Art-Union grew, so did the importance and popularity of the gallery. In 1844 the National Academy had to borrow paintings from the Art-Union's gallery in order to flesh out its own annual exhibition.[71] And three years later, when the Art-Union moved from rented rooms to its own, accessible first-floor gallery on Broadway, concerns escalated among the NAD leadership. Kensett noted that the accessibility and location of the Art-Union gallery had "taken away seriously from the interest of the Academy," which not only charged admission but located its own gallery on the fourth floor of the New York Society Library. So serious was the problem for the National Academy that in 1849 it began construction of its own Broadway building.[72]

Among artists, resentment toward the Art-Union focused not only on the prices offered for pictures, but also on their sense that managers were high-handed and disrespectful. Rapid growth of the organization during the 1840s made it more difficult for the managers to maintain the sort of correspondence that might have nurtured better relations with artists. In the end, even some artists who had been favored by the Art-Union came to resent the organization. William Sidney Mount, a full member of the National Academy, had sold at least five pictures to the Art-Union, and two of his paintings became the basis for Art-Union engravings. He was active in New York politics and a favorite among the Young Democrats. Nonetheless, Mount grew disenchanted with the Art-Union. Writing to his friend the writer and editor George Pope Morris in 1848, he complained that the Art-Union intends "to buy pictures at low *prices* to grind the *Artist* down." The system, he believed, would "produce poor pictures." Mount was angered that his brother's picture had been rejected for being "too shelly" after one of the managers had requested "a picture of that kind." Such treatment smacked of "impudence." Several months later, Mount's friend and fellow artist Charles Lanman wrote of a Washington, D.C., artist named

Boggs who sent the Art-Union "two very good pictures, and the other day was informed that the pictures *were not wanted*, the committee not condescending to give a reason." Though Boggs had ample means, Lanman noted that "this shabby treatment has disgusted him, and he will prevent hundreds from subscribing to the miserable concern again." For his part, Lanman sold pictures to the Art-Union and declared himself on good terms with the management, but nonetheless deemed it a "poor concern." Unlike Mount he was an associate rather than full member of the National Academy, but his loyalties remained with the older institution.[73]

Nonetheless, National Academicians were far from unified in their dispute with the Art-Union. In 1841, Daniel Huntington, among the city's most established and widely respected painters, was troubled by what he saw as the obstinacy of his own organization, and he expressed his frustration to fellow academician Francis Edmonds: "probably a little more concession on the part of the academy would have united them [the Apollo and the NAD] much to the benefit of both parties—but it has fallen through—leading only to bitter feelings."[74] Thomas Cole, who would later be honored by both organizations, let Edmonds know that he too blamed the National Academy in its dispute with the Art-Union. He declared his interest in the NAD would be "over" unless there was a "radical change" in the leadership.[75]

For all of the persistent tensions—described in 1847 as a "war"—strong ties also bound the leadership of the two organizations and prevented the rift from becoming a total rupture. The Art-Union's Committee of Management represented the sort of elite patrons that the National Academy unabashedly sought to cultivate. Bryant taught a course at the NAD, and twelve of the managers, including Philip Hone, were honorary members. Francis Edmonds was a full-fledged National Academician. In 1847, when the NAD was in crisis, artists donated pictures to be auctioned off in support of their organization. The Art-Union purchased all of them. At the same time, it featured works by the leading academicians. In 1849 the Art-Union acquired Henry Peters Gray's *Wages of War* for $1,500—more than it had paid for any other single painting. The following year it devoted an entire room to an exhibition of Huntington's work.[76] As public attacks on the Art-Union mounted in December 1851, Gray along with NAD president Asher Durand, Daniel Huntington, John Kensett, and Emanuel Leutze joined seventeen other mostly prominent and well-patronized painters in publicly supporting the Art-Union. In their public "card," they declared their "entire confidence in the honesty and integrity of the Managers of the institution." Durand, who followed Morse as director of the NAD, was an Art-Union favorite.[77]

The Century Association, founded in 1847 by former members of the Sketch Club, solidified social ties between leading figures in New York's two most prominent art organizations. The original membership, consisting of forty men, linked leading academicians such as Thomas S. Cummings, Durand, Gray, and Huntington to eleven Art-Union officials and managers.[78] Others joined thereafter as club membership grew to the one-hundred-person limit. The goals of the new association were clearly laid out in the constitution. The Century would "draw closer the bonds of social intercourse between those who should be better known to each other, and . . . do much to promote the advancement of art and letters . . . which is in accordance with the progressive century in which we live."[79]

The most vociferous attacks on the Art-Union came not from the ranks of the National Academicians, but from a second and third tier of artists who were excluded from the social circle represented by the Century. The *Bulletin* charged that these men were simply expressing private resentment over rejection, and to some extent this was correct. But challenges by artists also revealed deeper concerns about the Art-Union's control over the market for painting. Complaints by the landscape artist Thomas Doughty provide a case in point. Doughty, based in Philadelphia for much of his career, had been a leading artist of the 1830s, but he never rose from the ranks of honorary membership in the National Academy. By the 1840s, his reputation had waned. Although the Art-Union purchased about fifty of his pictures from 1839 through 1850, it bought nothing from him in 1851. That year Doughty published a letter charging the organization for giving him a "cold shoulder" during a fifteen-month illness. He denounced the Art-Union for spending "their means in a most prodigal manner on some half-dozen or so of pet artists" while refusing to give "even a crumb for others." The organization, insisted Doughty, was dictating "in matters which it knows nothing about." Yet Doughty's obvious dependence on the Art-Union gave the lie to his reminder that there were "other sources for the sale of pictures."[80]

During the 1840s, a group of New York artists attempted to construct an alternative system of patronage and exhibition. Most notable was John K. Fisher, a historical painter and copier of European masters who, like Doughty, never rose from the ranks of honorary membership in the

National Academy. As early as 1841 he wrote to the Committee of Management suggesting a plan that he thought would "coincide with the objects of the [Apollo] Association." Before the Art-Union had opened its own Free Gallery, Fisher proposed the establishment of a gallery to be paid for by the city and open, free of charge, to the public. He disputed the widespread assumption that voters would oppose such a plan, pointing out that it would require but a small amount from each taxpayer. "Without intending any disrespect to those who have labored to establish the different institutions now existing," he believed that they had "judged erroneously of the people's disposition; and to have adopted plans which cannot have the highest success because they cannot combine the means of all classes." Fisher suggested that public "agents," responsible for the purchasing, be required to pay no more than "half or a third" of the value of any work. Artists would have to return that amount if their artwork went unsold, but if a buyer bought the picture from the gallery, the artist would then receive the full price. Fisher also hoped that some of the artworks would become the property of the city and part of a permanent collection. It is significant that Fisher referred to the Art-Union as a "private Association," thereby countering the managers' identification of themselves with the public.[81]

Although Fisher's plan of 1841 shifted control from self-appointed stewards of culture to the city government, it allowed a place for the sort of elite amateurs who sat on the Committee of Management: "A private Association, like the Apollo, can do many things which, it seems, cannot be left to public officers." Whereas the Apollo (and later the Art-Union) concentrated on American scenes, Fisher suggested that the organization might use its funds to send artists "to Egypt and other countries to paint proper representations." He believed that such an Association "would watch over the interests of the public Institution, direct its operations & . . . aid it in procuring the higher class of works." And in an ambiguous statement he even suggested that Apollo's system of purchase and distribution might be continued if "the public agents cannot be entrusted with an independent management of funds." In that event, only the gallery itself would be paid for directly by taxpayers.[82]

Over the course of the decade, Fisher turned away from the Art-Union. That he sold only two small paintings to the organization and none at all between 1841 and 1849, must have contributed to his sense of alienation. By 1850 he was advocating a cooperative plan that would expand the market for painting while guaranteeing to all artists at least minimal support. Fisher joined Willis's *Home Journal* in arguing for the establishment of public galleries in big cities to house various collections, but he went further by formulating specific proposals designed to protect and encourage artists who lacked extensive patronage. He wanted galleries to display copies of European masters and works acquired by different art unions. Artists would "be allowed to deposit their works . . . if they had merit" in these institutions, and those who gave evidence of "having produced one work of merit" would be able to borrow against the value of an unsold work on exhibition in order "to produce another instead of being obliged to sell at any sacrifice to pay debts." (Fisher did not say how questions of "merit" would be decided, but it is reasonable to assume that he would have identified artists as the appropriate judges.) Paintings deposited in the galleries but not purchased might be sent out in traveling exhibitions "when enough had accumulated." Fisher believed that these "exhibitions for money" would "be successful in the smaller cities, where such attractions are not so numerous or frequent as to have palled curiosity." The provincial shows would expose paintings to potential purchasers, while the proceeds from the admission fees would be divided among the painters so as to provide them with "bread, if not butter."[83] Finally, Fisher joined Willis and others in promoting the distribution plan of London's Art Union, which, he hoped would be linked to the traveling exhibitions. This plan, he believed, "would be highly approved by artists who are not satisfied with the prices offered by the Art-Union."[84]

In September 1850 a group of artists met in Fisher's rooms not only to "inquire into the truth of the charges brought in public prints against the president and directors of the American Art-Union," but also to consider the creation of an alternative art union to be controlled by artists.[85] None of the seven officers of this short-lived "American Artists' Association" ever received substantial patronage from the Art-Union; nor were any of them associated with the National Academy. Fisher's characterization of the group cuts to the heart of the members' collective sensibility. Some, he observed, "do not enjoy that vulgar popularity which is got by oyster fed criticism, Academy and Art-Union influence and patronage, and other means that true artists regard with aversion."[86]

It is no coincidence that Doughty and eventually Fisher published their charges in the *Herald*. That paper became the Art-Union's principal antagonist, and a little-known British-born landscape artist named Thomas Whitley, as the *Herald*'s correspondent, issued a series of ringing denunciations. Whitley, an acquaintance of Bryant, had sold several paintings to the

Art-Union, but he became enraged by a series of rejections and channeled his wrath through the newspaper. Notably, he had a connection to Edwin Forrest, as manager of the actor's Kentucky vineyard. According to Whitley, Forrest fired him after he wrote a letter to the *Herald* that included positive references to Macready, but one has to wonder whether the letter actually followed the falling out.[87] In the pages of the *Herald* artists appeared as victims struggling to preserve their independent manhood in the face of Art-Union efforts to undervalue the product of artistic labor.

Charges in the *Herald* and several other penny papers were something more than a mirror of the artists' discontent. The papers had their own perspective—their own vision of cultural authority and their own construction of the art market. As scholars have pointed out, the penny press donned the mantle of republicanism by casting itself (or the reporter) as the incorruptible, unbiased critic of privilege. In their effort to attract the widest possible readership, these papers generally avoided aggressive or explicit partisanship. Instead, they marked themselves as the voice of the "public" and played out their struggle against privilege by challenging exclusivity in the realm of culture.[88] The *Herald*'s Catholic editor James Gordon Bennett was an immigrant from Scotland who learned about the newspaper business while working as a writer for the *Charleston Courier* in South Carolina. He presented the *Herald* as politically independent, but he was a virulently racist and misogynist anti-abolitionist whose sympathies lay with the Democrats until the Civil War. William Wells Brown, the author, abolitionist, and fugitive slave, referred to Bennett as "one of our most relentless enemies."[89] *The Herald* was also a staunch partisan of Edwin Forrest and sympathetic to the Astor Place rioters.[90] When Willis sued Forrest after the assault, the *Herald* provided its readers with a characteristically witty and revealing rejoinder. It pretended to summarize Willis's claims as follows:

Item—Damage to his face and left eye $1,000.49
Item—Injury to the top of the nose 565.56
Item—Disturbing three ringlets 464.45
Item—Deranging the moustache 125.75
Item—Dirt on the pantaloons 650.74
Item—Bursting a glove 45.67
Item—Driving a poem out of his head—
    copy-right worth 1,000.00
Item—Hurting his feelings .... 6,086.34[1]

Willis became Bennett's target not only because he tangled with Forrest, but also because his style of masculinity and affiliation with female literary culture was entirely out of step with the *Herald*'s cultural orientation.

Along with Willis, the *Herald* celebrated Goupil and Vibert, and charged that the American Art-Union fostered mediocrity in the name of art, but its point of view was markedly different from that of the *Home Journal*. Unlike Willis, the paper did not challenge the popularity of the Free Gallery. In fact, it focused its charge against Art-Union managers and gave little attention to the broader issues of exhibition and patronage. Rather than fostering a vision of feminized connoisseurship, the *Herald* adopted a masculine, plebeian voice. Instead of championing the cause of the National Academicians, it marked the National Academy as an exclusivist organization, and identified itself with artists who lacked the benefits of institutional privilege.[92] Unlike Willis, who located aesthetic authority in an artistic and literary elite, the *Herald* offered an unabashed vision of market democracy as the most appropriate mediator of artistic value.

Given the *Herald*'s ferocious anti-abolitionism—not to mention the deeply racist slant of urban commercial culture generally—it is not surprising that at least one abolitionist newspaper published several favorable notices on the Art-Union. By the late 1840s the map of New York culture was effectively fractured along the axis that pitted Macready against Forrest. A writer for the *National Era*, an abolitionist weekly, situated the Art-Union firmly with Macready, who had the advantage of representing restraint and gentility rather than the aggressive racism of Forrest's leading editorial defender. The 1848 article entitled "Rambling Epistles from New York" expressed concern about "the whole system of popular amusements." The author saw the theater, "almost without exception, [as] the very hot-bed of vice and indecency" and heaped particular scorn on the minstrel shows. Only Niblo's, where Macready was performing, was "conducted with great decorum." Similarly, the author looked to the crowded Art-Union gallery as evidence that an uplifted democratic culture was possible—that "the People are disposed to seek gratification and instruction from this department of Art."[93] The following year, Grace Greenwood contributed an essay to the same weekly describing her visit to New York. She had spent "some delightful hours . . . in the various picture galleries of the city," including the Art-Union. Only the exhibition of the International Art Union drew her disapproval for being "too distinctly French." She described the style of the French pictures as "meretricious," by which she seemed to mean tawdry. Attacks heaped on the Art-Union by Bennett's *Herald* undoubtedly raised its standing for Greenwood and her abolitionist friends.[94]

For all the managers' efforts to transcend the slavery question, they could not prevent Bennett from calling the Art-Union an abolitionist organization. The *Herald* described the managers as an "abolition clique" that secretly used the proceeds of its ostensibly public organization to further the supposedly nefarious goals of Henry J. Raymond in the founding of his own "abolition journal," the *New York Daily Times*. During 1850–1851, Raymond was serving in the New York State Assembly as an antislavery Whig. In order to expand the circulation of his new paper, he printed an Art-Union notice in an early issue of the *Times* and sent it out to a list of former Art-Union subscribers. On that basis Bennett charged the Art-Union with diverting funds to support the cause of abolitionism.[95]

Above all, the *Herald* challenged the Art-Union's identity as a public institution. It reviled the alleged duplicity of the managers, insisting that the organization promoted private, selfish interests. Managers, observed the *Herald*, made annual elections a sham by nominating themselves. In refusing to publicize the prices paid for paintings, they were, moreover, manipulating the lottery to their own interest. Spokesmen for the Art-Union insisted that this practice protected the pride and privacy of artists, but the paper suggested that managers, knowing the true value of the paintings, could swindle lottery winners by repurchasing paintings at low prices.[96] Another penny paper, the *Police Gazette*, later claimed credit for having opened the "eyes of the people" to the deceptions of the Art-Union; it echoed the *Herald*'s central point by observing that "the Art-Union is a swindle, and its whole result is to deplete the public purse to pamper the pockets of the few who secretly control it."[97]

The Art-Union's use of a lottery became the focal point of the dispute because the system was itself the target of escalating attacks during the 1840s. Licensed lotteries had a long history in the eighteenth century as a mechanism for raising revenue. They supported such varied projects as the building of canals, bridges, roads, schools, and churches. By employing the lottery, Art-Union officials were identifying their own institution with these widely acknowledged community projects. During the antebellum decades, however, lotteries acquired a new meaning. They sparked concern among reformers who associated recreational gambling with a raft of supposed urban sins from laziness to poverty, financial profligacy, and thievery.[98]

In directing attention to the Art-Union lottery, critics not only linked their cause to the reform movement but tacitly accused city and state authorities of employing a double standard. The underlying accusation was that the power and position of Art-Union managers had enabled them to subvert state authority. The *Herald* observed that city officials had, upon occasion, pressed for the dissolution of lotteries. Why then, should the Art-Union enjoy "an especial immunity?" The author speculated that the managers "rely on their high positions and influence to shield them from the penalties the law awards." "Is a Lottery a Lottery," queried another article, "or is a lottery not a lottery?"[99]

The Art-Union's postponement of the 1851 distribution was grist for Bennett's mill, and when the managers sued him for libel in January 1852, they played right into his hands. The action enabled the *Herald* to portray itself as the heroic public voice, challenged by the arm of privilege: "The Art Union might have swaggered through the world, with its lotteries and its humbug, a few years longer—but when it meddled with a clearheaded and independent journal, that knew its rights and would maintain them, it put its hand—nay, its whole arm into the fire, and has got burned to the very heart. A good warning to insolence and swagger!"[100] When the court squashed the case, a triumphant Bennett retaliated against his accusers by getting the court to issue an injunction against the Art-Union. Pressure from the press eventually prompted the District Attorney to bring two actions against the Art-Union in the State Supreme Court. Victory went to the prosecution. In December 1852 the managers auctioned off the organization's remaining artworks. The event, which was held in the Art-Union's gallery, took place amid considerable fanfare. Managers tried to maintain the organization by replacing the lottery with an annual auction, but that plan lasted only for one season.[101]

The fall of the American Art-Union signaled a decisive change in the patronage and exhibition of American art. The Western Art Union fell victim to the pen of Thomas Whitley and to many of the charges that engulfed its New York counterpart; none of the others survived past the early 1860s.[102] A painter who visited New York in the fall of 1852 "to see what could be done with pictures there" found "on account of the failure of the Art Union, every thing dull."[103] Lilly Martin Spencer, whose career never recouped following the demise of the various art unions, undoubtedly expressed the sentiment of many painters. "I suppose you have heard," she wrote in a letter to her

Figure 2.2. Stereograph, *Children's Art Union*, circa 1870. Author's collection.

parents, "of the downfall of the [American] Art Union which, although it was not a very good institution, still it was better than nothing."[104]

The Art-Union's lingering impact in memory and imagination is difficult to document. A commercially produced stereographic image, probably created in the 1870s, suggests that the organization had become, literally, child's play. Entitled *Children's Art Union* (see Figure 2.2), it pictures children, clearly well-to-do, posed in an elegant room among pictures and toys. A "Children's Art-Union" was also the subject of a short essay in the 1872 issue of the *Nursery: A Magazine for Youngest Readers*.[105] In 1881 a group of New York artists would form their own short-lived "Art-Union," modeled on the original but with very significant differences. Not only was it reinvented as an artist-controlled organization; it also shed the utopian hopes that had characterized its predecessor. Several surviving Art-Union managers would be involved in the founding of the Metropolitan Museum of Art, and the rhetoric of social uplift through art would echo in the museum's founding documents. But art enthusiasts of the postwar years also had new preoccupations.

The Art-Union appeared at a moment in the history of northern cities when it was still possible for upper-crust merchants and professionals to believe that shared culture, regulated by themselves, could become the foundation of social and ultimately national unity. That vision, shattered by the Civil War, was already under siege during the antebellum era. Prior to the construction of postwar art museums, antebellum urbanites were debating the relationship of art to commercial entertainment and the place of art in public life. Rather than serving as an exemplar of shared tendencies within antebellum urban culture as a whole, the Art-Union exposed fault lines that lay just beneath the surface.

CHAPTER 3

Art and Industry

Debates of the 1850s

With the demise of the American Art-Union, new questions rose to the surface in public conversations about art and popular taste, and it was New York's Crystal Palace exhibition that sparked the discussion. That event, which showcased contemporary art and manufactured products, brought American goods into direct competition with those of Europe and turned a shining light on the subject of aesthetic taste. Calls for the improvement of American products went hand in hand with renewed interest in the education of popular taste and the anticipation of new opportunities for artists. But as some commentators looked forward to a healthy alliance among art, industry, and consumption, others were more concerned about maintaining the role of art as a spiritual counterweight to modern materialism. Two journals, the *Cosmopolitan Art Journal* and the *Crayon*, emerged as the primary outlets for the debate surrounding these issues.

Art and Industry at Midcentury

By midcentury metropolitan industrialization was proceeding rapidly, transforming the face of New York City and the experience of living there. The city's population grew from about 313,000 to over 515,000 between 1840 and 1850. By the 1850s New York City was the manufacturing center of the United States, and in 1860 its population reached about 814,000. (That year Philadelphia, the nation's second most populous city, had about 566,000 inhabitants. Notably, the third most populous city in 1860 was Brooklyn.) The completion of the Croton Aqueduct in 1842 facilitated

expansion by giving New York a seemingly limitless supply of water compared to competing East Coast cities. Coal-fueled sugar refineries and
iron production grew apace. By the 1850s, Manhattan had 538 ironworks
employing about 10,600 people. Meanwhile, the manufacture of furniture, textiles, leather, and a vast array of other goods increased. By the
mid-1850s, about 90,000 workers were employed in the city's more than
4,000 factories, whose size ran the gamut from small shops to enterprises
that employed hundreds of workers. The garment industry was the largest
metropolitan employer. It grew with the supply of southern cotton,
demand for ready-made clothing, and the invention of the Singer sewing
machine. The business relied on armies of low-paid outworkers, who
transformed cut cloth into the finished products. The workday in the
garment industry could extend to sixteen hours, and most laborers could
not survive on their wages alone. At the bottom of the labor hierarchy
were single women—the seamstresses and embroiderers—who earned
substantially less than the men.[1]

If industrialization meant hardship for urban laborers, it opened new
vistas for more prosperous consumers. A survey of the city written in 1853
took note of the dry goods stores and warehouses that "spread with
astounding rapidity over the whole lower part of the city, prostrating and
utterly obliterating everything that is old and venerable."[2] Upper Broadway,
the city's main thoroughfare, became an upscale emporium, attracting new,
more luxurious stores. Tiffany's, which opened as a "fancy goods" shop in
1837, turned to the production and sale of silverware and jewelry and joined
other enterprises that moved farther up the avenue.[3] The most magnificent
and innovative of the Broadway establishments was A. T. Stewart's Marble
Palace. Located at 280 Broadway, off Chambers Street, the white marble
structure featured plate-glass windows on the ground floor. It was, according to one observer, second only to City Hall in appearance. The interior
was equally impressive. According to one observer, "The walls and ceiling
of this splendid apartment are very elegantly and chastely decorated with
paintings and the merchandise, to the sale of which it is appropriated."
Stewart innovated uniform pricing and organized the wide array of products into departments. His stock included "the most costly description of
silk stuffs and brocades" and carpets sold in the basement. During economic downturns, he put merchandise on sale. By 1853, the business of the
store was more than seven million dollars annually, and Stewart was among
the wealthiest men in New York.[4]

Stimulated by New York's industrializing economy, the city's art scene remained vibrant during the 1850s and continued to grow in size and diversity despite the economic instability that culminated in the Panic of 1857. The National Academy's spring exhibitions were now the focal point for the display of contemporary American art, but to sell their work, artists depended primarily on studio shows. Into the 1850s most artists still worked and exhibited in cheap rooms in or near the rather dingy building on East Tenth Street owned by New York University, but new buildings designed for artists began attracting tenants. Most notable was the Tenth Street Studio Building, completed in 1857, which accommodated twenty-five of the city's more successful artists. Not only did the new building foster a spirit of camaraderie; it also became a place where patrons and other potential buyers looked at artworks and mingled with artists. The smaller Waverly House, designed by the independently wealthy artist Thomas Rossiter, was a short walk away from the other studio buildings, and it functioned in much the same way.[5]

The number of artists in the city had also grown significantly since the founding of the Art-Union. In 1853, New York's self-described "artists" numbered 173. There were also six "portrait painters" and twenty-nine "sculptors." A sizable community of artists in Brooklyn took advantage of lower rents.[6] But even more significant than the growing number of painters and sculptors was the new sense of identity signified by their use of the term "artist." By the 1850s, producers of paintings and sculpture thought of themselves as members of a distinctive profession, with special moral significance. The founding in 1859 of the Artists' Fund Society, organized for the mutual aid of artists and their families, bespoke the sense of professional community. The group's annual exhibitions would become an important feature of New York's art scene in the later nineteenth century.[7]

Though European art did not begin flooding into the city until the 1870s, it was increasingly accessible to purchasers and spectators decades earlier. For twenty-five cents, visitors could see landscape, genre, and historical paintings of the "Düsseldorf school" not only by German painters but also by Americans who had studied in Germany. (The American Art-Union had featured some of these artists, most notably, Emanuel Leutze.) The Düsseldorf Gallery, which opened in 1849, initially showcased the collection of its founder, John G. Boker, a German-born wine merchant who had served as American consul in several European cities. The Gothic building, located on Broadway, had formerly been a Unitarian church. Gas lighting allowed it to remain open until ten o'clock at night and contributed to its popularity during the early 1850s. In 1852 Thomas Jefferson Bryan's Gallery of Christian Art opened at Broadway and Thirteenth Street, while European paintings could also be viewed at new auction houses and at smaller, short-lived venues.[8]

Meanwhile, the decade saw the rise of several prominent galleries that displayed artworks for sale. They were not yet organized to represent individual artists or to sell work on consignment. Rather they seem to have purchased paintings from artists and collectors. The showroom of the International Art Union was a magnet for art enthusiasts. Its director, Michael Knoedler, purchased it from the Goupil firm in 1857 and two years later moved the enterprise into a large building at the fashionable corner of Broadway and Ninth Street. It featured American and modern European pictures (mostly French) and a wide assortment of prints. Knoedler's gallery continued to operate through the twentieth century. Wilhelm Schaus, who also came to New York as a representative of Goupil, broke from the firm in 1852 and started his own gallery on Broadway. It also featured modern European and American art. Williams, Stevens & Williams, which began as a mirror shop, exhibited painting during the 1850s, including the celebrated *Horse Fair* by Rosa Bonheur. Other galleries were simply rental spaces leased to artists for exhibition. Most notable was the Dodworth Building on Fourteenth Street, which also housed a dance studio.[9]

The 1850s saw a significant expansion of opportunities for professional women artists, linked, in part, to new developments in publishing and eventually manufactures. New York's city directory, which listed only two female artists in 1854, does not accurately reflect the changing environment. As early as the 1830s the National Academy was offering a drawing class for women free of charge, and a small but growing group of women exhibited their work in the National Academy's shows. In 1851, Lilly Martin Spencer, whose work had been distributed by the American Art-Union and actively promoted by the Western Art Union, joined a small number of women artists awarded honorary membership by the National Academy. More significant was the establishment of the New York School of Design for Women, which merged with Cooper Union in 1857. Proponents of the School of Design believed that art-related fields could provide poor young women a respectable means of employment. By 1868 three thousand women had attended the school and sought employment not only as painters or sculptors but also as engravers, illustrators, colorists, and eventually as designers of manufactured goods.[10]

And yet, for artists and art enthusiasts of the 1850s, the relationship between art and industry remained a matter of discussion and debate. That artists were dependent on moneyed collectors and consumers was beyond dispute, but was their work a full participant in the world of business or an antidote to materialism? Would the circulation of low-priced artwork improve the taste of middle- and working-class consumers or drag it down? Did art need protection from the cheapening power of commerce or would popular markets be the means of disseminating taste? Could artists play a role in uplifting the aesthetic qualities of manufactured household products, and could those products acquire the attributes of art? In some ways these discussions extended the controversy that had swirled around the Art-Union several years before, but during the 1850s attention turned toward industrial goods, and female-oriented magazines played a direct role in shaping the conversation.

Art and Manufactures at New York's Crystal Palace

In the summer of 1853 New York hosted an international exhibition of "art and industry" modeled on London's successful Crystal Palace exhibition of 1851. The domed building, constructed out of iron and glass, was a smaller version of its British counterpart. Contemporaries described the American Crystal Palace as a "world's fair," though most of the international displays came from a handful of European countries and their colonial possessions. Nonetheless, visitors who made the trip uptown to the rather remote location on Forty-Fifth Street and Sixth Avenue were dazzled by the wide variety of articles on display. Goods ranged from agricultural machinery to displays of French tapestry, European paintings, bronzes, Sèvres vases, German toys and children's clothing, marble statuary, British silverware, various examples of European and American furniture, raw materials from around the world, foodstuffs, and much more.[11]

As a moneymaking venture, New York's grand exhibition was a failure. Even P. T. Barnum, an investor who reluctantly agreed to assume the directorship as a last resort, could not make it profitable. The fifty-cent admission fee and distance from the center of town had a chilling effect on attendance, as did delays in setting up some of the exhibits. The American

Institute rented the site for several years after the exhibition closed, but in 1858 the building went down in flames. Nonetheless, the Crystal Palace embodied a democratizing vision that celebrated the union of art and mechanical innovation and extended the qualities of art to objects of household use.

The Crystal Palace echoed the mechanics fairs, but also departed from that model. Unlike the fairs, it was a private commercial enterprise, organized as a joint stock company. The bankers, shipping merchants, and professionals who formed the majority of the board of directors sought to profit from the venture. The internationalism of the Crystal Palace also marked a departure from the mechanics fairs, as did the sheer scale of the enterprise. And whereas the early fairs located paintings among objects of household use and decoration, the Crystal Palace marked off the picture gallery. But sculpture, though concentrated in a place of honor at the center and naves of the structure, was interspersed with other objects, including a variety of bells, mantelpieces, cotton rope, Indian silks, a large ornamental mirror, and gas meters, among other things.[12] Although manufacturers were notably absent from the board of directors, the Crystal Palace, like the mechanics' fairs, functioned in the words of one contemporary "as an advertisement for the industrial and trading classes."[13] Proponents of the Crystal Palace exhibition also invested it with a higher social purpose. A statement from the board of directors declared, "If we effect our object, we shall . . . have given an impulse to mechanical skill and manufacturing industry; we shall have raised higher the standard of taste; we shall have extended and diffused the knowledge of the various families of the Old World; and, in so doing we shall have strengthened the bonds of peace and good-will."[14]

Among the exhibit's most committed supporters was Horace Greeley, founder and editor of the *New York Tribune*. After visiting London's Crystal Palace, he became an investor in the smaller exhibition planned for New York. He later published a book on New York's Crystal Palace composed of the *Tribune*'s extensive reportage. Greeley saw in both the London and New York exhibitions important lessons in political economy. Unlike most of his fellow Whigs, he was centrally concerned with alleviating the plight of workers, and, unlike most others of his class and political affiliations, he refused to blame poverty on the moral failings of poor people. At midcentury, he was the only editor of a major New York newspaper to give extensive and sympathetic attention to the labor movement. Having risen from the ranks of journeyman printers, he believed in the fundamental unity of interest between labor and capital and remained suspicious of unions and strikes. But Greeley was capable of imagining structural solutions to what he saw as the related problems of unemployment, poverty, and excessive competition, and he found comforting solutions to those problems in the great exhibitions of the early 1850s. Above all, Greeley saw the Crystal Palace exhibitions as a lesson in the dignity and value of the labor that produced the goods on view. He believed that the displays would imbue prosperous visitors with an appreciation of labor's value, while instilling pride in laboring people. As Greeley wrote during his trip to London, the exhibition would have a "beneficent influence . . . both in inspiring workers with a clearer consciousness of the quiet dignity of their own sphere, and in diffusing, deepening, a corresponding appreciation in the minds of others."[15]

Greeley also found hope and inspiration in the sheer number of products on display. They fueled his conviction that the modern era was bringing boundless opportunities for producers and consumers. There is, he declared after visiting London's Crystal Palace, "no such thing as Over-Production, and can be none," for "if each dwelling in wealthy and profusely manufacturing England alone were to be fitly and adequately furnished from the existing stores, the undertaking would very soon dismantle not merely the Crystal Palace but nearly all the shops and warehouses in the Kingdom." In other words, Greeley looked to a time when people in "every dwelling" would be able to fulfill their "legitimate wants" with the bounteous productions of industry and agriculture. Eventually workers would "afford a demand for each other's labor, a market for each other's products," while labor-saving machinery would limit the hours of daily toil.[16] In the course of his career Greeley offered different suggestions as to how production might be organized. He supported cooperative programs and statist interventions designed to give workers a just return on their labor and employers freedom from social strife. But for purposes here it is significant that he saw expanding production and consumption of industrially produced household goods as keys to solving the labor problem.

For Greeley, the bringing together of art and industry offered the opportunity to democratize art's refining influence. He seemed to echo the teachings of the British moral philosophers when he reminded readers that the "cultivation of the finer arts redeems society from its grossness, spreads an unconscious moderation and charm around it, softens the asperities of human intercourse, elevates our ideals and imparts a sense of serene enjoyment to all social relations." By "finer arts" Greeley meant not only painting and sculpture but also the array of "ornamental and elegant appliances." Industrial production made "luxuries of all kinds" widely accessible. Through "mechanical invention," wrote Greeley, "we have *universalized* all the beautiful and glorious results of industry and skill, we have made them a common possession of the people; and given to Society at large—to almost the meanest member of it—the enjoyments, the luxury, the elegance, which in former times were the exclusive privilege of kings and nobles." Greeley illustrated his point in the course of an enthusiastic discussion of a section of the exhibit devoted to porcelain. "The introduction of this material," according to the *Tribune*'s report, "is destined to effect for statuary what electrotyping accomplishes in the harder metals; it facilitates the reproduction of the works of the finest artists in material less costly than marble."[17]

Although some commentators saw the Crystal Palace as an argument for free trade, Greeley insisted that the exhibition supported the pro-tariff position promoted by the Whigs and later Republicans. For him, an undeniable lesson of both the London and New York exhibitions was that the United States lagged behind European nations in most areas of manufacture. The McCormick reaper might have saved the United States from embarrassment in England, and American daguerreotypes won compliments in New York, but the nation had "few fabrics equal to those of Manchester, few wares equal to those of Birmingham and Sheffield, no silks like those of Lyons, no Jewelry like that of Geneva, no shawls like those of the East, no mosaics like those of Italy." These were, Greeley insisted, "articles that we ought to have and must have, to give diversity to our industry, to relieve us from dependence upon other nations, to refine our taste."[18] The fair would give Americans and the people of other nations a chance to learn about foreign manufactures; and the tariff would enable American workers to benefit from the expansion of manufacturing at home.

It is telling that Greeley gave no attention to the picture gallery, which struck a curiously discordant note for American observers due to the sparse representation of American art. Of approximately seven hundred paintings on exhibit only thirty were by Americans, and most of those were by amateur or relatively unknown artists. Organizers of the exhibit dealt directly with artists who, apparently, withheld their work. The portrait painter Thomas S. Cummings, a founder and chronicler of the National Academy of Design, expressed the hostility that may have motivated other New York artists. As he observed, an "Art Exhibition, in connection with other and 'grosser material'—'*manufactures*'—has always been repugnant to the American artist, and even 'The Crystal,' with all the European example, did not form an exception to that feeling."[19] By 1850, the city's leading artists demanded affirmation of their special standing, particularly as new modes of industrial manufacture were cheapening objects of use.

New York's Crystal Palace did not entirely live up to the vision of its more enthusiastic promoters. The Reverend Edwin Hubbell Chapin, who spoke at the opening of the exhibition, was troubled by the absence of workers:

> I would have liked to have seen there a representation of the Laborers of all Nations. I would have liked to have had them line the galleries, and look down upon the spectacle from that magnificent dome . . . the men who have served before the furnace, and been blackened by the smoke, to make those rich utensils, and the women whose heart strings have been sewed into the fine linen and embroidered on the silk;—I would like to have had them come—from the factories of the free North, and the plantations of the South—from the mines and garrets of England—from the work-shops and labor fields of every land—to show us much, no doubt, that is cheerful and encouraging, but much, also, proving that it is a different thing to honor industry from what it is to honor the toiler.[20]

Even Greeley was disappointed that the organizers gave so little attention to the producers of the objects on display. He was sorry that during the opening ceremonies "no Artist was there. No Mechanic. No Laborer."[21]

An extensive catalog of the exhibition suggests that expensive luxury products, rather than affordable wares, garnered most of the attention. The editors presented readers with 504 engravings of objects on exhibition. They made their selections with the intention of teaching the lesson that "Americans most need to learn—the value and effect of an alliance of art with commercial industry." Where objects seemed lacking in aesthetic sensibility, the authors did not hesitate to comment. For example, with respect to the "works in precious metals," they observed that in "the American department and to some extent in the English, they are more remarkable for their value as bullion than as works of art." But overall, nothing appears to have been chosen with a view toward economy. In fact, the catalog creates the impression that manufacturers displayed their most lavish products in order to attract attention.[22] If the exhibition ignored laborers who produced the products, they also neglected all but the more affluent consumers.

In the end New York's Crystal Palace did much more to advertise manufacturing companies than it did to promote the welfare of labor, and it
featured products that were far out of reach for most New Yorkers. For
Greeley—and perhaps for readers of his paper—the exhibition offered a
vision of the future in which production, consumption, science, and art
became engines of democracy and solutions to "the labor problem." More
generally, the exhibition signaled a growing tendency to blur distinctions
between the taste for fine art and tasteful household consumption.

Women's Literary Culture and the Commerce in Art

Stories and articles, especially those oriented to female readers, helped to
broaden the meaning of art to include an array of manufactured objects. In
the process this literature not only paved the way for women's growing
employment in art-related occupations but also countered traditional
republican (and Calvinist) discourse on the dangers of luxury.[23] Even before
Godey's Lady's Book began hiring women as colorists, it was presenting
female readers with a bevy of stories and articles featuring art and artists.
From 1835 through 1860 the magazine published 174 such articles and stories
in addition to regular exhibition notices. Through the mid-1850s, readers
could follow the magazine's "Course of Lessons in Drawing," but they
could also find validation fur other expressions of artistic sensibility.
Increasingly, writers for *Godey's* suggested that tasteful consumption,
extending beyond the acquisition of painting and sculpture, was itself a
form of artistic expression.

Popular writers imbued consumption itself with artistic sensibility by
suggesting that artistic quality might be embodied within an array of household possessions. The author of a short biography of artist and banker
Francis W. Edmonds noted that "a principle of truth or beauty infuses
itself through the whole range of social wants, from the highest demand of
imagination to the most common of domestic necessities." For this writer,
Wedgwood china exemplified the union of beauty and utility. Another article in *Godey's*—a review of an exhibition at the Pennsylvania Academy—
made essentially the same point: "To costliness or elegance of furniture

there can be no objection;—only let it be real elegance. . . . House decoration is *an art*, and should be entrusted only to those who feel as artists or love as poets."[24]

Godey's was explicit in urging a closer relationship between the fine arts and the full spectrum of useful products. An essay published in 1848 suggested that "the principles of good taste" be extended to the "mechanic arts": "the highest ingenuity and the purest taste may be exercised in various and very different productions; and whether genius is exhibited in the composition of a fine picture, a noble piece of sculpture, a beautiful piece of cabinet work, a delicate and tasteful production of the loom, in a set of porcelain, or in a common stove, we give it our involuntary regard, and do honor to the mind which has designed, and to the hand which has wrought it into its perfect form." The author invoked Renaissance Italy where "the ornamental artisan was considered worthy of fellowship with the highest in the land" and suggested that American artisans would enjoy a comparable status when they became "more thoroughly instructed in the principles of taste, and raise the standard of ornament in the several branches of manufacture to which they belong."[25] An editorial published the following year extended the point by urging readers to recognize that "life is an art and not an accident; and that in all its phases, be it habitation, clothes, occupation or gastronomy, the artistic must be paramount."[26]

In 1854 a new organization mobilized female art enthusiasts on behalf of a distinctly commercial orientation to art and artists. The Cosmopolitan Art Association, based in Sandusky, Ohio, and New York City, was the creation of Chauncey L. Derby, a Sandusky book dealer and publisher. His stated goal was to "encourage and popularize the Fine Arts, and to disseminate pure and wholesome literature throughout the country." For an annual three-dollar fee, subscribers to the association received a chance to win one of the paintings or sculptures acquired by the organization. In addition, subscribers received an engraving of a work of art or a one-year subscription to any three-dollar monthly or quarterly journal published in the United States. The roster of choices included *Graham's American Monthly Magazine*, which was geared to a female readership, as well as *Godey's Lady's Book*. By 1856, Derby was having difficulty handling the distribution of the various journals and wound up substituting the association's new amply illustrated quarterly magazine. Derby hired Orville J. Victor, who would develop a career as an editor and writer of dime novels, to edit the New York–based publication. The Cosmopolitan Art Association held its annual distribution at its Sandusky gallery, but in 1857 it acquired a New York base when it purchased the Düsseldorf Gallery. That year subscribers numbered over thirty-three thousand, the high point of the association.[27]

The Cosmopolitan Art Association bore some resemblance to the American Art-Union and presented itself as a successor to the earlier organization, but it would be a mistake to overstate the similarities. Although it focused on American art and artists, it also purchased, distributed, and engraved European paintings. More significantly, the Cosmopolitan Art Association was a commercial enterprise, run by professionals in the publishing business, rather than an avowedly noncommercial enterprise run by wealthy amateurs. And, unlike the Art-Union, the Cosmopolitan oriented itself to a female market. The *Cosmopolitan Art Journal* actively promoted the work of female artists, most notably, the Ohio-born painter Lilly Martin Spencer. It also had regular female contributors, including Metta Victoria Victor, the prolific author of dime novels and wife of the editor. Honorary secretaries were men, but the *Journal* appealed to its "army of lady friends" by offering "the *fair* sex . . . a perfect *carte-blanche* permit to canvass for the Association" and promising a three-hundred-dollar prize to "the lady who shall send us the largest number of subscribers. *Three hundred dollars!*" Those who drew "even fifteen subscribers at one time" would receive smaller rewards in the form of an engraving and journal subscriptions.[28] The editor believed that the *Journal* would be welcomed "in the family circle" and urged the "daughter or mother [to] use it as a means to introduce the Association to her circle of friends."[29] In 1860, the *Journal* gave special attention to women artists represented at an exhibition of the National Academy by celebrating "the field of competition being thrown open by the genial spirit of the age, that seems to delight in conceding to woman a position which she never before has held."[30]

Unlike the American Art-Union, the Cosmopolitan Art Association generally chose images for engraving that featured female subjects. One notable example was based on a painting called *The Favors of Fortune* by the English artist Abraham Solomon. The eighteen-by-twenty-five-inch engraving, also produced in London, depicted a female fortune-teller with cards spread on a table before two sisters. The opulently dressed younger sister seems pleased by what she hears, but the other listener, "dressed in pure white, in fine keeping with her seemingly sedate and pure character," has a more sober expression. The image, as described in the *Journal*, evokes

Figure 3.1. The cover of the *Cosmopolitan Art Journal*, which depicts a female artist, writer, and reader, signaled its orientation to women and support for female artists. Among the journals depicted beside the globe (and initially offered along with the subscription) is *Godey's Lady's Book*. Courtesy American Antiquarian Society.

sentimental stories about virtuous womanhood and invites viewers to fill
in the gaps. The reference to the upright "cottage piano, to the right of the
first figure," would not have been lost on viewers. By the 1850s, pianos were
becoming more accessible to middle-class purchasers who recognized them
as a sign of refinement and elevated taste. In fact, prior to his full-time
engagement with the Cosmopolitan Art Association, Chauncey Derby took
up the sale of pianos along with his book business. As the *Journal*'s writer
pointed out, the instrument "serves to throw over the scene the presence of
music's refining influence." The association named the engraving *Manifest
Destiny*—a double entendre that emphasized the distinctive layer of meaning that attracted its "army of lady friends."[31]

Although the *Journal* featured painting and sculpture, it also gave attention to urban manufactures and retail as partners in the refining process. The
writer of the first entry in a series titled "The Department of Useful Art"
celebrated the rapid rise of manufacturing enterprises that required "palaces"
for the display of products. The subject of the piece was E. V. Haughwout, a
"manufacturing and sales establishment" on lower Broadway that "embraces
more in value and interest than any single building in the world if we except
the Crystal Palace at Sydenham, England." The company produced and sold
silverware "from the simplest to the most artistically elaborate," china and
porcelain "of richness and variety that challenge comparison for beauty, fitness, and excellence," and glassware "of such varied forms and exquisite
workmanship as almost defy description: chandeliers, of every imaginable
design and value—all manufactured under that one roof." The author
believed that people who shopped at Haughwout "must be refined, intelligent, energetic, prosperous; and we may well think our art—*American art*—
has a glorious future." Having seamlessly equated the taste for art with the
tasteful consumption of household products, the author signaled respect for
the skilled workmen who manufactured the goods. "Artisans," suggested the
article, "were the men most thought of and sought for . . . who are fast giving
character and tone to Metropolitan society."[32]

By collapsing the figures of the artist and the artisan, a story published
in the *Journal* drew comparable connections between fine art and decorative household display. "Palissy the Potter: An Art Romance," set in prerev-
olutionary France, was very loosely based on the life of Bernard Palissy,
widely known among British and American consumers as the inventor of
majolica pottery, which was highly popular in the mid-nineteenth century.[33] In the story, Palissy's identification as an artist is signaled not only

Figure 3.2. *Manifest Destiny*, engraving by Frederick Bacon after Abraham Solomon, printed by H. Peters. Dedicated to the members of the Cosmopolitan Art Association for the year 1857–1858. Courtesy American Antiquarian Society.

by his passionate creativity, but also by his "worship of Nature." Yet the pinnacle of Palissy's artistic work is the production of decorative tile for a noble patron who exclaims: "The stately, dearly prized Chateau d'Ecouen, a deserted castle of my fathers, thy fantastic genius hath transformed into a very realm of Eden."[34] The story not only celebrates the luxurious environment of Palissy's aristocratic client; it also extends the special qualities of art to manufactured household products highly valued by mid-nineteenth-century consumers.

Above all, the Cosmopolitan Art Association promoted popularity, reproduction, and commerce as keys to the dissemination of artistic taste. Derby and Victor had no apparent connection to the upper-crust social world that linked Art-Union managers to New York's leading artists, and they refused to accord art or artists a special noncommercial status. If the goods on sale at Haughwout's were a form of art, so too, suggested the *Journal*, were artworks distributed by the association a form of commercial product. An entry titled "The Dollars and Cents of Art" declared that "the great laws of demand and supply hold as good in the world of painting and sculpture as in the world of utilitarian art." The growing number of artists was indicative of growing demand. The author believed that "the more works produced the better, even if some of them *are* inferior." The result of competition among artists would be to lower the price of art and ultimately improve its general quality—"*good* works of the easel" would be "placed within easy reach of persons of small means and moderate pretentions."[35] The *Journal*, which on other occasions did not hesitate to criticize the English art critic John Ruskin, took the opportunity to quote him on the subject of "economy in art." Allowing that "art should not be made cheap beyond a certain point," Ruskin also suggested that "one of the principal obstacles to the progress of modern art was the high price given for modern pictures."[36]

For the Cosmopolitan Art Association, popularity, filtered by the tastes of middle-class women, was the paramount guide in selecting pictures for distribution and reproduction. In 1857 the journal announced the acquisition of Lilly Martin Spencer's *Shake Hands* along with the publication of a new engraving of the painting for distribution to subscribers. "Perhaps no picture painted in this country," declared the journal's essay on Spencer, "is better fitted for popular appreciation." The writer took the opportunity to note that *Shake Hands* was already "familiar from the Paris lithograph made of it, and from the exhibition of it in Cincinnati, New-York, &c. It is one of the few pictures whose popularity increases with every exhibition." The woman in the picture, with her hands covered in the mixture from the bowl, seems to reach out to a viewer who presumably shares in the joke. Whether Spencer intended the figure to be a servant or a young middle-class wife, she was drawing attention to her subject's confidence and competence. The scene as a whole portrays cooking not only as women's domain but also as a form of skilled labor. As an affirmation of shared female experience, the image is a far cry from the male-oriented genre pictures favored by the American Art-Union.[37]

Derby and Victor celebrated engraving and illustration as a means of disseminating art and artistic taste. And, like Greeley, they saw promise in those fields as means of employment. As one of the journal's writers observed, there was "such a constant and ever increasing demand for illustrations upon wood for every conceivable purpose . . . that it cannot but furnish remunerative and reliable occupation to all who excel in it. . . . Of course, the more genius is brought to its improvement and perfection, the more admirable will be the already delightful results. The popular taste will be moulded very much by its standard of merit."[38] Another entry noted improvement in several forms of reproduction, including the introduction of color through chromolithography and the transition from copper engraving to the more durable steel plates. As the author observed, "we now have beautiful engravings, executed in the first style of art, which reproduce and almost infinitely multiply the finest productions of native and foreign talent."[39]

The subject of photography drew a more measured response, but there, too, the *Journal* advocated on behalf of innovation and mechanical reproduction. The author of a lengthy two-part article argued that photographs could not replace paintings or engravings as works of art. However, the new technology could be an invaluable aid to artists and, with respect to miniature portraits, might well replace the work of lesser practitioners. The role of photography was "to give evidence of facts, as minutely and as impartially as, to our shame, only an unreasoning machine can give." In that capacity it would "supersede much that art has hitherto done, but only that which it was both a misappropriation and a deterioration of art to do." Customers were already turning to photography rather than commissioning miniature portraits. Although some artists would have to find alternative employment, the author insisted that "such improvements always give more than they take." The "self-styled artists" who struggled to make a

Figure 3.3. Thomas Phillbrown after Lilly Martin Spencer, *Shake Hands*, lithograph published in the *Cosmopolitan Art Journal* 2, no. 1 (December 1857). Courtesy American Antiquarian Society.

living by producing "inferior miniatures" could become photographers or find employment in photographic studios that employed artists "in touching, and coloring, and finishing from nature those portraits for which the camera may be said to have laid the foundation."[40]

In short, the Cosmopolitan Art Association, like the Crystal Palace exhibition, signaled a widespread movement to popularize taste and extend the qualities of art to manufactured domestic objects. It would be a mistake to characterize the organization or its journal as "democratic" without qualification. It did not address itself to laboring people for whom the three-dollar subscription fee would have been prohibitive. And the women's culture of which the *Journal* was a part promoted its own distinctive forms of class and racial hierarchy. Nonetheless, the association was notable for attempting to disseminate art and artistic taste without the mediating influence of cultural stewards. And, by celebrating the popular market in culture, the Cosmopolitan Art Association incurred the wrath of a young, energetic cadre of artists and self-styled critics associated with a competing journal called the *Crayon*.

Art Criticism and the *Crayon*

The *Crayon* began publication in 1855 as a weekly devoted entirely to the subject of art. Like the *Cosmopolitan Art Journal*, it promoted work by female artists and writers and sought female readers. According to one estimate, about one-third of the subscribers were women. In other respects, the two publications might have been designed in opposition to one another. Along with stories, reviews, biographical essays, and poetry, the *Crayon* carried philosophical and scholarly pieces that must have been difficult going even for engaged nineteenth-century readers. The editors refused to include illustrations, not only because reproductions were expensive, but also because they were loath to indulge popular preferences. Unlike the *Cosmopolitan Art Journal*, the *Crayon* sought to uplift taste by promoting high standards of art criticism. And, unlike its rival, the *Crayon* consistently celebrated art as the antithesis of modern materialism. During a period in which the nation's most successful monthlies exceeded 100,000 in annual sales, the *Crayon*'s circulation likely reached between 15,000 and 20,000—well below the numbers achieved by the *Cosmopolitan*. Yet the *Crayon* was significant not only because it articulated a position widely shared among artists and art enthusiasts of the 1850s but also because members of the group affiliated with the journal would reemerge after the Civil War as outspoken and influential critics.[41]

The creator of the *Crayon* was a twenty-seven-year-old New York artist and journalist named William James Stillman. He was born in Schenectady, the youngest of nine children. His father was a machinist-inventor and carpenter who lost all of his money in a Rhode Island business venture. Stillman described his father as a strict disciplinarian—"apparently a cold, hard man"—but also a devoted lover of nature. He recalled walks with his father "in the face of nature" and "botanizing excursions" with his brothers as enjoyable moments in an otherwise difficult childhood. Stillman was devoted to his mother, a devout fundamentalist Baptist, but later speculated that "only the absorbing activity of her daily life . . . prevented her from falling into religious insanity." Although he eventually turned away from his mother's orthodoxy, he gave her credit for his lasting "unconscious aspiration in prayer and . . . absolute trust in the protection of the divine providence." He also credited her for overseeing the education of her children and taking in laundry to help cover the cost of his tuition at Union College.[42]

By 1848, the year of his college graduation, Stillman had decided to seek training in art beyond what he had received in Schenectady. He followed his brothers and parents who had already moved to New York City and joined the burgeoning community of artists and intellectuals. Especially important to him during this period was the Brooklyn salon of the sculptor Henry Kirk Brown and his wife. There he became acquainted with artists and transcendentalist intellectuals not only from New York but also from Boston and Philadelphia. It may have been through these connections that Stillman met William Cullen Bryant, who hired him as the fine art editor of the *Evening Post*. For a brief period, Stillman turned to Frederic Church for training and, over the course of several years, sold three pictures to the Art-Union.[43]

Stillman credited his friends for recommending that he edit a journal. "It was," he later wrote, "a natural consequence of all this talking and writing about art." He believed that the *Crayon* would be sufficiently lucrative to support him in his career as an artist, and he turned to John Durand, devoted son of the eminent painter Asher Durand, to coedit, raise funds, and handle the marketing. Stillman's brother Thomas, partner in the Novelty Ironworks—the largest ironworks in New York—contributed half of the necessary capital. Stillman proceeded to win support from the close-knit Boston-area literary and scholarly community. The group included the young Charles Eliot Norton, who would become Harvard's first professor of fine art, Louis Agassiz, the Harvard scientist who promoted the racial theory of polygenesis, Thomas G. Appleton, the publisher, Edwin Percy Whipple, a prominent literary critic, and the poets James Russell Lowell and Henry Wadsworth Longfellow. Ralph Waldo Emerson, who was a towering public figure by the mid-1850s, was also a supporter of the journal and an increasingly important figure for Stillman. The transcendentalist writers Brownlee Brown and Justin Winsor would become regular contributors. Stillman and Durand also secured contributions from other prominent writers such as Lydia Sigourney and Lucy Larcom, whom Stillman referred to as "the truest poetess of that day in America." The artists Daniel Huntington, Asher Durand, Horatio Greenough, and William Page would publish in the *Crayon*. William Rossetti, the English critic whose brother was the Pre-Raphaelite painter Dante Rossetti, was also a regular contributor through 1856.[44] But it was Stillman who wrote more than half of the first two volumes and most of several early issues. After two years, he resigned the editorship in exhaustion but continued to send contributions. At that point, the *Crayon* became a monthly.[45]

From the outset Stillman and Durand built the *Crayon* around the ideas of the British critic John Ruskin, whose writing appeared in the journal not only in reprinted essays but also in answers to questions posed by readers. Many of the writers recruited by Stillman shared his engagement with Ruskin's work, though not necessarily the same level of passion. As he later wrote, "The art-loving public was full of Ruskinian enthusiasm and what strength I had shown was in that vein."[46] He had met Ruskin, who was eleven years his senior, in 1850 during his first European trip, and the two men developed a friendship that would last for twenty years. Stillman's religious background and reverential connection to the natural surroundings of his youth prepared him for the encounter. Years later he recalled, "Ruskin held very strong Calvinistic notions, and as I kept my Puritanism unshaken we had as many conversations on religion as on art, the two being then to me almost identical and to him closely related."[47]

By the time the *Crayon* began publication Ruskin was approaching the high point of his reputation in the United States. He had published the first three volumes of *Modern Painters* (1843–1856), *The Seven Lamps of Architecture* (1849), and *The Stones of Venice* (1851). American tourists were using his books to guide them through European churches and galleries, and artists were turning to his work for inspiration. Ruskin built on the work of Reynolds and the British moral philosophers, developing their argument that art, distinct from luxury, served a higher public purpose. But he put religion at the center of his discussion. Ruskin saw divinity in nature and argued that all beauty in art derived from that source. "I have," he wrote, "but one steady aim in all that I have ever tried to teach, namely—to declare that whatever was great in human art was the expression of man's delight in God's work."[48] He celebrated the work of the painter J. M. W. Turner not only because Turner observed natural phenomena—the "facts" of nature—so closely but also because he was able to move beyond imitation to the communication of deeper emotional and spiritual truths. Ruskin celebrated the artist's imagination not as a form of *self*-expression, but rather as the expression of feelings and ideas evoked by nature itself. In some ways Ruskin echoed the nature worship of American transcendentalists and landscape painters, and his deep religiosity spoke more generally to many Americans of Stillman's generation and cultural background.[49]

With respect to modern manufactured products, whether made by machine or through the division of human labor, Ruskin presented a stinging critique. He believed that "no machine yet contrived, or hereafter contrivable, will ever equal the fine machinery of the human fingers," and he insisted that the very uniformity of manufactured products reflected the dehumanization of the labor that produced it. As Ruskin famously wrote in *The Stones of Venice*, "We have much studied and much perfected, of late, the great civilized invention of the division of labour; only we give it a false name. It is not, truly speaking, the labour that is divided; but the men:—Divided into mere segments of men—broken into small fragments and crumbs of life."[50] Ruskin recognized the value and necessity of mass-producing some goods, but he urged that industrial production be kept to a minimum. Whereas manufactured products bore the mark of workmen turned into machines, artisanal products, with all their irregularity and imperfection, could embody human inventiveness and feeling. In Ruskin's view, Gothic cathedrals contained all of the qualities that he missed in modern industrializing society. They united the soaring designs of educated architects with the thoughtful inventiveness of skilled workmen; they embodied close attention to organic forms and profound religious feeling.[51]

For Ruskin, London's Crystal Palace embodied much that was wrong with modern society. If, as he argued, "the value of every work of art is exactly in the ratio of the quality of humanity which has been put into it, and legibly expressed upon it forever," the Crystal Palace was sorely lacking. He admitted that "the quantity of bodily industry which the Crystal Palace expresses is very great," but he found the building deficient in ideas, much less feeling. The architect Joseph Paxton expressed but a single thought—namely, "that it might be possible to build a greenhouse larger than ever greenhouse was built before."[52] Ruskin focused most of his criticism on the building, but his outlook on the contents was also dismissive—"the petty arts of our fashionable luxury—the carved bedsteads of Vienna, and glued toys of Switzerland, the gay jewellery of France."[53]

Ruskin's critique of modern manufactured products carried somewhat contradictory implications. On the one hand, his insistence that the mode of production shaped the moral and aesthetic quality of products opened the door to the more systematic socialist critique later developed by the British textile designer, writer, and social activist William Morris. On the other hand, it is possible to read Ruskin simply as a guide to high-end consumption and critic of the cheaper manufactured goods that middle- and working-class purchasers might afford. The tension is apparent in his comparison of modern machine-made glass to old Venetian glassware. "Our modern glass," wrote Ruskin, "is exquisitely clear in its substance, true in its form, accurate in its cutting. We are proud of this. We ought to be ashamed of it." The modern glassworker had become "a mere machine for rounding curves and sharpening edges." By contrast, old, irregular Venetian glass embodied beauty derived from workmen who cared little for uniformity and accuracy but made each glass a unique form reflective of a "new fancy." The very imperfection of Venetian glass bespoke the humanity of its creators. According to Ruskin, it was "so lovely in its forms that no price is too great for it."[54] Good design, he admitted, could transform manufactured products from "mere drugs on the market" into "educational instruments," but he also implied that those goods would be directed toward "the humble and the poor." In manufactured goods, wrote Ruskin, "we require work substantial rather than rich in make; and refined, rather than splendid in design. Your stuffs need not be such as would catch the eye of a duchess; but they should be such as may at once serve the need, and refine the taste, of a cottager." He immediately proceeded to identify as "the prevailing error in English dress, especially among the lower orders," an "awkward imitation of their superiors."[55] In short, Ruskin's profound critique of industrial production and persistent interest in the uplift of public taste went hand in hand with acceptance of class hierarchy.

The most comprehensive scholarly account of the *Crayon* points out rightly that the journal was far from slavishly devoted to Ruskin and that it reflected multiple intellectual influences. Durand, who did far less writing than Stillman, was a member of the Swedenborgian New Church, which held that that humans lived amid an unseen spiritual reality and that the millennium—the revelation of new truths and unification of matter with spirit—was already in process. In fact, Durand and Stillman shared a fascination with spiritualism. Durand was also interested in historical and social analysis, and after Stillman reduced his own role at the *Crayon*, more articles began appearing on those subjects. Durand was probably responsible for including reprints and contributions from German and French writers.[56] But Ruskin's ideas formed the initial intellectual foundation upon which Stillman and Durand built the journal's distinctive point of view.[57]

The editors announced their mission in the journal's first issue by defining their task as the "glorious work of art-cultivation," and they introduced their central theme by juxtaposing Art and Nature to materialism and trade. Noting the economic downturn of the mid-1850s, they declared it "fitting . . . that we should enter this action at this very crisis, when trade has shown its hollowness, and money-pride its brittleness, for after trials and sorrows come humility and love, and with these Beauty enters the heart."[58] In the midst of the Panic of 1857, the journal intensified its critique. "Need we be surprised," observed the writer, "if the commercial machinery should occasionally explode and go to pieces from the innate putrefaction of its own sins." Commerce, whose true object was to be "a convenient passage-way between the laboring producer and industrious consumer," had been disregarded in the interest of "individual avarice and selfishness."[59]

If trade fostered sin, art and nature offered the possibility of redemption. The journal's introductory essay, made that point by noting the impact of some marigolds on "a group of boys rollicking through the street, after the fashion of the candidates for Bowery distinction." When the boys saw the quantity of flowers, "they made a simultaneous rush for them, not with pushing and squabbling, as they would have done for coppers or 'valuables,' but with eagerness. . . . Their voices were softened, and their bearing harmonized."[60] An entry, probably written by Durand, identified merchants' clerks as a group especially "in need of the influences of Art, and a basis of thought about Art." Such young men were "lost in two ways, either drawn into sensual excesses, or, what is equally to be deplored, lost in successful selfishness." As a first step, Durand urged such men to "Go to Nature. Study human nature, humanity, and the world of beauty which surrounds you. . . . Take leisure to go into the country."[61]

Having imbued art with redemptive power, the *Crayon* held to strict standards of criticism. An entry, probably written by Stillman, established the journal's position by insisting that "knowledge of, and love for, Nature" was a necessary but insufficient qualification for would-be critics. Also necessary was education in the "mechanical and merely intellectual elements" of the artist's education. The entry went on to bemoan the "plethora of half-fledged social and newspaper critics who, with their senseless babbling and scribbling, cloud public judgment and confuse public feeling."[62] The author of another entry pointed out that the "cultivation of taste is not so easy a thing that it may be effected carelessly, nor has taste itself so great native vigor that it can resist false influences, and remain correct in spite of sophisms." Ruskin would make the same point several years later when he declared, "Everybody is talking about art, and writing about it, and more or less interested in it; everybody wants art . . . and few who talk know what they are talking about."[63] For the editors, as for Ruskin, good criticism was of utmost importance because art had moral and spiritual implications.

Unlike the *Cosmopolitan Art Journal*, which at times seemed almost antagonistic toward artists, the *Crayon* presented itself as an inspirational beacon, particularly for landscape painters. Its tone was respectful. "If he [the artist] has a right to exist," declared one writer, "then he has a right to that consideration and position which make existence easy. . . . We owe him attention and respect, not favor; and we ourselves suffer most deeply from neglecting him." Letters to the editors suggest that artists responded in kind. One young painter from Oxford, Ohio, having read a few issues of the *Crayon*, ordered a subscription despite his "very humble circumstances." He described Oxford as "a country village where the value of everything is estimated by its *usefulness*." Feeling "shut out from the world of art," he declared, "nature is my only teacher." The young man believed that "the Crayon would be of great service to me, that it would encourage, stimulate and learn me things that I ought to know. That it would be a friend and companion."[64] Another aspiring artist wrote Durand from

Rhode Island, requesting professional advice. Having been pressured by his parents to take a job as a painter of jewelry, he longed to pursue a less practical career as a landscape and portrait painter. He had become "almost irritated" when his parents spoke of alternative pursuits. "Now what shall or can I do?" he asked Durand. His more specific request was for Durand to recommend a teacher and estimate the cost of lessons.[65] Both Stillman and Durand were embedded within New York's artist community and sought to make their journal an inspirational companion to artists. The subscription list included not only young aspiring painters but also leading American artists of the 1850s, including Jasper Cropsey, Albert Bierstadt, Frederic Church, and Jerome Thompson.[66]

The work of Lilly Martin Spencer came under fire in the *Crayon* about six months before the *Cosmopolitan Art Journal* began actively promoting it, but a critical review that appeared in the *Crayon*'s May 1856 issue highlights differences between the two publications. It was likely that Stillman himself wrote the extensive critique of Spencer's contributions to the annual exhibition of the National Academy of Design. He acknowledged that the artist had "a truly remarkable ability to paint," but went on to say that she "ruins all her pictures by some vulgarism or hopeless attempt at expression." He reviled her "ambitious attempts at humorous painting," reflecting that "the most pitiable of all people is some one who attempts to be funny and only succeeds in being ridiculous." But the "most radical difficulty," argued the reviewer, was Spencer's choice of subject: "Being a woman, she should have some deeper, tenderer conceptions of humanity than her brother artists, something, at all events, better worth her painting and our seeing than grinning house-maids or perplexed young wives." Not only had Spencer's humorous genre scenes overstepped Stillman's notion of appropriate female subjects; perhaps more important, the images seemed to violate the *Crayon*'s vision of art as a means to Christian transcendence. That end, Stillman suggested, was better served by "the sobriety and dignity of calm thoughtfulness" than by "mere humor and jesting."[67]

That the Cosmopolitan Art Association embraced Spencer's genre scenes must have infuriated Stillman and Durand, who saw the entire enterprise as a threat to art, art criticism, and taste. They made their position clear in 1855 when they published an article that challenged the association for distributing mainly "French copies of Claude, Jardin, Teniers, and other old masters whose pictures have been reproduced hundreds and hundreds of times." These pictures, declared the writer, "should never be looked upon by those who desire to cultivate a taste for the arts."[68] The problem, as a later entry put it, was that the association was "one of those fungus inspirations that are entirely supported by the corruptions of commercial life." The prizes distributed by the association were, with few exceptions, "poor copies, bad originals, and false objects of Art called Art by commercial courtesy—but in reality nothing more than Art trash, made to sell, and no more worthy of consideration in relation to Art than Mormonism is to religion, or wooden nutmegs to genuine spice." The *Journal*, declared the writer, was nothing more than "a well printed mass of verbiage." Rather than fostering the distinction between art and commerce, the Cosmopolitan Art Association dragged art down. It was "a gross humbug" that injured art by "thus using the cause as a cloak to conceal operations carried on solely for private gain."[69]

William Rossetti articulated comparable concerns in a journal entry on the Glasgow Art Union. Like Stillman, he believed that good criticism was necessary in order to guide the uneducated public to an appreciation of true art, and he feared that art unions were fostering mediocrity. Rossetti complimented the Glasgow Art Union for having a committee select prize pictures, and he compared the organization favorably to the Art Union of London, which allowed prizewinners to make their own choices. But in Rossetti's view, even the committee could not be trusted because its collective judgment was "only ordinary." He wished that the selection could be "delegated to some single man, the most competent of the day—say to John Ruskin."[70]

The *Crayon* had little to say about the arts of design with respect to household products and other objects of use. That relative silence bespoke the editors' insistence that the taste for art transcended material concerns and that art itself had to be protected from crass commercialism. Thus, an essay sarcastically titled "The Poetry of the Crystal Palace" declared, "It does not appear that many persons have gone from the exhibition of the Crystal Palace better than when they entered it."[71] Another writer, in a series titled "The Family as a Work of Art," condemned extravagant consumption by observing, "True Art has nothing to do with extravagance. It has nothing to do with the adulations of men's vanities or conceits, as they interpret themselves through the medium of gaudy houses, gaudy furniture, or gaudy dresses." It is telling that Stillman objected to the inclusion of that series, warning Durand that it was "very much laughed at." Apparently he found the subject unworthy of a journal devoted to the philosophical discussion of art and nature. And perhaps he saw the series as too blatant an effort to attract female readers.[72]

And yet, when the *Crayon* deigned to discuss manufactured products, it joined the widespread call for improvement in the arts of design and endorsed the employment of women in that arena. Most notable was an essay reprinted from the *Independent* and authored by Clarence Cook, a young Ruskin enthusiast whose reputation as a critic would grow over subsequent decades. "We look," he wrote, "to the kitchens of Pompeii and wonder to see pans and skillets whose shape and ornament make them fit for the tables of the gods; we can find no such kitchen utensils at Berrians or Windles, nor anything in that line that suggests divinity." He believed that the source of the problem was disrespect for manual labor. It was "no longer possible for a 'gentleman' to be a tinman or brazier. He may learn to read inscriptions on Greek vases, but he must not soil his hand with potter's clay." Cook believed that many young men would find satisfaction in craft production and argued that lighter work would provide a good source of employment for artistically inclined women who wanted to avoid the drudgery of sewing. Such occupations, he admitted, "are the lesser of the Fine Arts . . . but nothing can come of their culture but grace and goodness, and peaceful hours."[73] Several years later, another essay expanded Cook's point on the employment of women. The author declared that the "fine taste of women, if directed and nourished by a good education . . . could be substituted for the taste of men in certain branches of industrial art. Jewelry offers them a vast field." The author saw other possibilities in the ornamentation of wood sculpture, upholstery, lithography, and engraving, all of which "would gain in quality by passing from men's hands to the hands of woman."[74]

Where the *Crayon*'s editors and writers refused to follow Ruskin was into an analysis of labor relationships, and in this regard they shared far more with the editors of *Cosmopolitan Art Journal* and *Godey's* than with Horace Greeley and the *Tribune*. When Cook called for improvement in the design of pots and pans, was he envisioning an artisan shop or a factory? The question appears not to have occurred to him. He referred to "handicrafts" but ignored the subject of the division of labor. Even an essay that compared modern art unfavorably to the art of the Middle Ages attributed the difference solely to the profound spirituality of medieval artists and made no reference to the extensive discussion of labor that appeared in Ruskin's *Stones of Venice*. At one point, when a writer, likely Stillman, approached the subject of the nineteenth-century labor question, he immediately dismissed it. He recognized that "We talk fluently, in these times, of the right of labor, and say, truly, that society has no right so to organize itself that it shall cut off its humblest members from their dues of sunlight and bread. Labor has rights, and will enforce them, or, at least, exact a terrible penalty for its disinheritance." Labor, in other words, would take care of itself by pressing its needs on the public. The point of the article was that artists, by comparison, suffered from neglect. For the editors of the *Crayon*, the labor question was marginal to the subject of art—a mere aspect of the bread-and-butter material world that true artists sought to transcend and, ultimately, redeem.[75]

Although the *Crayon*'s editors and writers occasionally included labor's woes among the evils of materialism, they expressed no concern for southern slaves. Despite Stillman's sympathy for abolitionism, the journal took little interest in the brewing national political storm. It echoed the Art-Union's claim that art would somehow resolve political tensions, but gave little attention to the subject. When Durand assumed sole editorship, several entries implied that abolitionism was itself a form of materialist agitation, intrinsically antagonistic to the spiritualizing mission of art. An 1859 article suggested that artists had the power to assuage the nation's "strife of races and an amalgamation of nationalities" by revealing their "picturesque significance." Thus artists had the opportunity to depict "the feudal barons of the Middle Ages ruling in the South, and the thrifty business man of the 19th century asserting his power in the North. The one full of sentiment and chivalric notions, the other tremulous with activity, and palpitating with speculative enterprise."[76] By 1861, with the journal on the brink of financial failure and the political crisis escalating, Durand's vision darkened. "We cannot push back the legitimately flowing currents of a young nation or shed tears over the imaginary woes of the Southern slave, while the northern laborer and his family are threatened with starvation." But Durand's solution for the worker, as for the nation, was "the study and reverence of Art" which would not make people rich but would "give them the taste to make better use of their riches and their time, and draw them aside from the many national and local delusions which are constantly springing up amongst us like epidemics."[77]

For all of its antimaterialism and despite Durand's growing negativity about the state of national politics, the *Crayon* displayed considerable optimism about the prospects for industrial America. That optimism arose with the conviction that Christian art would redeem modern society. Redemption would involve changes of heart rather than labor relationships. As an 1857 entry put it, "the industrial era is in full bloom. Let us thank God that it is so. But the creation of a nobler life-philosophy, of a nobler sympathy with the refining influences of the higher powers of civilization, Art, and literature, based upon a high moral standard, is required to prevent that spirit of industry which is now a blessing by its diffusion of wealth and comfort and, at least material happiness, from becoming a curse, by its exhalations of lucre, and profligacy, and reckless immorality."[78]

Durand and Stillman linked their vision of national redemption to the modern, racialized, scientific study of the history of art and civilizations. It is telling that the *Crayon* devoted considerable space to studies of antiquity. Mostly under Durand's editorship, the journal became a conduit for French and German scholarship that acquainted readers with new forms of historical thinking that made race a central category of analysis. Of course, Ruskin was also centrally interested in the history of art and its relationship to the cultures that produced it, but the continental historians were far more invested in charting supposed racial differences. They were far less interested than Ruskin in labor or, for that matter, in art per se. Once Durand became sole editor, the *Crayon* began foregrounding studies that emphasized race as an explanation for the psychological, moral, scientific, and artistic capacities of nations, continents, and peoples.

Ernest Renan, the French historian and scholar of Semitic languages, was among the *Crayon*'s early contributors. He referred to his method as the "comparative history of civilizations" and invoked racial difference in discussing the art and progress of peoples. China, he suggested, "offers the remarkable phenomenon of a people who have never been other than practical . . . [and] never had anything that deserves the name of art." By contrast, the "superior races," which were "so superior to the Orient in religious and poetic instincts," initially lagged behind Asia in the area of industry, but eventually surpassed it.[79] The particular object of Renan's negative judgment was the "Semitic race," which, he argued, had far less to do with the history of Christianity than most people assumed. "We have no desire," demurred Renan, "to draw invidious distinctions as to races, the comparative study of them having not yet reached that point of maturity which would warrant us in doing so," but he believed that "modern research" was sufficient to demonstrate "that there is a manifest difference; that while some have proved themselves to be really progressive in the order of moral and intellectual culture, others have proved themselves to be stationary."[80] The *Crayon*'s glowing review of Renan's *General History of the Semitic Languages* summed up the author's point of view by suggesting that he was "the first to recognize that the Semitic race, compared to the Indo European race, really represents an inferior combination of human nature. It has neither the high spiritualism of the races of India nor Germany, nor that sentiment of proportion and perfect beauty which Greece has bequeathed to the neo Latin nations; nor that delicate profound sensibility which is the dominant trait of the Celtic races." The work, concluded the reviewer, exemplified "the happy results of historical studies, carried out in the right direction."[81]

The *Crayon*'s engagement with the new "history of civilization" extended far beyond Renan's contributions. The German scholar Adolf Stahr contributed a six-page article in which he argued that ancient Greece was, in part, the product of "Orientalist influence." This was a challenging argument because it threatened to diminish the singular excellence of Grecian culture and its difference from the neighboring cultures of the eastern Mediterranean. Stahr dealt with the conundrum by invoking a racial explanation. He observed that the "Semitic races . . . appear to be full of brilliant imagination and endowed with fine intuitive perceptions of natural beauty, while they lack the steadiness required for slow and gradual progress; but the Greeks and Romans, the great historical representatives of the Hindoo-European races, possessed the genius of adaptation, instead of invention, the faculty of infusing their genius into the thoughts and works of others, rather than a genius that shines by the vigor and splendor of new creation."[82] Not even the study of Shakespeare was immune from the scholarly obsession with race. In 1861 the *Crayon* carried a long, highly favorable review of *A New Exegesis of Shakespeare*. The thesis of the book was that "the great dramatist, intuitively if not with premeditation, delineated his masterly characters on the principle of a distinction of races."[83]

The *Crayon* ignored peoples generally regarded as too low on the racial hierarchy to merit consideration as producers of art. One contributor was explicit in drawing the line. Professor Hart, in his second "Lecture on Painting," made only a passing reference "to India, Mexico, China, New Zealand and other aboriginal countries . . . [because] the Arts of these nations . . . do not come within our scope as elementary forms in the history of the progress of Fine Art proper." The value of artworks from Asia and the eastern Mediterranean would remain matters of

STILLMAN & DURAND, EDITORS AND PROPRIETORS.

February, 1856.   Vol. III.—No. 2.

THE CRAYON

AMERICAN JOURNAL OF ART.

OFFICES OF PUBLICATION,
F. W. CHRISTERN, 763 BROADWAY, N.Y.   TRÜBNER & Co., LONDON.

Figure 3.4. The *Crayon*'s short-lived cover illustration identified the magazine with the progress of civilization from savagery (beneath the feet of the muse) to Christian redemption, with the figure of art playing the central role. Courtesy American Antiquarian Society.

dispute within nineteenth-century American and European scholarship, but at midcentury the creations of African and aboriginal peoples were beyond the realm of consideration as art.

The new "comparative history of civilization" was part and parcel of the editors' millennial vision—a vision that found visual expression in the only cover illustration ever to appear on the journal. In 1856, in response to complaints from readers, Stillman and Durand included the image on the cover of several issues. The image, analyzed by Janice Simon, features a seated woman in Renaissance dress, looking heavenward. She holds a stylus in one hand and a tablet in the other. In front of her bare foot lies a small, speared, distorted aboriginal figure. To the right of her seated figure is the head of an Egyptian sphinx. On the left is an Egyptian sacred bull. Higher up on the left is an allusion to the Islamic Alhambra and, to the right of the woman, a figure of the Greek Athena. At the top of the image, extending up from either side of the woman's head, are two Gothic spires. Simon suggests that the female figure is modeled on Raphael's painting of Theology and represented "the redemptive spirit, moral truth, and divine inspiration that *The Crayon* sought to convey in its pages." The *Crayon*'s cover pictured the progress of art and civilization from its primitive phase to ancient Semitic culture, followed by celebrated exemplars of Islamic and pagan Greek art, culminating in the triumph of Christian theology. Here was a picture of racial hierarchy that mapped a vision of human progress.[84]

The millennial faith in America's potential as the world's leader in art *and* industry gained traction during the Civil War, as did the belief that the nation was approaching its providential position at the apex of the long history of civilizations. Those convictions fueled the creation of New York's first museum of art. Backed by industrialists, the museum would chart a new relationship between fine art and American manufactures, while also presenting visitors with an art historical narrative extending back to antiquity. From the outset, the museum would expand its holdings beyond painting and modern sculpture to include antiquities and arts of design. In this way, the debates of the 1850s marked the distance between the American Art-Union and the Metropolitan Museum.

CHAPTER 4

The Art of Decoration and the Transformation of Stewardship

The Making of the Metropolitan Museum of Art

The 1870s saw the founding of New York's Metropolitan Museum, Boston's Museum of Fine Arts, the Philadelphia Museum of Art, and the Art Institute of Chicago; the 1880s followed with art museums appearing in Cincinnati, Detroit, St. Louis, San Francisco, and Pittsburgh. Founders and early trustees were wealthy men whose donations of time and money underwrote the new enterprises, but the municipal art museums also depended on assistance from city governments in the form of land and subsidies. All of these projects distanced themselves from the commercial accumulations of curiosities most successfully embodied by P. T. Barnum's American Museum, but they included objects among their displays that would have been wholly out of place in most prominent antebellum art galleries.[1] In different ways and to greatly varying extents, the postwar art museums expanded beyond painting and sculpture to include objects ranging from ancient pottery and glassware to jewelry, metalwork, textiles, furniture, and musical instruments, not only from Europe and the United States but also from countries of the Near and Far East.

If we consider the postwar museums in relation to the antebellum institutions from which several of them actually emerged, this reorientation comes into focus as the elephant in the gallery. Eighteenth- and early nineteenth-century Anglo-American art promoters had insisted that the taste for art would improve the quality of American manufactures, but they assumed that graphic art and sculpture (primarily casts) would best serve the purpose of art education. The National Academy of Design, the

Art-Union's Free Gallery, elite men's clubs, and counterparts to those venues in American cities beyond New York confined themselves to the "fine" as distinct from the "useful" or "mechanical" arts, defined almost exclusively as graphic and sculptural work.

For museum builders of the 1870s, London's South Kensington Museum served as an important referent, and the early history of that institution sheds light on some of the concerns that animated American museum projects. Founded in 1852, the South Kensington (renamed the "Victoria and Albert Museum" in 1899) was the direct descendent of London's Crystal Palace exhibition. That international emporium, far more successful than New York's imitation, had sensitized British visitors to the elegance of France's luxury craft productions and fostered a competitive effort to upgrade the aesthetic quality of British manufactured goods. The stated purpose of the South Kensington was to educate consumer taste and to improve the quality of the nation's manufactured products; the museum grew out of a school of industrial design with which it remained affiliated. Founders hoped that improved taste would create a demand for better goods, while uplifted design would educate popular taste. By the time the South Kensington began attracting interest on the part of American museum builders, its collections were eclectic, including displays of medieval and Renaissance luxury objects, as well as original paintings, copies of masterworks, and a large collection of plaster casts. Its most distinguishing feature was the focus on "industrial art." Unlike "decorative art" (the term used rather loosely to connote objects of use and beauty, mostly in reference to luxury goods), "industrial art" encompassed contemporary objects of general use and implied attention to productive processes. It also signaled an interest in providing art education for workmen and a form of display that organized objects according to type and material rather than according to national or regional schools.[2] Henry Cole, the South Kensington's founding director, was committed to making the museum as accessible as possible to working-class visitors. He sought to make labels intelligible and did his best to facilitate transportation to and from the museum site. Charles C. Perkins, the wealthy, independent scholar who played a central role in the founding of the Boston Museum of Fine Arts, declared that the South Kensington had demonstrated its "power to bring industry up to a high artistic level."[3]

Founders of the Metropolitan Museum, the largest and most ambitious of postwar museums, were no less captivated by the South Kensington than were their counterparts in other cities, but they also drew on other models and moved quickly, if often inadvertently, in new directions. The distance traveled away from the South Kensington has obscured the multiple ways in which the Metropolitan, almost from the outset, became enmeshed within the burgeoning world of manufacturing, middle-class consumption, and, more particularly, the late nineteenth-century fascination with home decoration. Underwriting these connections was the belief that products of home decoration were, or should be, objects of art. Because the museum's founders had roots in the Art-Union movement and related institutions, the trajectory of the Metropolitan reveals much about the transformation of art culture in the late nineteenth century. To recognize the Metropolitan's engagement with the arts of personal and home decoration is to resituate the museum within the international consumer world of which it was inevitably a part.

Precursors: Art, Exhibition, and Nationalism

Despite the relatively recent experience of the Crystal Palace exhibition, none of those developments were evident when the United States' museum movement began to take shape. The first proposals for the creation of an American art museum coincided with the Civil War and linked the project to the millennial vision of democratic, statist nationhood unleashed during the war years. The American expatriate critic, editor, and collector James Jackson Jarves, who would advise the founders of the Boston and New York museums, published his call for an American "art gallery" in 1862. His vehicle was the popular Boston-based *Christian Examiner*. That Jarves had an interest in selling his own collection of early Italian paintings to such a gallery undoubtedly shaped his dream of an American institution modeled on the Louvre, but he also looked to the Louvre as a symbol and educator of democratic citizenship: "Let it be borne in mind," wrote Jarves, "that the greatest Museum of Europe was thus founded by republicans. It was not until the people had won political power that the rulers threw open to them the treasures of art which had hitherto been enjoyed in selfish privacy or displayed only as reflections of the aristocratic taste and magnificence of the few." Now the United States was living through a comparable revolutionary period. As Jarves put it, "The success or failure of democratic freedom, as opposed to aristocratic domination, is the great point which we are now determining. More than ever do we require the refining and ennobling influences of high art to counteract the too rigid strain of the mind tending almost exclusively toward the development of material strength." Through art, national values would be communicated to future generations: "We are making history anew, based upon the loftiest principle of civil government,—justice and freedom alike to all. Heroic action is ripening out of heroic thought. If we would perpetuate the trials and triumphs of our time in forms of living beauty, we must bid Art do it." Invoking familiar antebellum arguments, Jarves reminded his audience that art flourished "in proportion to the freedom of the people. . . . Hence our hope for the spread of high art on this continent rests in great degree upon our faith in the ultimate triumph of a true democracy."[4]

Jarves, who was part of the social and intellectual circle associated with the *Crayon*, drew on long-standing intellectual linkages between art and sociability, suggesting that taste would serve as a counterweight to capitalist competition and individualism, thereby strengthening the nation's post–Civil War democracy. His vision was democratic insofar as it identified taste explicitly as a universal potentiality. God, declared Jarves, "has implanted in every human soul the instinct of the beautiful, and faculties for its guidance and cultivation." Museums, by stimulating that instinct would foster national goals: "The vice of our civilization . . . is the intense egotism it fosters. Success to one person too often means loss to many." In terms reminiscent of Art-Union promoters, he declared that art galleries, like religious institutions, would be a "means of infusing a more neighborly spirit among men" while discouraging "exclusiveness among the rich and covetousness among the poor."[5]

What sort of museum would best serve this grand, national purpose? Jarves made a case for the Louvre's system of historically organized collections, divided into distinctive "schools" and organized in such a way as to foreground progress and decline in "technical, intellectual, and moral value": "A gallery of art is the summary . . . of the imaginative, inventive, and imitative aesthetic faculties of one generation or nation against another. It is furthermore a record of its mental and moral life, its pictorial or plastic literature,—an incarnation of its loves and hopes, or that subtle transmutation of ideas and feelings into form and color, by the sight of which we inwardly mark, learn, and digest the spirit of the age and artist."[6] Thus, Jarves held to the notion of art as a teacher of moral lessons, embedded in history, and in this regard it is telling that he used the phrase "pictorial or plastic literature." His imagined museum, featuring European painting and sculpture, would present a narrative of the rise and decline of nations, a story within which the United States would be the culmination.[7] As Jarves wrote in *The Art-Idea*, a book that went through four editions between 1864 and 1877, art and civilization had progressed from the "classical Pagan, or sensuous-mythological," to the "Roman Catholic, or ascetic-theological," and, finally, into the "Protestant, or democratic-progressive, founded upon the elevation of the people into a power of state." Jarves acknowledged that "art now loses in intensity of sacred symbolism and princely grandeur" but claimed that it gained an ability "to express the religion of humanity: praise to God alone and good-will to all men, as distinguished from the two previous phases of misguided religious thought and misinterpreted Christianity."[8]

Like all other American museum promoters of his era, Jarves believed that properly constituted art museums would have the effect of improving the aesthetic quality of American manufactures. He suggested that displays include not only paintings and sculpture but also "specimens of every kind of industry in which art is the primary inspiration, to illustrate the qualities and degrees of social refinement of nations and eras." "What utensil is there," he queried, "with which we may not, as did the Greeks, connect beauty of form and color, and which we may not make suggestive of hidden meaning, pointing a moral or narrating a tale." To "stimulate the art-feeling," he favored free public access to museums and referred approvingly (if briefly) to the South Kensington. But it was clear that the type of museum he envisioned would not center on industrial art displays. Jarves's preference was for an American Louvre whose many galleries would present visitors with a rigorously organized "mental and artistic history of the world." A great museum would enable visitors to "broadly survey the entire ground of art, and make ourselves, for the time, members, as it were, of the political and social conditions of life that gave origin to the objects of our investigations." Only such deep historical understanding would facilitate the interrelated goals of moral and aesthetic awareness. When he and others claimed that the South Kensington was "more devoted to artistic education" than other great museums, he was referring not to art education in general but to a particular sort of education that gave primacy to industrial art and what he saw as the technical education of artisans.[9]

For Jarves, it must have seemed obvious that the New-York Historical Society would constitute the foundation of an American art museum. The Historical Society, having moved in 1857 to a new building on Eleventh

Street and Second Avenue, included a large gallery that housed artworks transferred from the recently defunct New York Gallery of the Fine Arts created from the collection of the deceased merchant Luman Reed. Jarves tried, without success, to sell his own collection of Italian paintings to the Historical Society, which put them on temporary exhibit in 1863. By that time, it had acquired a donation of fourteen Assyrian marble sculptures ("the Nineveh Sculptures") from the merchant James Lenox and had purchased a large collection of Egyptian antiquities, amassed by the British-born physician Henry Abbott during his twenty-year stay in Egypt. These collections were not exhibited within the gallery, but were on display in the library of the same building.[10] The Egyptian and Nineveh collections were central to the Historical Society's proposal, formulated in 1860, to establish "a grand museum of antiquities, science and art" in the New York State Arsenal building near the southeast corner of Central Park. It would be "a public institution, whose collections in all departments may be accessible to all classes, subject only to such regulations as may be essential for security and preservation." Less than two years later the state legislature granted the request, with the caveat that the Historical Society would be responsible for renovations to the building.[11] Andrew Haswell Green, head of the Central Park Commission, was a strong supporter of the project, believing that the proposed museum and Central Park shared a common mission of cultural uplift.[12]

For purposes here, the New-York Historical Society's proposed museum is significant because the social group that ran the organization had many ties to both the Art-Union and the Metropolitan and because it marked an important evolution in that group's vision of a "public" art gallery. The Historical Society, founded in 1804, was a stronghold of New York's mercantile upper crust. Its six-member Art Committee, formed in 1856, included five former Art-Union officials or managers. Among them was Jonathan Sturges, formerly the business partner of Luman Reed. Prosper Wetmore was also an active member of the society, as was Evert Duyckinck. On the walls of the society's gallery hung portraits of the Art-Union's four presidents along with Daniel Huntington's *Sibyl*. Those canvases, once the property of the Art-Union, had come to the Historical Society through the transfer of paintings from the New York Gallery of the Fine Arts.[13]

And yet the inclusion of ancient artifacts and European paintings in the museum plan represented a substantial evolution away from the Art-Union and related antebellum institutions. Not only was the Historical Society beginning to measure its own collections against the great museums of Europe; it was also using ancient artifacts to construct a progressive historical narrative, extending back to biblical times. The fourteen colossal sculptures composing the Nineveh collection had been excavated by the widely known British archaeologist Austin Henry Layard. As the society proudly noted, other pieces from the same collection were housed in the British Museum and in the Imperial Museum of France. They represented "the culminating point of Assyrian art"—a period of biblical significance just before the destruction of Nineveh by "the father of Nebuchadnezzar."[14]

The framing of the Egyptian collection had a more pointed message. Prior to selling his "Egyptian Museum," Abbott had tried to run it as a commercial enterprise, but the catalog is notable for its nonsensationalist tone, in keeping with the noncommercial character of the Historical Society. Each of 1,118 articles had a separate entry. Abbott, who invoked scholarly authority, tried his best to identify the temporal and geographical location of the objects and to indicate their original use and/or historical meaning. The first and last entries, reinforced by the introduction, constructed a Christian framework that linked antislavery to moral progress and, by implication, to the United States. The first reference is to an enormous

> Head in sandstone, the face painted red the colour the ancients always used to represent a native Egyptian. This fine head was brought from Thebes by I. Perring, Esq., and is a portion of a colossal statue of Thothmes III, who, according to Sir Gardner Wilkinson, was the Pharaoh of the Exodus, which event took place during his reign, in the month of Epiphe, 1491 years before the birth of our Saviour. This Pharaoh is wearing the "ouabsh" or white crown of Upper Egypt with the "uraeus" or sacred serpent, emblem of royalty, in front.

The very last entry refers to "a wooden figure of a Slave, with his hands bound behind him, and his face upturned, as though imploring his conquerors to grant him liberty."[15] In this way the catalog evokes Jarves's vision of a historically organized museum designed to illustrate the progressive unfolding of religion, art, and democracy.

Museum projects of the war years could not get off the ground largely because they lacked backing from a sufficiently broad representation of the city's upper class. To put it another way, neither merchants nor industrialists alone were yet capable of bringing the museum into being. In 1864 the Park Commission rescinded its offer of the Arsenal building to the Historical Society, probably due to displeasure with the Society's architectural plan for refurbishing the building. Instead the city offered to provide land in Central Park between Eighty-First and Eighty-Fourth Streets, eventually the location of the Metropolitan Museum. The Historical Society objected strenuously but to no avail. Unable to raise funds for the building, it eventually abandoned the project.[16] In 1864 manufacturers, under the auspices of the American Institute, put forward their own plan for the building of a "permanent national depository for inventions and museum of art." The project fizzled after the Institute failed to win a gift of land from the city.[17] The unified wealth and power of the city's elite would be necessary to realize so ambitious and expensive a project.

Efforts to create a New York art museum testify to the city's increasingly lively art scene, which, in turn bespoke the growing wealth and ambition of the city's upper class. By 1864 New York artists and art promoters were abuzz with efforts to deploy art on behalf of the Union. While the war years signaled economic depression for much of the city's population, wealthy men were making money, buying pictures, and apparently thinking anew about connections between art and public life. The war created opportunities for merchants, but was even better for bankers and especially industrialists who profited from high tariffs and wartime production. The more New York wealth invested in the war effort, the greater its commitment to the Union and determination to win.[18]

In April of 1864, the Metropolitan Fair opened in New York for the benefit of the United States Sanitary Commission, the organization created for the support of Union soldiers. During the first two days of the three-week event, it attracted 13,000 visitors. In addition to raising money, the goal was to foster political unity within the politically divided city by providing uplifting entertainment capable of cutting across class lines. In many ways, the fair as a whole anticipated the world fairs of the later nineteenth century. It was the largest of thirteen such events organized throughout the wartime North, and it was the only one that had a significant international component, with donations orchestrated by ambassadors and fair committees abroad. New York men usurped the leadership position of female organizers, but the "Ladies Committee" nonetheless played a critical role in planning and operating the massive event. Attractions included a "Floral

Temple," "Indian Department," exhibitions of the New York Police and
Fire Departments, a restaurant, children's department, "Knickerbocker
Kitchen," an exhibition of "Farmers Implements," and an "International
Hall." Manufacturers contributed hats and furs, among other things.
Church groups donated handmade items, and wealthy women donated
jewelry. At a "Fancy Goods Hall" visitors could purchase "costly perfumes,
elegant bronzes worsted work and fancy articles too numerous to mention
. . . at prices below the market value."[19]

The most popular department at the fair was the picture gallery, which
was housed in its own building and required twenty-five cents for entry in
addition to the one-dollar general admission ticket. American artists were
eager to participate in the event, which, unlike the Crystal Palace, had a
clear patriotic purpose. The approximately 350 pictures that hung on the
walls included some that were donated by artists for sale and others loaned
by the city's major collectors. In addition, visitors could purchase photographs of "our most eminent men" by Matthew Brady and engravings
donated by the firm of Goupil. Directing the fair's art gallery was the ardent
Republican John Kensett. His cochair, representing the "Ladies Committee," was Mary Sturges, wife of the merchant Jonathan Sturges. The exhibition simultaneously evoked the Art-Union's Free Gallery and pointed in
markedly different directions. Unlike its predecessor, the display was carefully curated, drawing almost exclusively from work of the city's best-
known artists. Most important, the special charge of admission signaled the
organizers' expectation that the art gallery would be a relatively elite venue.
The inclusion of European artworks delivered a message rather different
from that of the Art-Union—namely, the sophistication of American collectors and the ability of leading American artists to compete in a transatlantic forum. In any case, the throngs of visitors could hardly have missed
the galvanizing nationalist message of the exhibit. Emanuel Leutze's widely
celebrated painting *Washington Crossing the Delaware* (from the collection
of Marshall O. Roberts) occupied one end of the room (see Figure 4.1). The
catalog entry, nearly two pages long, left little doubt as to the moral message
of the work or its relevance to the current crisis: "The darkest hour of that
protracted night of peril had then overshadowed the noble spirits who held
in their keeping the welfare of their country—the freedom of the world."
Other places of honor went to Albert Bierstadt's *Rocky Mountains*, Frederic
Church's *Heart of the Andes*, and well-known paintings by Asher Durand,
Daniel Huntington, and Kensett himself.[20]

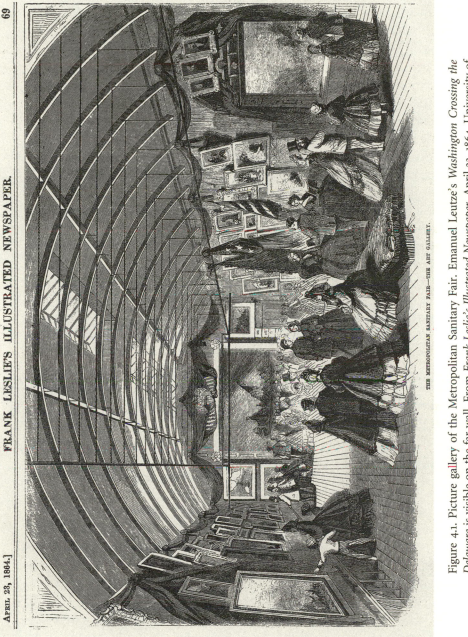

THE METROPOLITAN SANITARY FAIR.—THE ART GALLERY.

Figure 4.1. Picture gallery of the Metropolitan Sanitary Fair. Emanuel Leutze's *Washington Crossing the Delaware* is visible on the far wall. From *Frank Leslie's Illustrated Newspaper*, April 23, 1864. University of California Libraries, Annex.

The Union League Club, which sponsored the fair, would play a major role in the founding of the Metropolitan Museum. The club was formed in 1863 to foster the Union cause, the goal of emancipation, and a strengthened nation-state. Its founders were Frederick Law Olmsted, architect of Central Park, and the Unitarian minister Henry Whitney Bellows, who was also president of the Sanitary Commission. Leaders of the New-York Historical Society were well represented among the Union Leaguers. Indeed, almost all surviving Art-Union officials, including former Democrats, were members. But the club cut a far wider swath among New York's elite than the Art-Union and signaled growing political and social ties between merchants and industrialists. With the municipal government under the control of Democrats, and with support for a negotiated settlement on the rise, wealthy Republicans saw the club as an avenue through which they could exert political and cultural influence. They were quite explicit in their effort to rally the economic, intellectual, and artistic elite of the city—what Olmsted referred to as the "American aristocracy" in support of the Union. The club also signaled the radicalization of many powerful New Yorkers not only on the subject of the nation-state but also on the issues of slavery and emancipation. Among the first acts of the Union League was the fitting up of an all-black regiment. In November 1863 the club had a membership of 530 men. By the end of the war, membership had grown to 800. As Bellows later recalled, "almost from the very beginning the Union League Club had become a center of all movements having a patriotic impulse in the city of New York."[21] Among those movements was the Sanitary Fair presided over by Union Leaguers and their wives.

Founding: Leadership, Precedents, Access

It was also the Union League Club that successfully shepherded the museum project. In 1866, the new president of the club was John Jay, an attorney, diplomat, and grandson of the first chief justice. Although he never served as a manager of the Art-Union he gave an invited speech before the organization in 1844. Prior to becoming a Republican, Jay was a Whig whose active membership in the New-York Historical Society testified to his identification with New York's old mercantile families. He famously renewed the call for an art museum during a Fourth of July speech that he delivered to fellow Americans in Paris in 1866. Ignoring prior proposals, he later recalled that "the simple suggestion that 'it was time for the American people to lay the foundation of a National Institution and Gallery of Art and that the American gentlemen then in Europe were the men to inaugurate the plan' commended itself to a number of the gentlemen present, who formed themselves into a committee for inaugurating the movement." The group presented its request to New York's Union League, which had its art committee write a formal proposal. In November 1869, about three hundred men met to discuss and launch the plan.[22] With the venerable William Cullen Bryant presiding, invited speakers gave voice to the various concerns that animated the museum project: It would be a point of pride for the city, an attraction for tourists, a place where the wealthy could donate private collections, an educational resource for artists and manufacturers, a source of general moral uplift, and a special benefit to the poor. Bryant struck the central note when he declared that the meeting had been assembled "to consider the subject of founding in this city a Museum of Art, a repository of the productions of artists of every class, which shall be in some measure worthy of this great metropolis and of the wide empire of which New York is the commercial center."[23]

Before the end of 1870, the imagined museum had an administrative structure; one year later it had the promise of a new building, and in 1872 held its first exhibition. A committee of fifty men, appointed at the November meeting, elected a subcommittee that proceeded to draft a constitution providing for the election of trustees and officers. In addition, the museum would welcome members—an honorary position costing ten dollars per year. In April 1870, the state legislature granted an act of incorporation for the purpose of "establishing and maintaining in the said city a museum and library of art, of encouraging and developing the study of fine arts, and the application of art to manufacture and practical life, of advancing the general knowledge of kindred subjects, and to that end, of furnishing popular instruction and recreation." Andrew Green, of the Department of Parks, had long envisioned Central Park as a cultural center, and he led the effort linking the museum to the space formerly promised to the Historical Society. Promoters of the Metropolitan were far more successful than the New-York Historical Society in their negotiations with the city. Municipal authorities agreed to provide not only the land extending from Eighty-First to Eighty-Second Streets on Fifth Avenue and Central Park, but also a new building. Taxpayers would foot the bill. Prior to 1880 when the structure was finally completed, the museum would be housed in rented quarters, first at the former Dodsworth Dancing Academy, located far uptown on Fifth Avenue between Fifty-Third and Fifty-Fourth Streets and then at the more generally accessible Douglas Mansion on Fourteenth Street.[24]

Former Art-Union managers and officials were actively involved in the planning and early development of the Metropolitan. In addition to Bryant, William J. Hoppin and Marshall O. Roberts attended meetings that preceded the opening of the museum and survived to sit on the board of trustees. Jonathan Sturges, who died in 1874, never served as a trustee, but he participated in the planning. Other early trustees were part of the same social and political circle: The painters John Kensett, Frederic Church, and Daniel Huntington, favored by the Art-Union, were among the museum's first trustees.[25]

But the museum's founders and early board of trustees also reflected changes in the social class from which it was drawn. While the Art-Union's leadership had been more or less restricted to old money merchants and professionals, the museum's trustees also included industrialists. Robert Hoe Jr., a member of the board from 1870 until 1892, inherited his father's printing press factory and expanded the business into an international concern. William T. Blodgett, active on the board from 1870 until 1875, inherited a varnish-making business but made his fortune in railroads. John Taylor Johnston was a lawyer who made and lost a fortune in the railroad business. He became the trustees' first director. Henry Gurdon Marquand, member of the board from 1871 until 1902, was the son of a prosperous silversmith and made his fortune as a banker and railroad speculator.[26] Joseph Choate, a major player on the board from 1870 until 1917, was New York's leading corporate attorney. He also represented individuals in civil cases. Among his most notable clients were the Standard Oil Company and the American Tobacco Company. It was Choate who negotiated the terms of the museum's relationship with the city. In 1895, he argued successfully before the Supreme Court against a proposed federal income tax. Cornelius Vanderbilt, grandson of the railroad magnate, joined the board of trustees in 1878 and served until his death in 1899. Marshall O. Roberts, who was a shipping merchant during the period of his involvement with the Art-Union, made a fortune during the war through the purchase of United States bonds and by supplying naval supplies and assistance to the Union. After the war he turned his attention to railroads.[27]

Trustees were more widely traveled than their Art-Union predecessors, not only in Europe but more particularly with respect to the eastern Mediterranean. They were eager to make New York a repository for Old World antiquities being unearthed at accelerated rates during the later nineteenth century. Bryant traveled to Egypt, Palestine, Turkey, and Greece in 1852, and Johnston was in Egypt when he received a telegram inviting him to be the president of the board.[28] William Cowper Prime, the wealthy evangelical lawyer and journalist, appointed to the board in 1873, wrote two books on his travels, *Boat Life in Egypt and Nubia* and *Tent Life in the Holy Land.* The latter, published in 1857, became a standard travel guide for Americans. It also served as fodder for Mark Twain, whose *Innocents Abroad* mocked Prime for his sentimentalism, gullibility, and ostentatious chauvinism.[29] An avid collector of pottery and porcelain, Prime also published a lengthy guide for collectors entitled *Pottery and Porcelain of All Times and Nations* (1878).

At the time of its founding, the Metropolitan's relationship to living American artists was not a foregone conclusion. Some museum promoters believed that the display of American art should be the central concern of the institution. Nonetheless, the focus on European art accelerated over the course of the Metropolitan's first decade. Museum trustees, more cosmopolitan than their predecessors, were poised to take advantage of bargains (real and imagined) in the wake of the Franco-Prussian War. Although the long-lived artist Daniel Huntington remained on the board until 1903, the deaths of artist-trustees John Kensett in 1872 and Sanford Robinson Gifford in 1880 diminished further the museum's engagement with contemporary American art, as did the expansion of artist-run societies that were singularly devoted to the promotion of work by living American artists.

Promoters of the museum mentioned a number of European precedents, but the Louvre and South Kensington predominated as models. (Sometimes, in referring to historically oriented art collections, founders invoked London's National Gallery instead of the Louvre.) In 1872, the first year in which the museum opened to the public, the trustees were quite explicit in declaring their plan to unite the rather divergent programs of the great European institutions. They hoped, "in the first place, to collect and publicly exhibit adequate examples of the ancient and modern schools of painting and sculpture, and, secondly, to provide as large and complete a collection as possible of objects which, without coming within the class just mentioned, derive their chief value from the application of fine art to their production—in short, a representative Museum of Fine Art applied to Industry."[30]

The trustees' initial acquisitions reflected their ambition, their investment in European models, and their interest in the eventual creation of a comprehensive art historical display. During a European tour, William Blodgett bought 174 mostly Dutch and Flemish paintings for which the trustees subsequently reimbursed him. These paintings constituted the bulk of the museum's holdings when, in 1872, it opened for the first time. Their second major acquisition also reflected the trustees' focus on European art and their interest in matching—or besting—major European collections. Purchased for $60,000 in 1872, it consisted of thousands of antiquities, including monumental sculptures, unearthed on the island of Cyprus. It would be named the "Cesnola Collection" after Luigi Palma di Cesnola, the man who orchestrated the excavation, claimed the plunder as his own, and sold the collection to the Metropolitan. In 1876 the trustees purchased a second Cypriot collection from Cesnola, who, soon thereafter, accepted a position as the museum's first director.[31]

At the same time, trustees sought to incorporate elements of the South Kensington model. As Joseph Choate observed at the opening of the Central Park building, it was "a prominent feature of the Trustees' plan . . . to establish a Museum of Industrial Art, as distinct from the beautiful in art, for the direct and practical instruction of artisans, showing the whole progress of development from the raw material, through every artistic process to the most highly wrought product of which art is capable." Toward this end, the trustees set aside the basement of the Central Park building as the future site of the industrial art exhibitions. In 1880, they also took the first steps toward the establishment of an "industrial Art-School." The following year, funded by a $50,000 donation from an anonymous New York City merchant, the museum's school was in operation on East Thirty-Fourth Street, offering night classes in "Drawing and Design," "Modeling and Carving," and "Carriage Drafting and Constructing." An afternoon class was designed specifically for female students, who received training in "artistic decoration of leather, silk, satin, glass, etc., and the use of oil and water-colors in preparing designs for industrial ornamentation." Teachers gave special consideration to "the composition of designs for wall-papers, carpets, etc., and for cards and vignettes in color." Trustees looked forward to a time in the not too distant future when an array of tradespeople, including silver, bronze, and other metal workers, would collaborate with the museum school in offering classes of their own.[32]

Both the Louvre and the South Kensington would persist as referents, but, almost from the outset, it was clear that the neither one could serve as an entirely comfortable model. During the 1880s, the Cesnola collections would overwhelm other displays, fueling a conflict that consumed the trust-ees' attention. Within two decades the schools would be abandoned, their functions usurped by other institutions, notably Cooper Union. Industrial art displays promised for the basement never materialized. In practice, trustees were dependent on the acceptance of loans and ad hoc gifts from wealthy donors. Not until the beginning of the twentieth century would a huge bequest and new management facilitate the implementation of a systematic program of development.

The distance between the Metropolitan and its primary models derived as well from the trustees' vision of their audience—a retreat from the rela-tively inclusive vision that initially shaped their ideas about both the Louvre and the South Kensington. Although the act of incorporation cast the museum as a project geared toward the education and enjoyment of a broad public, the decade of the 1870s saw an escalation of class anxiety and antidemocratic sentiment among wealthy New Yorkers. Between 1866, when Jay made his speech in Paris, and 1880, when the museum reopened at its permanent location at Central Park, the Union League and the social class of which it was a part underwent a significant ideological reorienta-tion. The draft riots of 1863 had heightened antagonism between the city's Republicans and the Irish working class, but it was the proliferation of unions and labor unrest after the war that eroded Republican faith in a key component of free labor ideology—the fundamental unity of interest between labor and capital.

With the depression of 1873, the industrial and mercantile wings of New York's upper crust found common cause in their defense of property and opposition to labor mobilization. Those efforts gained traction as non-Protestant immigrants began changing the shape of the city's working class. "Slowly, but persistently," as Sven Beckert writes, "workers were cast as 'the other.'" In this climate, wealthy New Yorkers found growing appeal in social Darwinism—the belief that wealth was a sign of immutable superior-ity and that interference with market mechanisms would slow the progress of civilization. Even those who eschewed the more radical articulation of laissez-faire ideas embraced antidemocratic efforts under the banner of anticorruption. During 1870s the sort of men who joined the Union League and who served as museum trustees pressed for strengthened police forces, police and military intervention to subdue strikes, and tougher anticrime legislation; they also looked for ways to muffle the political voice of laboring people. In 1877 the Union League joined an array of business organizations and leading newspapers by endorsing an ultimately unsuccessful plan that would have transferred much of the city's administration from elected to appointed officials. The same plan would have imposed a stiff property requirement on voters.[33]

During the first decade of its existence, the museum became embedded within the social world of New York's upper crust, a process that contributed to a sense of proprietary entitlement among the trustees. A "hanging committee" physically placed pictures on the walls, and trustees packed and unpacked boxes when the museum moved. Given the role of dedicated officials in funding the institution, it is hardly surprising that they came to regard it as their own. In addition, the reliance on loan exhibitions to supplement regular collections and the trustees' unrestricted acceptance of artworks donated by members of their own circle contributed to the sense that the institution was the possession of the city's wealthy donors. Elegant receptions honoring lenders and donors became part of the fabric of the city's elite social life. As a reporter for the *Daily Tribune* observed in December of 1874, "the reception at the Metropolitan Art Museum last night brought together the wealth and beauty of the metropolis. Year by year these receptions are growing into an institution which promises the best result for the art culture of our people."[34] (See Figure 4.2).

Ambivalence on the matter of access was apparent during the 1870s in the trustees' approach to municipal financing. While the museum was taking shape, some of its promoters pressed for taxpayer support as a way to foster broad public commitment to the institution. William J. Hoppin, veteran of the Art-Union, made this point in a letter read at the November meeting of 1869. According to Hoppin, "the strongest reason why the taxpayers should themselves build and support the contemplated Museum is, that in this way only can they be brought to take an interest in it. . . . If they could say: 'We own this ourselves; it cost us so much money; it is finer than anything in Boston or Philadelphia'; can we doubt that they would visit it often?" Hoppin envisioned a time when people would "throng the halls" of the museum "on holidays (and perhaps on Sundays)."[35] The report of the "Committee of Fifty" appointed to follow through on proposals made at the November 1869 meeting declared that "it should be a principle that the Institution should not attempt to derive a revenue by admission fees, but that from the first it should identify itself with the public." True, the Union League's art committee had looked to create a museum "free alike from bungling government officials and from the control of a single

NEW YORK CITY.—OPENING RECEPTION OF THE METROPOLITAN MUSEUM OF ART, AT THE TEMPORARY HALL, NO. 681 FIFTH AVENUE, FEBRUARY 20TH. -SEE PAGE 411.

Figure 4.2. Depiction of the opening reception of the Metropolitan Museum of Art at its temporary quarters, presenting the museum as an uplifting upper-crust space, welcoming to women and children. From *Frank Leslie's Illustrated Newspaper*, March 9, 1872. Author's collection.

individual," but the issue of municipal support was still alive in 1871 when museum promoters struck their first deal with the city government. At that time, there was every indication that trustees would have been pleased to receive more from the city than the funds allotted for the land and the building at Central Park. The annual report invited a change in the structure of the funding arrangement by noting that, "for the present," private subscriptions would fund the acquisition of museum objects.[36] In 1873 trustees enumerated the extensive contributions of the British Parliament to art projects including the British Museum and the South Kensington. They solicited contributions from the city to their "ordinary expenses," although they made no explicit request for municipal help with respect to acquisitions. An anonymous writer for the *Daily Tribune* got to the nub of the matter when, in 1873, he declared himself "anxious to see the museum supported not by private persons but by the public; not by forced contributions, nor even by generous gifts from individuals, but by the State, that is, by the whole body of citizens rich and poor." The writer may have been disingenuous in claiming to take it "for granted that the trustees are as anxious to have this brought about as we are." Six years later a writer for the *Herald* made essentially the same point: he urged the trustees to "bring all their influence to bear on the Legislature," among others in order to secure funds "adequate to all purposes of proper maintenance and acquisition."[37]

Yet, by 1881 trustees allowed no room for doubt concerning their attitude toward taxpayer funding. They believed that it was "unnecessary to show . . . that in a country with political institutions like ours, a Museum of Art would be more certainly useful to the people if independent of municipal or legislative grants." In addition to the building and lands at Central Park, they welcomed the city's annual stipend of $15,000 for "ordinary expenses"—a sum that rose to $25,000 in 1890. However, they were satisfied to keep the acquisitions independent of municipal assistance and thereby free of external interference.[38]

Whereas Art-Union managers had insisted that theirs was a "public" institution, trustees and other promoters of the Metropolitan Museum began to characterize their organization as "private."[39] The arrangement with the city made the museum beholden to municipal politics and public opinion, but it also gave the officers and trustees full control over collections; in the process, it fostered a sense of ownership among the trustees of an institution that was, in fact, dependent on taxpayer dollars. James Jackson Jarves, who remained a staunch supporter of the museum throughout his life, went so far as to claim that it was "virtually . . . a private institution owned and governed as such." Far from criticizing this situation, Jarves urged others to appreciate the "gifts and labors of a few patriotic gentlemen" who had created an institution for "public entertainment and instruction.[40] In 1880 Cesnola informed a reporter for the *Tribune* that "'one point generally lost sight of in regard to the Museum is that it is a private institution. People come here and ask for the restaurant, the bar, and want to eat their lunch in the picture galleries; all because they say it is a public institution—which it is not.'"[41] When John Taylor Johnston addressed the board in 1885 he referred to an "erroneous idea" that had "gained some currency"—namely, that "your Museum is a public institution."[42]

Unlike Art-Union managers who eagerly drew people into the Free Gallery, Metropolitan Museum officials were conflicted in their efforts to attract visitors. When the museum opened at its first temporary location trustees decided that cramped quarters militated against general, much less free, admission of the public. Instead subscribers, who had paid the ten-dollar annual fee, received tickets, which they, in turn, were free to distribute to friends and family. When the museum moved to temporary quarters on Fourteenth Street, trustees established a fifty-cent admission fee that they dropped to twenty-five cents soon thereafter. They designated Monday as the only admission-free day. In response to pressure, they experimented with evening openings but found that low attendance failed to justify the expense of the gaslight and the paid attendant. In 1876, John Taylor Johnston rejected a proposal to forgo admission fees on Washington's Birthday. "Our general policy," he observed, "has been to avoid making free days of holidays. When a holiday *comes* on a free day I would let it go, but I would make no addition to the free days such as is proposed." By 1880, when the museum opened at its permanent home in Central Park, trustees had already established four admission-free days—a requirement of their 1878 agreement with the Parks Commission. On two additional days, visitors had to pay the twenty-five-cent fee. By all accounts, the majority of visitors came to the museum on free days, but working-class visitors were not, for the most part, among them. As a reporter noted in 1879, "Ladies have been known to hire a carriage at a dollar and a half an hour—on a free day. That is to say, they have paid a livery stable keeper three dollars, but the museum not one cent."[43] Until 1890, strong-willed Sabbatarians on and off the board of trustees resisted efforts to open the museum on Sundays—the only day available to most of the city's working class.[44]

During decades of escalating class conflict, when as many as eighteen dailies, as well as weekly and monthly publications competed for readers, it is not surprising that the Metropolitan and its admission policy became the object of intense critical scrutiny. Almost from the time the museum opened, a wide array of city publications pressured the trustees on the matter of access and accused them of exclusivist practices. In 1873 a writer for *Scribner's Monthly* challenged the trustees of the "weanling Museum" for "trying to make it not a public possession, enjoyed, studied, taken pride in by all the citizens, but a mere extension of their own comfortable and luxurious private parlors." Seven years later, on the eve of the Metropolitan's move to Central Park, the *Tribune's* reporter declared that the museum "from the very beginning . . . has been an exclusive social toy, not a great instrument of popular education." Echoing those charges the *Police Gazette* declared, in 1883, that the museum, "though inaugurated by private parties, has been richly endowed by the State. Yet it is run as an essentially aristocratic and exclusive institution . . . and the American public only obtain admission to the museum at all because the charter provides for it."[45]

Cesnola's disdainful attitude toward working-class visitors and high-handed implementation of decorous spectatorship, widely reported in the press, bespoke the Metropolitan's elitist orientation. In 1880 trustees received an angry response after Cesnola notified police to "turn out of the building anyone caught spitting on the floor." Editors of the *Evening Post* sided with the trustees by noting that the "tone of the address is appropriate to the breeding of persons capable of committing such an offense" and that a "milder" injunction "had proved ineffectual."[46] Cesnola's commentary on working-class visitors would remain a source of contention throughout his tenure as the museum's director.

Consuming Visions and Retail Connections

It would, however, be a mistake to suggest that the Metropolitan remained an isolated bastion of high art, wholly removed from popular interest. Attendance records for the early years are difficult to decode, in part because turnstiles were not installed until 1880 but also because the trustees had some incentive to inflate the figures. They offer a mixed picture. Trustees claimed that on February 22, 1875, a public holiday, nearly 7,000 people visited the museum. The same year only 42, on average, attended during evening openings, so trustees abandoned that experiment.[47] According to the museum's annual report, 353,421 people visited the museum from 1873 to 1879. Of those attendees, 94,000 came during the year in which the Metropolitan cosponsored a Centennial Loan Exhibition with the National Academy of Design. The great majority came on free days. In 1877 and 1878 attendance fell precipitously to 41,674 and 26,674 visitors respectively, but the opening of the Central Park building generated an upsurge. According to official figures, 1,200,000 people visited the museum from its opening at

Central Park on April 1 through April 30 of the following year. After that year, the number of visitors declined. Average yearly attendance from 1880 through 1890 was 391,729. As we shall see, attendance rose significantly during and after May 1891, when the museum finally began offering free Sunday admission.[48]

Widespread reportage on the Metropolitan derived not only from class resentment but also from the extraordinary depth and breadth of popular interest in the arts. In fact, the museum was part and parcel of a network of art-related institutions described by the historian J. M. Mancini. The last quarter of the nineteenth century saw the emergence of new artist-run associations, the establishment of schools for artists that welcomed female students, the proliferation of amateur art societies across the country, and an organized movement that promoted the teaching of drawing in secondary schools. Most significantly, Mancini suggests that we should consider the print media as a critically important player in the art field of the post–Civil War decades. Not only were newspapers and journals granting greater attention to the arts—even to the point of hiring specialized art critics—but the period also saw the publication of new specialized art journals. These publications were not confined to New York or even to the East Coast. Just as the museum movement spread to Syracuse, Cincinnati, Chicago, and places farther west, so too did the publication of art journals, art schools, and amateur art societies.[49] Nor was this interest in art confined to highbrow publications. The *New York Times* and the *Nation* attended to art-related matters, but so did cheap daily papers, including the *World*, the *Continent*, and the illustrated *Daily Graphic*. Publishers and journalists regarded print media not only as a source of criticism but also as an important agent for the dissemination of artistic knowledge—a partner, in many ways, to the new art schools and museums. Thus, when the Metropolitan opened at Central Park, the popular *Daily Graphic* published a long, illustrated account of the new displays (see Figure 4.3).

With notably mixed success, trustees made a concerted effort to woo journalists, and several prominent editors sat on the board. William Cowper Prime was editor and part owner of New York's *Journal of Commerce*, and George William Curtis, a fellow trustee from 1870 to 1889, edited *Harper's Weekly*—a publication that reached a circulation of over 200,000 during the 1870s. Curtis, who also wrote for *Harper's Monthly*, achieved renown as a proponent of civil service reform and an opponent of New York's Democratic machine politics.[50] That the trustees kept official scrapbooks of

1—ONE OF THE GALLERIES, THE AVERY COLLECTION. 2—EXTERIOR OF THE MUSEUM. 3—ANTE-ROOM TO MAIN HALL, THE CESNOLA COLLECTION. 4—THE MAIN HALL. 5—GALLERY OF MODERN PAINTINGS. 6—SCULPTURE GALLERY. 7—GALLERY OF OLD MASTERS.

VIEWS OF THE METROPOLITAN MUSEUM OF ART, CENTRAL PARK, NEAR EAST EIGHTY-FIRST STREET.

Figure 4.3. That the *Graphic* gave readers a full-page illustration of the new Central Park museum suggests that interest in the Metropolitan extended beyond the ranks of New York's upper crust. The gallery of paintings is relegated to the bottom right and left corners of the image. *Views of the Metropolitan Museum of Art*, from *New York Daily Graphic*, February 7, 1880. New-York Historical Society.

newspaper and periodical clippings is an indication of their sensitivity to publicity, and they did their best to shape reportage by inviting journalists and editors to museum receptions.[51] That so many working-class people flocked to the museum as soon as it became available to them suggests how enmeshed it already was within a broad public discourse. Whether complimentary or critical, the press effectively made the museum an object of fascination, familiar, in some ways, to people who never entered its galleries.

Unlike the Art-Union, which had been particularly focused on attracting male subscribers and visitors to the Free Gallery, the Metropolitan presented itself as (and seems to have actually been) a distinctly welcoming environment for prosperous women—a place, akin to the department store, where women could go unaccompanied by men. Early images of the Metropolitan's interior tend to feature female visitors in sparsely attended, elegant surroundings. As the *Evening Post's* writer had inadvertently pointed out, prosperous women were hiring carriages to attend on free days.[52] When, in 1885, Joseph Choate wrote to the director requesting special Sunday tickets for some "importunate female friends," he exposed the museum not only as a place of class-based privilege but also as a comfortable place for women.[53]

Contributing to women's interest in the museum was its engagement with the subject of interior decoration. The museum movement of the 1870s and 1880s coincided with a period of growing interest in home decoration and in decorative objects from around the world. Interest in the decoration of domestic space had deep roots in the antebellum era, as did the conviction that home decoration was an art in its own right. But these preoccupations deepened after the war when interest in interior design burgeoned. Evidence of this excitement could be found not only in the lavish mansions of the nation's wealthiest families but also in the "cozy corners" of more modest households where families surrounded themselves with decorative art from foreign places. In fact, part of the explanation for the explosion of interest in home decoration can be traced to the opening up of the international market in art objects. The 1870s and 1880s saw the publication of advice books on the subject of home decoration, and in 1879 the *New York Herald* could reflect that "house furnishing twenty-five years ago was something to strike terror to the aesthetic heart; now-a-days it is a thing of beauty; or if it is not it should be, the demand for good things having brought about a supply, and by a little care and taste one can make a very tasteful room with very limited means."[54]

It would be difficult to overestimate the impact of Philadelphia's Centennial Exhibition in promoting American fascination with an international array of "artistic" products for the home. In 1876 more than ten million people visited the exhibition, where they encountered not only an enormous gallery of European and American painting and sculpture but also enticing displays of decorative objects, sometimes presented with price tags in simulated domestic settings. Those who could not make the trip were able to read about the exhibition in the vast and often illustrated reportage. Japan's Meiji government was particularly effective in promoting its goods, and its pavilion created a sensation. By the end of the 1870s Japanese products were the subjects of widespread conversation, and Japanese aesthetic references could be found in many American homes, shops, and factories. Overall the fair spoke to widespread anxiety about the aesthetic appeal of industrially produced goods and the competitiveness of American products. Handmade objects (and objects presented as handmade) appealed to growing nostalgia for preindustrial life. It was at the Centennial that many Americans became acquainted with textiles and pottery associated with the British decorative arts movement, an encounter that sparked the development of a comparable movement of largely female, small-scale, and amateur production within the United States.[55]

The Metropolitan not only directed its attention toward the display of art objects other than painting and sculpture; it also established links to high-end retail markets. In 1878 the trustees authorized the exclusive Fifth Avenue firm of Tiffany and Co. to make reproductions of jewelry from the second Cesnola collection. The museum appears not to have received any financial payment from this arrangement, but the connection with Tiffany publicized the collection and enabled the trustees' boast that "these old forms of beauty, thus revealed to modern eyes, were sources of general gratification."[56] The following year's annual report observed that "the windows of the establishments on our principal shopping streets afford to everyone who possesses a ten year old memory, the evidence of what this Museum of Art has accomplished for commerce, for industry, for the value of real estate, for the business-interests of New York . . . and abundant indications of civilizing, refining and ennobling influences which have been introduced into homes." When Joseph Choate addressed President Rutherford B. Hayes and other assembled guests at the opening of the Central Park building, he speculated that the museum was wielding indirect influence upon "the taste of the community and the trades" and thereby contributing to the "splendid display of articles of artistic beauty in our shops."[57]

Choate articulated hopes, expectations, and connections that interested observers had long held out for the museum. A writer for the *New York Times*, captivated by the loan collections when the museum opened at its temporary Fourteenth Street location, suggested that its primary function was to acquaint consumers and producers of goods with choice possessions from the homes of wealthy families. Noting that the "treasures of art, which have been loaned by numerous millionaires of the city" composed "the chief glory of the museum from an artistic stand-point," the author went on to describe the "sweet things that have crept from dusky corners in the houses of the wealthy, into the glare of day." The collections, "completely strange to the majority of visitors," included "objects carved in jade, belonging to Edward Matthews; the cloisonné enamels of Meredith Howland; the garden lace ware of S. Whitney Phenix; the exquisite pottery and faience of Samuel P. Avery; the specimens of rare and delicate book-binding of Robert Hoe, Jr.; the Sevres ware of the Prime collection; the Japanese collection of pottery belonging to Russell Sturgis." One can easily imagine how the description might have tempted curious readers, but the writer's primary concern was that the collections "furnish mines of ideas in decoration to manufacturers and artisans." In other words, the exhibitions would help to improve the quality and variety of manufactured domestic goods by offering producers an opportunity to study heretofore hidden and unfamiliar art objects.[58] Thirteen years later, the reporter, as well as Choate himself, might have been pleased to learn that a firm was producing enameled gold and jeweled ladies' pins based on photographs taken in the Metropolitan Museum of General Grant's sword.[59]

Undoubtedly Choate and others exaggerated the museum's impact on manufactures, but it is significant that museum promoters did their best to draw such connections. In 1874, an article in *Harper's Weekly* portrayed the upscale firm of Starr & Marcus almost as an extension of the museum:

A quarter of a century ago the number of persons even in our great capitals to whom it would have occurred to think of seeking for an artistic charm and an aesthetic meaning in a tea-urn or a soup-tureen, a coffee-pot or a set of knives and forks, when they set about supplying themselves with "household stuff," was about equal to the number of students of Parsee theology or Sanskrit poetry among us.

A business house which should have devoted itself then—as the house of Starr & Marcus, at 22 John Street (up stairs), in this city, now does—to meet and develop an educated demand for "beauty in use," would soon have reached the limits of its market. . . . Yet [today] the work of this house is fast outrunning the capacity of its warerooms. . . . The Metropolitan Museum of Art is worthy of study, because it shows us what has been done in this direction in other lands and other ages. Warerooms such as those of Starr & Marcus are not less worthy of a visit, because they show you what is doing now in our own country.

A writer for the more expensive *Harper's New Monthly Magazine* elaborated—and exaggerated—the same point by crediting the museum for having stimulated "the market for beauty" and the demand for "the finest classes of table porcelain"[60] (see Figure 4.4).

Trustees shared in the excitement over the Centennial Exhibition, and made some effort to draw the museum into its orbit. They joined with the National Academy of Design in arranging an exhibit of American art to coincide with the Centennial and boasted that some of the tourists who traveled to Philadelphia also took time to visit the museum. They were not entirely off the mark. According to their records, attendance at the Metropolitan reached 94,000 in 1876, whereas only 66,663 people had attended in 1875. In 1877 the Metropolitan exhibited a collection that had been the subject of great admiration at the Centennial.[61] Owned by the Italian Alessandro Castellani, it consisted largely of fifteenth-and sixteenth-century Italian ceramics, but also included jewelry, marbles, and other artifacts from that period. Ultimately, the Boston Museum of Fine Arts acquired the Castellani collection, but its showing at the Metropolitan—as well as its reception—highlights the ties that bound the museum to the growing market in ceramics and tableware. In particular, the thickly glazed, heavily molded, deeply colored majolica style (created in central Italy during the Renaissance and well represented in the Castellani collection) was immensely popular in the United States and Europe as new processes of ceramic production lowered prices.[62]

At least one writer, reporting on the exhibit for *Harper's Weekly*, invited readers to view the Castellani collection with a consuming gaze that flattened distinctions between age-old artifacts and contemporary consumables. He was impressed by the ceramics, which included specimens of "the

THE South Gallery of the Metropolitan Museum is most interesting for its exhibition of Cyprian glass and the unique
specimens of ancient jewellery and gems found in the treasure-
chamber of Curium. Among
other noticeable cases, in addition, are those containing examples of mediæval silver-work—
Dutch, German, French, Italian, and English, as well as old
watches and enamels; a collection of mediæval glass; and
one of English plate, compris-
ing specimens of work from
Elizabeth to Victoria. In the
North Gallery, which is shown
in the lower portion of our illustration, may be seen the splen-
did Avery collection of Oriental porcelain—Chinese and Japanese—the Pruyn collection of Oriental ivories and lacquer-work,
some of the gold lacquers from the Phœnix donation, as well

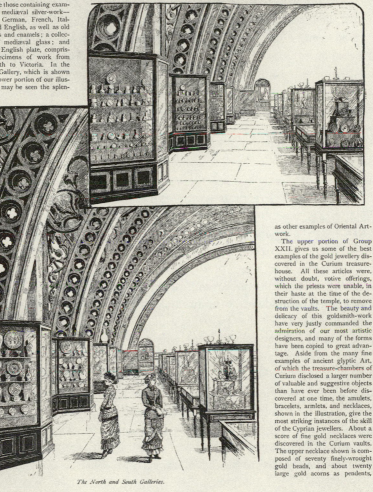

The North and South Galleries.

as other examples of Oriental Artwork.

The upper portion of Group
XXII. gives us some of the best
examples of the gold jewellery discovered in the Curium treasure-
house. All these articles were,
without doubt, votive offerings,
which the priests were unable, in
their haste at the time of the destruction of the temple, to remove
from the vaults. The beauty and
delicacy of this goldsmith-work
have very justly commanded the
admiration of our most artistic
designers, and many of the forms
have been copied to great advantage. Aside from the many fine
examples of ancient glyptic Art,
of which the treasure-chambers of
Curium disclosed a larger number
of valuable and suggestive objects
than have ever been before discovered at one time, the amulets,
bracelets, armlets, and necklaces,
shown in the illustration, give the
most striking instances of the skill
of the Cyprian jewellers. About a
score of fine gold necklaces were
discovered in the Curium vaults.
The upper necklace shown is composed of seventy finely-wrought
gold beads, and about twenty
large gold acorns as pendents,

Figure 4.4. Women view the china exhibit at the museum. From L. P. Cesnola,
ed., *The Metropolitan Museum of Art, Illustrated by Charles Gibson* (New York:
Appleton, 1882). The Huntington Library, San Marino, California.

most gorgeous effects in ruby, gold, silver, emerald, and copper lustre" and noted "these wares are now so highly prized" that one of the best examples was "worth a thousand dollars." Equally impressive were the "articles of ladies' toilet use, and many exquisite little things," along with "magnificent necklaces of shining gold, rings of delicious workmanship, bracelets that are fit for any white arms of ancient or modern times." The writer noted the "rich dressing-cases" whose contents were "exhibited to modern ladies' eyes to show how much alike are all ages and all peoples."[63]

Descriptions of the MacCallum collection of laces, on loan at the museum in 1877, evoked similar consumerist associations. Reporters located the specimens in time, but focused on their aesthetic and technical components as if writing for potential buyers or producers of fine needlework. A reporter for the *New York Times* pointed out that the objects were arranged "with reference rather to picturesqueness of position than to system" and was moved to compare the Persian designs to the "sampler of our grandmothers." The writer concluded that there was a "fancy displayed which our somewhat prosaic grandmothers never could have so much as dreamed about." The *World*'s reporter saw the exhibit in the same light, noting that "in one case, directly in front of the windows are arranged on crimson velvet twenty-six pieces each worthy of study on account of the design or the work upon it. Among the more remarkable of these is a strip of needle lace representing French 'Point d'Alençon' of the latter half of the eighteenth century. In this an arrangement of inverted semicircular garlands rests upon a groundwork of buttonhole stitched hexagons, known to the initiated as 'reseau.' " The reporter saw in a Venetian needlepoint "a coiffure not unlike in fashion that of the present day."[64]

The period of museum building coincided with the proliferation of urban commercial art galleries, and it was with respect to these new venues that the Metropolitan's retail connections were most clearly drawn. When Jarves issued his call for the establishment of American art museums, he took the opportunity to note: "Every shopkeeper can become, through the means of his wares, if he but comprehends the elementary rules of beauty, a teacher of good taste to the public. Especially this is true of establishments devoted to art."[65] In addition to Avery's Art Room, New York's leading establishment devoted to the sale of expensive paintings and other artworks was the firm of Goupil and Co. (formerly Goupil, Vibert and Co.'s International Art Union), which, by the start of the Civil War, had been purchased by the French-born Michael Knoedler. By the time the Metropolitan

Museum opened on Fourteenth Street, the gallery had moved from Broadway to the uptown location of Fifth Avenue and Twenty-Second Street. Like Avery's, Knoedler and Co. exhibited and sold work by contemporary American as well as European artists and included decorative objects among its merchandise. Among Knoedler's clients were many of the collectors who sat on the Metropolitan Museum's board of trustees.[66] The architect and trustee Russell Sturgis designed the Twenty-Second Street gallery, which featured a large plate-glass window through which strollers could view the elegant display of art objects for sale.[67]

Several of the museum's early trustees signaled the direction toward which the museum was moving. Born in 1803, Alexander Turney Stewart was of the generation that built the Art-Union, but his immigrant, nouveau riche status distanced him from the Art-Union's social group. He was notably absent from the roster of Art-Union managers. In 1869 the Stewarts moved into a fifty-five-room mansion on Fifth Avenue that featured a large picture gallery and decorative objects from around the world. By 1870, his wealth and reputation as an art collector were sufficient to win him a place on the museum's board of trustees. Stewart died in 1876, but his role in the museum was significant despite its short duration.[68] He embodied more enduring ties between retail magnates (most notably the department store owner Benjamin F. Altman) and the Metropolitan's board.

The career of Samuel Putnam Avery, one of the most active and long-lived of the early trustees, exemplified and fostered these connections. He was engaged in the business of high-end retail as a dealer in art objects. As a member of the Union League's art committee he helped to promote the museum project, and he served as a trustee from 1871 until his death in 1904. Avery, who was born in 1822, began his career as an engraver—an occupation that fostered contact with painters. By midcentury he was collecting American art and by the end of the Civil War he had opened his first gallery. During the 1870s, he traveled extensively in Europe, acquiring artworks for American clients, including a number of his fellow board members. Avery specialized in the work of living academic artists but did not confine himself exclusively to paintings. His diaries indicate that he also purchased a variety of objects ranging from silverware to jewelry and glassware for clients. Avery's Fifth Avenue gallery specialized in work by living European and American painters but also featured Chinese and Japanese porcelain. Its general decor offered affluent visitors an opportunity to envision the artworks for sale as elegant household ornamentation. This aspect of the gallery's presentation drew notice in the city's press. A writer for the *Evening Express* referred to the gallery as "a dainty and cozy little house" in which "everything has the look of comfort and culture." The *Home Journal*'s correspondent referred to it as "a fitting house of the arts," noting among other things that one of the rooms was "devoted to the display of very fine and ancient specimens of the porcelains of China and Japan, as well as various other choice objects of art." Through the 1870s, it was possible to walk from the Metropolitan Museum's temporary quarters to the gallery and to imagine objects—or reproductions—in a "cozy" household setting. In the words of yet another writer, Avery's "cunning display of good taste . . . enables the buyer to see how any particular picture would look if hung upon the wall of a correctly furnished parlor or drawing room."[69]

The trustees' commitment to the encouragement of tasteful consumption helped them to justify the purchase of two major collections on the eve of the 1880 opening at Central Park. Convinced of "the importance of Ceramic Art with regard to the manufacturing and commercial industries of our country," they paid $35,000 for Avery's "Oriental Porcelains," which had been on loan to the museum for several years; they also spent $2,445 on the MacCallum collection of laces and accepted from their fellow trustee Henry Marquand a donation of a collection of Venetian glass. With respect to the latter, they noted that "the industry of glass making and decoration is becoming important in this country."[70]

The museum's handbook to the collection of "Oriental Porcelains" scripted readers as "artists" involved in the production of modern-day objects, but also as collectors and connoisseurs. The language of moral uplift was entirely absent, but the writer also eschewed pure aestheticism. Instead, he suggested that appreciation required a high level of knowledge and grounded the handbook with information about historical development, symbolic meaning, and, above all, stylistic differences. The pamphlet addressed its readers directly, pointing out that "American students, artists, artisans, and that large portion of the American public whose life is more or less dependent on the arts as subjects of commerce, may find ample instruction in the works of the Oriental potters. The American potter, like the European potter, can have no higher ambition than to equal these superb products." But if the writer imagined the works on display as offering inspiration and instruction to producers, one can easily imagine consumers as an equally receptive audience. Much of the discussion was purely descriptive, as if written from the perspective of educated connoisseurship. Thus the commentary on the blue and white porcelain included the following observation: "the fineness of the blue and clearness of the white ground determine the artistic value of this description of Porcelain. One very rare variety is a soft clouded blue ground, realizing the tint of a spring day, and may be the 'blue of the sky after rain." A writer for *Harper's Weekly* got to the heart of the matter. When the Central Park building opened in 1880, he could note that "here the china-hunter will find his paradise."[71]

That the museum should serve the end of home decoration seemed obvious to one writer as early as 1879. An article in the *Evening Post* suggested that the trustees designate rooms and halls of the new museum building to be "decorated by genuine artists, so that each one shall be a mute but effective teacher of the characteristic styles of house decoration from the beginning to the present day." Recognizing that artists would need to be paid for their labor, the writer urged wealthy men to foot the bill. "What better monument could a rich man leave behind him than a room in the new building decorated in the way suggested at his own expense, so that, for example, if one read of the style of house ornamentation in vogue in the time of Louis XIV, he could straightway repair to the Central Park and there see with his own eyes . . . a real room decorated by a real artist, precisely as it would have been had it been constructed in France during the time mentioned."[72] Here was a vision of the museum as an aesthetic beacon for home decorators, an educator in the history of interior design, and a monument to the taste of the donors. Not until the early twentieth century would the museum begin to display objects of art in period rooms, but almost from its inception the Metropolitan was oriented to the consuming gaze, enmeshed within a broader art world in which domestic decor played a central role.

The Metropolitan Museum's leadership cultivated connections to the movement that some contemporaries referred to as the "decorative arts craze." Cesnola, along with the trustees Joseph Choate, William Prime, and Russell Sturgis, appeared on the masthead of the biweekly *Art Interchange* when it made its first appearance in 1878. The magazine, subtitled *A Household Journal*, began publication as an arm of Candace Wheeler's Decorative Arts Society, which aimed to raise the status of decorative arts and to make them a source of income and independence for genteel women. The journal offered lessons in the making of decorative art objects (including pottery), advice on interior design, reviews of art exhibitions, biographical accounts of contemporary artists, book reviews, and notices about art-related events. It also gave readers an opportunity to write in questions. The *New York Times* condescendingly described it as a journal devoted to "various subjects more or less related to bric a brac, decoration of interiors, or to the household generally."[73] At a cost of thirty-five cents per issue, the journal was within reach of the sort of struggling, middle-class and genteel women whom Wheeler hoped to reach. Prime, Cesnola, and Cesnola's American-born wife published articles in the *Art Interchange*, and the Choates served on the advisory board of the Decorative Arts Society. Caroline Choate, a onetime artist, was a personal friend of Wheeler's. In 1880, Wheeler joined with Louis Comfort Tiffany in forming an interior design company, and in 1883 she established her own all-female company (also named the Associated Artists) that enabled her to focus on the design and manufacture of textiles.[74]

By 1880, forces within and without the museum linked it to the burgeoning consumer world that celebrated decorative art, fostered aesthetic consumption, and located the home as the principal site of aesthetic improvement; yet the Cypriot sculptures, the centerpiece of the museum's holdings when it reopened at Central Park, rested uncomfortably within that network of assumptions. Within months following the museum's move to its permanent location, it became enmeshed in a controversy that pitted the museum's historical or archaeological project against its aestheticizing consumer orientation. The conflict, which centered on the Cypriot sculptures, was born of the racial thinking that shaped intellectual life in late nineteenth-century Europe and America. It would shadow the museum through the 1880s and for years thereafter.

CHAPTER 5

Metropolitan Museum on Trial

Cypriot Antiquities, Expertise, and the Problem of Race

When the Metropolitan Museum reopened at Central Park, the Cesnola collection of Cypriot antiquities overwhelmed the other displays (see Figures 5.1 and 5.2). Monumental sculptures, organized in chronological order amid cases of pottery and smaller statues, dominated the cavernous first-floor exhibition areas. The collection extended to the second floor, where visitors could view Cypriot glassware, metal receptacles, and jewelry in gold, silver, bronze, and alabaster. There were, of course, other objects on display. Examples of mid-nineteenth-century American sculpture greeted visitors in the Fifth Avenue entryway; the large collection of mostly Dutch and Flemish paintings could be seen in the second-floor galleries. Loans of paintings, laces, and Chinese ceramics and Japanese lacquers were dispersed throughout the museum along with tapestries, carved ivories, old books, Limoges enamels, Venetian glassware, European chinaware, and other "numerous pretty bibelots."[1] But the Cypriot antiquities constituted the museum's largest and most prominent display. For the Metropolitan's board of trustees, the Cesnola collection was a triumphal acquisition. At a time when European nations and museums were competing for archaeological sites and laying claim to the imagined legacy of ancient Greece, it was no small achievement for the fledgling Metropolitan Museum to have acquired a huge and widely celebrated wealth of antiquity.

For all the fanfare that accompanied the Metropolitan's primary acquisition, it came under attack within a few months of the Central Park opening. During the summer of 1880, Gaston Feuardent, a dealer in coins and antiquities whose London gallery had temporarily housed a part of the Cypriot collection, charged that several of the sculptures had been deceptively

1. Statues of Cypriote Kings.   2. Growing Sphinx.   3. Ancient Pottery.   4. Exterior View of Museum.   5. The Main Hall.   6. Cypriote Sarcophagus.   7. One of the Art Galleries.

NEW YORK CITY.—ATTRACTIONS IN THE METROPOLITAN MUSEUM OF ART, OPENED MARCH 30TH.—SEE PAGE 86.

Figure 5.1. The Cesnola collection, in the right half of the image, overwhelms the picture gallery (lower left). *New York City.—Attractions in the Metropolitan Museum of Art, Opened March 30th,* from *Frank Leslie's Illustrated Newspaper,* April 10, 1880. Fales Library, New York University.

Figure 5.2. Objects from the Cesnola collection surround the image of the Main Hall of the Metropolitan Museum of Art. *The Metropolitan Museum of Art, in Central Park, New York*, from *Harper's Weekly*, April 10, 1880. University of California Libraries, Annex.

altered in order to enhance their appearance and archaeological significance. Feuardent, who had seen much of the collection in London and again in New York prior to 1880, charged that museum workmen had transformed several pieces through the adhesion of unrelated or entirely new parts.[2] The dispute escalated in the press, and eventually Feuardent sued Cesnola for libel and defamation of character. The ensuing trial, which began in October of 1883, lasted for more than three months and became a cause célèbre. Even after the jury vindicated Cesnola, it took several years for the conflict to dissipate.

In retrospect, the most notorious episode in the protracted controversy was the exposure of several pieces to public scrutiny during March of 1882. Cesnola and the trustees, desperate to quell the escalating crisis, removed

two controversial statues from their glass casings and placed them on accessible tables in the museum's Grand Hall. They invited the public to do an
inspection. For an entire month professional sculptors, amateurs, scholars,
and editors, along with the general public, enjoyed unrestricted access. They
scraped, filed, chiseled, hammered, and applied acid in order to determine
whether museum workmen had made alterations. Augustus Saint-Gaudens,
one of New York's leading sculptors, was unable to come to a determination, but others declared the pieces to be sound. Those results failed to
convince Feuardent and his allies.[3]

What was at stake for the protagonists in this battle? Until recently,
that question garnered remarkably little attention in part because Cesnola's
personality seemed to overwhelm the conflict that swirled around him. He
was charming, energetic, and capable of eliciting diehard loyalty from
friends; but he was also brittle, defensive, and quick to anger. Throughout
his life, Cesnola was a magnet for controversy, and he had a gift for inciting
enemies. One has to wonder whether the affair would have fizzled out
quickly if early on he had admitted to the carelessness that he finally
acknowledged at the trial.[4]

But the episode was not simply the product of Cesnola's personal volatility
and carelessness. It also spoke to ongoing debates that extended back over
three decades. As was the case during the Art-Union controversy, class tensions fueled the dispute. During a decade of escalating strife in both the city
and the nation, the Cesnola controversy offered an opportunity to ridicule
the wealthy trustees who, ostensibly, fell for the fraud.[5] Struggles over cultural
authority were also central to the crisis at the Metropolitan, though the partic-
ulars of the argument were a far cry from those that bedeviled the Art-Union.
Cesnola had the misfortune of presenting his collection at a time when the
field of archaeology was on the cusp of professionalization. Standards of
expertise were in flux, and the Cypriot collection became a battleground in
the effort to define norms of excavation, restoration, and museum display.[6]

Perhaps most important for purposes here, the Cypriot collection
evoked new disputes about aesthetic taste and the most appropriate means
of fostering taste through museum displays. The antiquities, as presented
by Cesnola, told an uncomfortable historical story that seemed to undermine their value as art. The relics appeared to reveal a process of racial and
cultural amalgamation that compromised the supposed purity of classical
Greece. In the context of growing interest in the lineage of "Western civilization," the Cesnola collection provoked anxiety. In the process, it tapped

festering tensions between the archaeological narrative that gave meaning to the collection and the more consumerist or aestheticist orientation that celebrated the transcendent beauty of decontextualized objects. Through the 1870s the Metropolitan's promoters and trustees, including Cesnola himself, assumed that the two approaches were compatible and that the museum could and should develop along both axes. The Cypriot collection, by its very magnitude, brought these ways of seeing into an explosive conflict.

Cesnola and the Cypriot Collection

Luigi Palma di Cesnola was born in northern Italy in 1832, the second son of an aristocratic family. He was educated for military service, but left school at the age of fifteen to join the Sardinian Army and fight for Italian independence. Five years later, the army dismissed him for reasons that remain unclear, and he joined the Anglo-Turkish army in the war against Russia. Cesnola moved to New York in the late 1850s and suffered through several difficult years. For him, the Civil War was a godsend. After opening a cavalry school for wealthy New Yorkers, he volunteered for service in 1862. By that time, he had married Mary Isabelle Read, the daughter of a prosperous New York family, over her parents' objections. When the war was over, Cesnola parlayed his military exploits, including seven months of incarceration at the Confederate Libby Prison, into a postwar appointment as American consul in Cyprus. He used the title of "General" after the war, maintaining that President Lincoln promoted him to that rank just prior to being assassinated. No one, including Cesnola's biographer, was able to substantiate the claim.[7]

Cyprus, under Ottoman control when Cesnola arrived in 1865, might have been known to educated people in England and the United States as the site of Shakespeare's *Othello*, a stop in the travels of Saint Paul and Saint Barnabas, and, perhaps, as a place conquered by King Richard during the Crusades. It had already attracted some attention from antiquarians and amateur archaeologists, and British leaders were eyeing Cyprus for its potential value as a colonial outpost and pathway to Egypt. In 1878 Britain took control of the island as part of a complex exchange with the Ottomans. For all that, the new American consul was the first person to organize massive excavations.[8] According to his own account, he employed diggers who unearthed hundreds of sites before making their most significant discovery in 1870 in the ancient town of Golgoi. To protect his prizes Cesnola had them transported to warehouses close to his house in Larnaca. Tour groups from England would visit the buildings and some of those visitors helped themselves to souvenirs. With no sign of intentional irony, Cesnola wrote that it was "a strange truth that there are people, apparently respectable, who think nothing of pocketing antiquities not belonging to them, or of breaking off pieces of sculpture in order to carry them away as trophies to their homes."[9]

In the early 1870s Cesnola was an international celebrity, though not quite on a par with his rival Heinrich Schliemann, the famed excavator of Troy. He had sold pieces to the Berlin, Vienna, and British Museums and, by 1870, was negotiating with the Louvre and the Hermitage Museum for much larger sales. The Franco-Prussian War disrupted discussions with the French and, for reasons unknown, the Hermitage backed off. In 1871, Cesnola turned his attention to the British Museum and then to the fledgling Metropolitan as alternatives to selling his collection piecemeal at auction in London. By then Turkish authorities were growing uneasy about Cesnola's activities. The sultan banned further excavation on Cyprus and the island's governor-general prohibited exportation. Nonetheless, with assistance from a friendly Turkish official, Cesnola managed to ship nearly two hundred cases, including "the most and best" of the collection, to London. The New York trustees, eager to win a collection that had attracted attention throughout Europe, acquired it for $50,000. By the start of 1873 it had been shipped from London to the United States, and Cesnola had negotiated for expenses and a monthly stipend to oversee the unpacking and installation. Meanwhile, an Austrian ship, bound for New York directly from Cyprus and loaded with more than sixty cases of Cesnola's plunder, caught fire and sank shortly after leaving the island. That event appears to have had no impact on Cesnola's relationship with the Metropolitan.[10]

Emboldened by the sale and encouraged by his new friends in New York, Cesnola returned to Cyprus to pursue his archaeological project. To his friend Hiram Hitchcock he wrote with characteristic exuberance: "Here I am once more in the island of Venus, in good spirits and ready for more *work, glory* and *money!*"[11] It is testimony to Cesnola's reputation that John Ruskin gave him $2,500 for a claim on the new excavations, but also notable that Cesnola reserved the most valuable discoveries for himself.[12] On this expedition he put together a new collection of artifacts that was quite different from the first. It was, he suggested, "worth more than that at New York . . . for while that in New York is poor in gold, precious stones, silver, bronze, and alabaster, and rich in heavy bulky stone sculptures, this collection is just the opposite."[13] He seemed especially pleased to report that his discoveries included "*many* gold things . . . the quantity and quality of which throws into shade Schliemann's so called Treasure of Priam."[14] Cesnola claimed to have found many of these objects in a remarkable single tomb at Curium dating from the sixth century BC, but no one else was ever able to verify the existence of the site, and subsequent archaeologists pointed out that the "Treasure of Curium" included items from widely disparate periods. Cesnola invented the story of the single vault in order to enhance the value of his discoveries. The Metropolitan's trustees, competing with the British Museum and the Louvre, acquired the bulk of the second collection, including the "Curium Treasure," for an additional $60,000. Cesnola returned to New York in 1876 and worked at the Metropolitan Museum for several years with the title of "secretary." In 1879 he received a formal appointment as director, a position he would hold until his death in 1904.[15]

Cesnola sold his collections by embedding them within stories not only about himself but also about Cyprus and its relationship to the celebrated world of ancient Greece. He related fanciful tales that linked Cypriot kings to Homer's Agamemnon and Menelaus, but unlike Schliemann, he did not have the benefit of excavating (or claiming to excavate) a single mythic site associated with the widely known and revered Homeric tales. Instead, he gave significance to his collection by locating the objects within a narrative of historical progress that gained currency during the mid and later nineteenth century. According to this narrative, Greece represented the apex of ancient civilizations understood simultaneously as a cultural counterweight to modern-day materialism and as the source from which "Western civilization" supposedly grew.[16] Cesnola presented his collection as a record of the progressive social and art-historical development that culminated in Hellenism. As John Taylor Johnston, president of the Metropolitan's board of trustees put it, the collections formed "the most complete illustration of the history of ancient art and civilization" and were the "key to the origin and development of Greek civilization . . . [illustrating] the manner in which the civilization, religion, and arts of the East were transmitted to and adopted by the Greeks."[17]

The island of Cyprus, only forty miles from the coast of Asia Minor, appeared in Cesnola's narrative as an important meeting place where the presumably "Western" Greeks encountered the "East" in the form of Phoenicians (who came from the region of present-day Lebanon), Assyrians (of Mesopotamia, or present-day Iraq), and Egyptians. The artifacts unearthed on the island could reveal the process by which Greek people shaped foreign influences into their own superior artistic style and civilization. In 1872 Hiram Hitchcock, owner of the elegant Fifth Avenue Hotel and Cesnola's close friend, galvanized support for the acquisition by publishing a celebratory promotional article in the relatively highbrow *Harper's New Monthly Magazine*. Hitchcock had visited Cesnola on Cyprus and personally delivered his friend's gifts of wine and artifacts to select museum trustees.[18] The value of the collection, he declared, could "hardly be overestimated." There were, he continued, "islands of the sea—sepulchers of the ages—which can unfold the history of ancient civilization to one who searches their dark recesses with a heart for classic memory, and who can read their language of death; and Cyprus, from its history and position, is pre-eminently one." It was in Cyprus that "the West first met the East, and Greece first knew the wonder of Eastern art. Here Greek and Oriental idolatry met."[19] This was the lesson received by Joseph Henry, director of the Smithsonian Institution, upon reading Cesnola's book. In an appreciative letter to the author, Henry observed that the "great migration passed from the East to the West . . . gathered up the materials of the separate civilizations and in this way produced the civilization of ancient Greece, a combination and improvement of all other civilizations." Cyprus, he continued, was "a resting place in this progress," and Cesnola's collection "exhibits, as it were, the transient state of art which finally culminated in Greece."[20]

Yet Feuardent had been suspicious of Cesnola's practices as early as 1871 when he began checking sculptures at his London gallery against an illustrated catalog of the collection assembled by the Hermitage Museum in preparation for the acquisition that never occurred. Upon inspection of the Metropolitan's display, he raised questions about several sculptures. At first he spoke privately to the Metropolitan's staff, but when Cesnola issued a furious public response, Feuardent responded in kind. He declared that the statuette designated *Venus* had appeared at the museum's temporary Fourteenth Street building without the carved mirror (see Figure 5.3). The "antiquity of the mirror," insisted Feurardent, "dates from the year A.D. 1879." He also raised questions about other pieces,

STATUETTE NO. 157.
FRONT VIEW.

STATUETTE NO. 157.
SIDE VIEW SHOWING MIRROR.

Figure 5.3. Gaston Feuardent charged that the mirror, visible on the profile of the figure, had been carved into the statuette at Cesnola's direction. From Feuardent, "Tampering with Antiquities," *Art Amateur* 3, no. 3 (August 1880). Library of Congress.

including a large sculpture that he referred to as "that dreadful monstrosity, the bearded Venus," insisting that the head and arms did not belong to the torso and that the dove was a recent addition created by an "ornithological manufacturer working under Mr. DiCesnola's eyes"[21] (see Figures 5.4 and 5.5).

Cesnola issued his own public response, furiously denying all charges, demanding that the trustees conduct an investigation, and dismissing his accuser as "a French Jew dealer." He insisted that Feuardent's motivation was that of an angry, disappointed businessman. Had the Cypriot collection

Figure 5.4. Cesnola in Cyprus posing beside the sculpture that he suggested might represent a "bearded Venus." Feurardent used that term to ridicule the sculpture. Cesnola's workmen later constructed a dove and attached it to the figure's left hand. The base is also a late nineteenth-century addition. Louis Palma di Cesnola, Golgoi, Hagios Photos, 1870. Cambridge University Library.

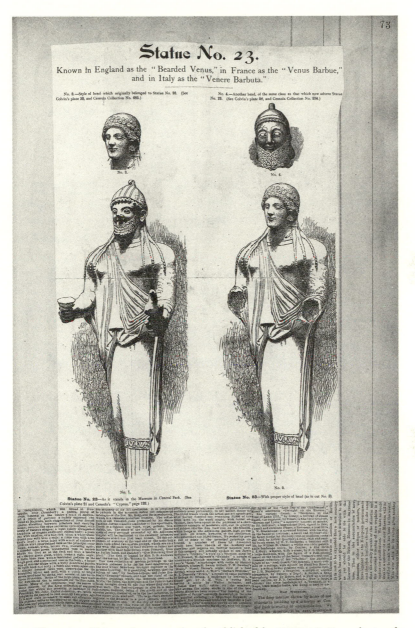

Figure 5.5. This card, prepared and published by Gaston F. Feuardent, referenced the "Bearded Venus." It suggests that the sculpture was a hodgepodge of unrelated parts. Metropolitan Museum of Art, Archives.

sold in London at auction, Feuardent, by the terms of his contract, would have earned a commission. Feuardent's attack, according to this argument, was his way of getting back at the man who had cost him dearly. When a committee of investigation, carefully chosen by the trustees, provided the requisite vindication, it did little to quell the escalating controversy. In the spring of 1882, Feuardent sued Cesnola for libel and defamation of character.[22] The trial would begin over a year later, but in the meantime, Cesnola drew the wrath of another, more powerful adversary—the *Daily Tribune*'s art critic Clarence Cook.

Cook's attacks echoed those by Feuardent but went even further. In 1881 he published a series of articles entitled "Our Mismanaged Museum," followed in March of 1882 with a pamphlet called *Transformations and Migrations in Certain Statues in the Cesnola Collection* (see Figure 5.6). Using images of the collection published by Cesnola and others created prior to 1880, he charged that additional statues had been deceptively altered. Equally damning was his claim that the Tomb of Golgoi was nothing more than the product of Cesnola's opportunistic imagination.[23]

Aestheticism, History, and the Problem of the Cypriot Statues

By the time Clarence Cook joined Feuardent in the assault on Cesnola, he already had a considerable reputation as the *Tribune*'s opinionated and sometimes vitriolic writer on art-related matters, a terror to many artists, and a staunch defender of professionalism and independence in art criticism. Raised as a Unitarian, his intellectual and personal roots lay in the reformist world of antebellum New England. His father, director of a Boston insurance company, served in the Massachusetts House of Representatives and founded the state's Horticultural Society. Cook graduated from Harvard in 1849 a staunch abolitionist and aspiring poet, but without the family wealth that might have sustained a literary career. Troubled by the "barbarism" he found in New York City, he moved in 1852 to the Hudson River Valley town of Fishkill Landing and worked in the office of the celebrity architectural reformer and landscape designer Andrew Jackson Downing. He would later marry Downing's eminently upper-crust sister-in-law, the granddaughter of President John Adams, described years later in Cook's obituary as "the daughter of John P. Dewint, one of the old settlers of Dutchess County and of Knickerbocker stock." The architect Calvert Vaux,

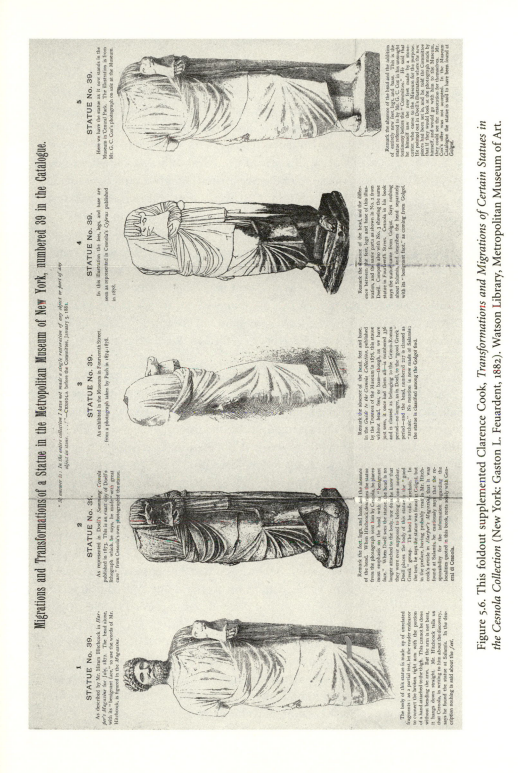

Figure 5.6. This foldout supplemented Clarence Cook, *Transformations and Migrations of Certain Statues in the Cesnola Collection* (New York: Gaston L. Feuardent, 1882). Watson Library, Metropolitan Museum of Art.

codesigner of Central Park, also worked with Downing, and Cook's first book was a respectful account of the park project. By the mid-1850s, Cook was earning his living as a journalist, writing for an array of publications that included the abolitionist *Liberty Bell* and *National Anti-Slavery Standard.* (A portrait of Cook painted in 1861 includes a picture of John Brown in the background.) During this period Cook was an impassioned devotee of John Ruskin and cofounder of the Society for the Advancement of Truth in Art, dedicated to the promotion of Ruskin's ideas and to the support of a small group of artists who identified themselves as the American Pre-Raphaelite Brotherhood. In line with Ruskin, the society celebrated the art culture of the Middle Ages and minute observation of nature as the route to moral truth in painting. In 1863 Cook became editor of the *New Path*, the group's journal, only to leave one year later when he took a position as a staff writer for the *New York Daily Tribune.* He would spend two years in Europe as the paper's foreign correspondent, but eventually left the *Tribune* due to a falling out with the editor, Whitelaw Reid, over the Cesnola controversy.[24]

Cook's retreat from the progressive political engagement of his abolitionist youth mapped his growing celebration of the decorative over the didactic, moralizing element in painting. Like others of his ilk, he came to celebrate the "poetry" of art, emphasizing the importance of its ineffable, spiritual impact. Later in life, he wrote that a painting that was "only moral or didactic . . . slips over from art to literature."[25] By the 1870s, he had moved away from Ruskin's influence, drawing distinctions between art and "scientific illustration" while giving greater attention to "originality" and "independence" in artistic vision. As French impressionist artists became known in the United States, Cook was among their most enthusiastic champions.[26] A picture, he believed, should "address itself to something in us higher than our senses; but it ought to do that and be decorative too."[27]

Cook was consistent in his dedication to the uplift and education of popular taste, but for him the goal of aesthetic education was increasingly personal and domestic. After the downfall of the Art-Union, he proposed that the building be maintained as a free gallery, and throughout his life he insisted that galleries, museums, and parks should be broadly accessible. He was also committed to his work as a journalist for affordable publications and believed that tough, honest, independent criticism would foster the dual causes of popular education and the improvement of art. But by the time he issued his attack on Cesnola, his most well-known and probably most widely read work was a collection of essays on interior design that focused attention on urban apartments. Initially published as a series for *Scribner's Monthly*, the essays were republished in 1878 and again in 1881 as a volume entitled *The House Beautiful*. Cook also wrote the introduction to a promotional pamphlet published in 1881 by Warren, Fuller, and Co., a producer of wallpaper.[28] Several years later he coauthored a series of essays entitled "The Modern Home" for the *Art Amateur*. Cook invested these projects with great significance because he believed that household decor simultaneously expressed and shaped the character of the inhabitants. The living room, he argued, "ought to represent the culture of the family, what is their taste, what feeling they have for art." But he also looked upon that room as "an important agent in the education of this life," which would "make a great difference to the children who grow up in it, and to all whose experience is associated with it." It was, he pointed out, "no trifling matter, whether we hang poor pictures on our walls or good ones, whether we select a fine cast or a second rate one. We might almost as well say it makes no difference whether the people we live with are first-rate or second-rate."[29]

Though he struggled to make a living through journalism, Cook's education, marriage, and Unitarian background provided considerable cultural capital; his social and likely political ties were to the self-styled "Independents" or "Liberals" who included a number of former abolitionists. These were men who sought to cleanse the country of corruption by pressing for political reform, professionalization of the civil service, and moral improvement through cultural education. While condemning venality in business and vice in the Republican Party, they pinned more blame on Democratic machine politics, labor radicals, immigrants, and "ignorant" voters generally. Their commitment to democracy was, as Thomas Bender aptly writes, "conditional." William Cullen Bryant counted himself among this group, and one suspects that other Art-Union promoters would have joined him had they lived as long. Cook wrote about art rather than politics, but he was part of the Liberals' intellectual milieu. His commitment to aesthetic education and his mission to purge the Metropolitan of corruption were consistent with the group's core values.[30] He also counted among his friends two liberal members of the Metropolitan's board of trustees, the editor George William Curtis and the architect and critic Russell Sturgis, who worked with Cook at the *New Path* and later became art critic for the Liberals' leading journal, the *Nation* magazine. Sturgis had also written for the *Crayon.* In many ways the intellectual evolution of Cook and Sturgis ran on parallel tracks. Sturgis wrote books on painting, sculpture, and furniture, hoping to educate the taste of middle-class readers. Like Cook, he came to embrace decorative over explicitly didactic elements in art, and when his friend came under fire for his outspoken, negative art criticism, Sturgis issued a strong defense.[31] When Cook leveled his attack on Cesnola and the Metropolitan, he did so not only as a self-styled professional but also as a man with confidence in his own social connections and class.

It is no coincidence that Cook's "Our Mismanaged Museum" appeared in a journal that was called the *Art Amateur.* This was also the journal that published Feuardent's initial charges, and its editor, Montague Marks, was a staunch critic of the Metropolitan. The *Art Amateur* (1879–1903) was a leader (in longevity and circulation) of the bevy of late nineteenth-century illustrated periodicals whose purpose was to bring art and artistic taste into the home. The carefully worded subtitle, *A Monthly Journal Devoted to the Cultivation of Art in the Household,* speaks to this mission. It provided encouragement to amateur artists for whom the household was the site of production, but it also offered advice on making the household an artistic space. Readers could learn about art exhibitions in the United States and Europe; they could find accounts of artists living and dead; and they could garner advice on home decor (see Figure 5.7). At the core of the journal were illustrated instructions on the creation of art objects with features ranging from Japanese fans to ceramic bowls. The journal, along with others in the same genre, conveyed the sense of a seamless link not only between graphic and decorative art but also between creators of art objects and decorators of interior spaces.

Cook allowed a legitimate place in art museums for artifacts and artworks whose significance was entirely archaeological, but he was much more interested in the museum's role as an improver of American domestic taste and design. The alleged fraudulence of Cesnola's collection was especially galling to Cook because, in his view, it had no value apart from what it could say about the ancient world. "The Cesnola collection," Cook insisted, "contains, with one single exception, no statuary of any value as art. Its sole value lies in the supposed antiquity of the objects, in their integrity, and in the alleged fact of their having been found in a particular spot."[32] Tampering with objects and lying about their provenance destroyed whatever historical and archaeological value they might have had.[33]

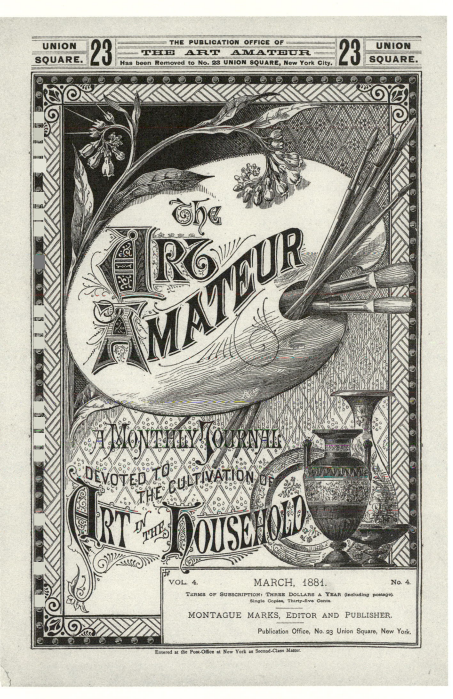

Figure 5.7. The *Art Amateur* 4, no. 4 (March 1881). The magazine, edited by Montague Marks, was aligned with Clarence Cook and Gaston Feuardent. Author's collection.

But there were even deeper objections. It was one thing to include antiquities that represented great civilizations of the past, but from the perspective of critics, Cesnola's antiquities did no such thing. As Cook observed, "the art of Cyprus, so far as it had an aboriginal character, was of a piece with the art of all the islands that fringe the coast of Asia Minor, and was distinctly of a rude almost savage character." Cesnola's Cyprus, presented as a window onto the development of ancient Greece, was also firmly rooted in the part of the world that nineteenth-century Americans and Europeans deemed Eastern, Oriental, Semitic, and decidedly other. In the nineteenth century, American scholarly interest in the "Near Orient" was linked to biblical studies, and Cesnola capitalized on those connections by suggesting that ancient Cyprus was "the Chittim" of the Old Testament. His focus on the Phoenicians as early traders and settlers on Cyprus also had biblical implications. Nineteenth-century readers of Cesnola's book would have recognized Phoenicians as the Canaanites of biblical times.[34]

Both Cesnola and Hitchcock emphasized the indebtedness of Greek art to peoples of the Near East and identified the Cypriot antiquities as windows onto those cultural exchanges. Cesnola's discussions of specific objects highlighted the theme of cross-fertilization between Asiatic/Semitic peoples and the Greeks. A giant sarcophagus appeared to him "as a clear illustration of the development of Greek from Asiatic or Assyrian art. The resemblance between the lions at the four corners of the lid and the bronze lions found at Nineveh by Layard" was "very striking," while the carved image of a bearded man appeared to be of "Asiatic style." But Cesnola identified warriors sculpted onto the sides of the sarcophagus as "Greek."[35] From this point of view, the artifacts unearthed on the island could reveal the process by which Greek people shaped foreign influences into their own superior artistic style and civilization. As Hitchcock wrote, Greek pottery represented the "culmination" of ancient ceramic art: "she [Greece] learned of Phoenicia." And, "when the source of Greek art is reached, a full, rich, ornate stream will be seen issuing from the mother Egyptian fountain." The Metropolitan's handbook to the Cypriot sculptures, written by Cesnola's young assistant A. Duncan Savage, developed this historical narrative, emphasizing the indebtedness of Hellenism to Phoenicia in particular. When the Greeks first settled Cyprus, "they were in a primitive stage of civilization," while their "new neighbors" the Phoenicians, having learned from the Egyptians, "were much further advanced." As Savage put it, "when these two currents had done their work of fructification, the foreign

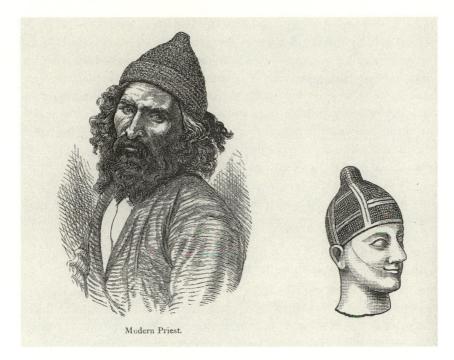

Modern Priest.

Figure 5.8. Cesnola noted a "resemblance" not only between the hats of the contemporary Cypriot priest and the ancient statue but also between their "features." From Cesnola, *Cyprus: Its Ancient Cities, Tombs, and Temples* (London, 1877). Geisel Library, University of California, San Diego.

elements were fused and the mixture transmuted into an independent national and Greek art.[36]

The artifacts, most of which did not embody the celebrated Grecian style, also acquired meaning as ancestors—even stand-ins—for the people who populated modern-day Cyprus. Cesnola, whose account of his excavation was riddled with contemptuous commentary on the island's residents, observed that the "priests . . . who work in the fields like the peasants wear a conical hat, not unlike those represented in the statues discovered at Golgoi." He also saw "a resemblance between the features of the priest . . . and his sculptured predecessors." Cesnola, who speculated that the cone was a symbol of fertility associated with the ancient Aphrodite, implied a linkage between modern wearers of canonical hats and their forebears[37] (see Figure 5.8). Hitchcock made a comparable point with the illustration that opened his *Harper's* piece. The image draws a visual analogy between the statue and the Turkish digger (see Figure 5.9). If, as was widely believed, Americans and Europeans were the inheritors of classical civilization, so the darker skinned, supposedly degenerated people of the modern Mediterranean had racial and cultural affinities with exotic artifacts of more remote antiquity. The unavoidable implication of this narrative was that the majority of the Cypriot artifacts were the products of lesser people. Their primary significance, in the view of nineteenth-century commentators, was as a measure of the superior civilization that flowered elsewhere.

By linking ancient Cyprus to the East, Cesnola was able to woo readers and audiences with Orientalist fantasies. In a sense, he had no other choice: Larnaca is located barely 130 miles from Beirut. Most of the artifacts in the collection looked decidedly un-Greek or at least unlike the classical and Hellenic objects widely regarded as the apex of ancient art. Cesnola presented Cyprus as the tantalizing site of Eastern luxury and sexual promiscuity. "There is no doubt," he wrote, that "under the original Greek settlers and for centuries after them . . . Cyprus had maintained a high character among the Greek Islands." But, he continued, "the intercourse with the East rendered the people of Cyprus proverbial as the happiest beings on earth as far as luxury and pleasure could make them . . . there was no excess or refinement or indulgence which they did not practice."[38]

Cesnola attributed degenerate Cyprian cultural practices in large part to the worship of Aphrodite, whom he identified not as the idealized, classical goddess revered by philhellenic Europeans, but rather as one of the primitive Eastern female deities whom the Greeks presumably surpassed.[39] In Cesnola's view, Aphrodite derived from the "Tyrian goddess Astarte," and he suggested that "the Asiatic side of her religion" promoted prostitution among her worshippers at the Cypriot temple at Paphos. Cesnola also evoked notions of sexual monstrosity. He opened the door to Feuardent's ridicule by suggesting that the statue of the man (eventually) holding a dove might be a representation of the "Bearded Venus," traditionally identified as a Cypriot figure. Describing the statue, Cesnola observed that "the great development of the breasts and the quasi feminine features have led more than one archaeologist to believe that the statue might represent the goddess herself, who, according to Macrobius, was at Amathus conceived as having a beard."[40] Hitchcock drew these connections as well when he linked the sin of the Cyprian ancients to Aphrodite worship and referred to sculptures in and around the temple of Golgos as "*Nana*, the Chaldaean Venus;

THE EXPLORATIONS OF DI CESNOLA IN CYPRUS.

THE COLOSSUS OF GOLGOS.

AMERICA is a long way off from the ancient historic world, and our people who do not visit Europe and make acquaintance with antiquity in the great museums there have little opportunity for perfect realization of the oneness of the race in all ages. We are not often brought into direct contact with the results of ancient thought and handiwork, and hence we are comparatively strangers to the men and women who lived in Asia and around the eastern shores of the Mediterranean two and three thousand years ago. Within a few years, however, we have begun to see more of the long past, and it has at length occurred that an American citizen and representative abroad has conducted a series

Figure 5.9. Hiram Hitchcock, "The Explorations of Di Cesnola in Cyprus," *Harper's New Monthly Magazine*, June 1, 1872, 188. Author's collection.

Ishtar, the Assyrian; *Mylitta,* the Babylonian; *Astarte,* the Phoenician (the strange goddess *Ashtoreth* that beguiled Solomon); *Aphrodite,* the Greek; and *Amathunta,* the bearded Venus."[41] From this point of view, Aphrodite signaled the luxury, exoticism, sexual profligacy, and transgression that linked Cyprus to the East.

Among the anxieties that festered beneath the surface was the fear that Cesnola's claims cast aspersions on ancient Greece itself and on the developing racial narrative of Western superiority. The late nineteenth century was the period when European scholars were beginning to fixate on the notion of Greece as an Aryan civilization that developed without significant input from Semitic or Oriental peoples. The German art historian Wilhelm Lübke, whose multivolume work Cook edited and translated for publication in the United States, insisted that an invasion from the northern mountains by "the powerful race of Dorians" had "laid the foundation of that pure and beautiful art which henceforth we designate as Greek." And Cook argued in the same vein when he declared: "It would be a serious mistake on the student's part . . . were he to believe that the pure and graceful forms, and lines of Greek pottery of the best period were 'derived' from these crude, grotesque, and often purely naturalistic and imitative productions, of the native potter's art. As was said of the sculpture of Cyprus, so it must be said of the pottery: We must be content to learn from it what it can teach us about Cyprus." "As to the 'origin and development of Greek civilization,'" Cook concluded, "the antiquities of twenty Cypruses could help us little in solving that mystery."[42] One can find a hint of these concerns even in a positive review of Savage's handbook to the collection of Cypriot sculptures. The author noted that "the gradual transition from Orientalism to Hellenism in Cyprian art, which Mr. Savage clearly brings out by means of skillful grouping, is in the highest degree interesting, showing how much, and yet, artistically speaking, how very little, Greece owed to older nations."[43]

In fact, Assyrian and especially Phoenician artifacts had negative connotations in the late nineteenth century. For many students of antiquity, these were the racialized others of biblical history. As early as the 1840s, artifacts from Mesopotamia were on view at the Louvre and the British Museum where they attracted a great deal of negative attention on the grounds that Assyrians were a violent, crude people incapable of producing great art. The Phoenicians had an even worse reputation as traders and Semites, given to sensuality.[44] Lübke, who shared this perspective, declared that "the plastic art of Assyria" never achieved greatness because "its narrow realism was forever employed to serve the material uses of despotism." And Lübke was at pains to argue that the Greeks, whatever they may have owed to the Phoenicians in the way of technical skill, owed them nothing in the way of art. He believed that Phoenician remains showed "extreme clumsiness" compared to those of other ancient people.[45] A writer for the *American Journal of Archaeology* offered an even more extreme assessment:

> The Phoenicians, so far as we know, did not bring a single important fructifying idea into the world. Nor, as the inventors of technical processes, by which moral ideas and emotions may be expressed, were they remarkable. Their most important contribution to higher civilization, the adaptation of the alphabet, was, so far as concerned themselves, quite a mechanical and unexpressive one, an accident of business. Their arts of dyeing purple, of pottery, of making glass, of carving ivory, of casting and beating metals hardly deserve to be called arts; they were for the most part only trades. Their architecture, sculpture, painting were . . . of the most unimaginative sort. Their religion, so far as we know it, was entirely an appeal to the senses.[46]

The editor of the *Art Amateur* agreed with this damning assessment, noting that "the Cesnola collection is undoubtedly of great archaeological interest, but the objects, for the most part, are entirely out of place as models in an *art* museum; for, excepting a few of Greek importation into Cyprus, they are truly Cypriote, the work of rude barbarians."[47] Similarly, a writer for the *Century* noted "a large part of the [Cesnola] stone collection consists of amorphous and hideous objects of archaic or provincial workmanship."[48] From this perspective, the alleged fraudulence of the restorations simply added insult to the deeper injury.

Here was the central point of dispute with Cesnola, who, in an effort to legitimize his collection, adopted a historical and archaeological argument for its significance. No one, including Cesnola, promoted the collection on aesthetic grounds, but while detractors emphasized this negative assessment, defenders pointed to the collection's historical and archaeological significance. A writer for the *New York Times* suggested in 1873 that the statues "artistically are worthless, but archeologically they have a high value." Similarly, William H. Goodyear, whom Cesnola would soon

appoint as the Metropolitan's first curator, declared that "the two principal
features of the [Cesnola] collection are its ugliness and the confusion it is
likely to leave in the mind of the spectator." Goodyear believed that "this
confusion will disappear when we study the position and history of Cyprus
with a view to what we may expect to find there."[49] The British archaeologist Reginald Stuart Poole wrote in 1878 that the antiquities of Cyprus were
"interesting alone to the serious student of the remote annals of the Mediterranean . . . [as] a precious connecting-link between Egypt, Assyria and
Early Greece and the less attractive they are to the artistic eye the more
valuable they are to his comparative vision."[50] Cesnola got to the nub of
the matter when he charged that his critics did not understand that "Art is
one thing and Archaeology is another and quite different thing." He
believed that Cook's pamphlet exemplified "the muddle" by failing to recognize that "in all discoveries of ancient sculpture there are a thousand
poor works of art to one good one."[51]

The museum's annual report for 1883 elaborated upon that point and
elevated the distinction between archaeology and aestheticism to the level
of a mandate. The trustees declared that the purpose of a museum of art
should be "not to teach what its founders think ought to be admired, but
to teach what men and women, under the varied circumstances of age,
country, education, religion, have admired and have utilized." A similar
argument had justified the acceptance, in 1882, of a loan of "ancient American Works of Art, chiefly Mexican." In defense of the collection, the annual
report observed, "every object is a thought, or a group of thoughts, a sen-
tence, a page, sometimes a long story. A museum of such art will thus
become a library, which arranged by studious archaeologists will be a price-
less restoration of the lost history." Archaeology, according to this line of
argument, was an analogue of the new field of anthropology and the art
museum an appropriate site for the study of comparative cultures or
civilizations.[52]

By contrast, Cook's inclination was to aestheticize artworks. Like many
artists and critics of the 1870s and 1880s he was captivated by Japanese
design. He urged artists and home decorators to study it, and he recommended that Japanese artworks be incorporated into household decor (see
Figure 10). Yet, he professed little interest in the culture that produced the
admired objects. "The Japanese live in moon-land," Cook declared. "Their
ways are not ours, and it is impossible for us to put ourselves into sympathy
with them." It satisfied him to note that "their art comes out of themselves,

Much in Little Space.
No. 40.

Figure 5.10. Cook recommended the use of Japanese elements such as the pictured wall hanging. Other illustrations featured Japanese fans decorating mantel pieces. *Much in Little Space*, from Clarence Cook, *The House Beautiful: Essays on Beds and Tables, Stools and Candlesticks* (New York: Scribner, Armstrong and Co., 1878). Geisel Library, University of California, San Diego.

and they are producing it now in our day on the models they have been following for centuries and with much of the spirit of antique time. And therefore it has a vitality for us, and knocks at little secret doors in our own nature and gets some sort of response, though, for the most part it is but the wind whistling through the key hole."[53] This is an odd passage in part because Cook obliquely raised questions with which he was unwilling to engage. He seemed to wonder whether the very capacity to appreciate the delicacy of Japanese imagery signaled some commonality between the admirers and producers. How could inhabitants of "moon land" create works capable of uplifting the inhabitants of American living rooms? Did respect for the art require respect for the people? Clearly, Cook was disinclined to open the door to these questions. Along with many other proponents of Japanese design, he attributed the aesthetic vitality of Japan's art to the persistence of time-honored practices. He suggested that the very advancement of modern society increased the longing for preindustrially produced or "antique" crafts. But Cook did his best to confine his interest to the objects themselves.[54]

Cesnola's antagonists, including Cook, tended to favor the acquisition and display of casts over what they deemed to be unworthy, overpriced originals. They argued that casts served the interest of education, by which they meant not only the education of artists but also the more general uplift of public taste.[55] William Stillman, a supporter of Cook's position, argued that "what was wanted in New York was an art-museum in which public art-education could be forwarded. Any collection of casts of Greek statues would have done what was wanted better" than the Cesnola statues. In 1883 he still believed that the sculptures had archaeological significance "showing certain connections in civilization, mythology and art which were never brought out by any other work," but he insisted that they had "no value whatever as art."[56] Stillman contrasted the Boston Museum to its New York counterpart when he complimented the former's "five Greek rooms devoted to casts."[57] Similarly a writer for the *Century* suggested in 1884 that "a great American Museum" required "a collection of casts of all the great Greek sculptures." And the *Art Amateur* declared that the acquisition of a complete set of casts and molds from major art museums "would be incalculably more valuable to the Museum for educational purposes than the two Cesnola collections."[58]

Cook seemed to regard his own writings on home decor in much the same way as he envisioned art museums—as educational tools for the improvement of American taste and manufactures. He hoped that his essays would uplift taste by acquainting readers with exemplars of fine design. To those readers who complained that the engravings in *House Beautiful* depicted unaffordable pieces, he responded without apology: "I think we need in this country to be made as familiar as possible with the look of beautiful things of this sort." Once readers were familiar with the best pieces, they would be in a position to improve their lives by choosing tasteful but economical furnishings. In "Our Mismanaged Museum" Cook revealed his expectation for art museums and his opinion as to where the Metropolitan fell short. He observed that "the Philadelphia Centennial Exhibition . . . gave the impulse to our taste, and filled us with the desire for more artistic surroundings, which in turn have set in motion all the wheels of trade to satisfy the popular need. The one institution to which we owe absolutely nothing is the Metropolitan Museum."[59]

It is telling that Cook and others were far less critical (at least initially) of the second Cesnola collection—the so-called "Curium Treasure" (see Figure 5.11)—than they were of the Cypriot sculptures. By the mid-1880s, European archaeologists were questioning the existence of the Curium tomb, but before that time the relentlessly critical Cook allowed himself to be gullible. He declared the collection "found in a tomb near the site of Curium" to be "remarkable in its beauty, and value."[60] Similarly, a writer for the *Century*, who doubted Cesnola's honesty and believed that "a large part of the [Cypriot] stone collection consists of amorphous and hideous objects of archaic or provincial workmanship," believed that the "jewelry, gems, and glass are of considerable value."[61] The point is that critics found it easier to credit decorative objects that had meaning to contemporary viewers, particularly women, as objects of use and beautification.

In fact, the second Cesnola collection, particularly the jewelry and other precious metalwork, was incorporated rather easily into the museum's aestheticizing project. It was from among these objects that Tiffany's created reproductions for sale. William Prime's 1877 article for *Harper's Monthly* introduced the "Kurium Treasure" and presented choice pieces as exemplars of timeless taste and luxury. It urged the museum visitor to "dismiss from his mind all notions of the early history of Greek art which books and museums have heretofore given him." Claiming that the treasure had been "buried for some six centuries before Christ," he suggested that "no modern work in jewelry is any finer in design or more exquisite in delicacy of execution than are the large number of these articles." Similarly, an ancient

PLATE XXVII

GOLD ORNAMENTS.—FROM CURIUM

[To follow Plate XXVI.

Figure 5.11. Gold jewelry supposedly found in a tomb at Curium. From Cesnola, *Cyprus: Its Ancient Cities, Tombs, and Temples* (London, 1877). Geisel Library, University of California, San Diego.

silver cup "must have belonged to a man of finished taste, as it was the work of an artist who has never been surpassed."[62]

But the bulk of the Cesnola collection was out of step with the museum envisioned by Cook and others. Its sheer size and accompanying narrative put it at loggerheads with efforts to construct the museum as an exemplar of beauty for the education of consumers and artisans. A slim but lavishly illustrated overview of the museum, edited by Cesnola and published in 1882, embodied that tension. The volume, entitled *The Metropolitan Museum of Art*, is remarkable for neglecting even to mention the collection of paintings. Twelve of its thirty-two pages deal with decorative art objects outside of the Cesnola collection. Descriptions convey a sense of luxury, and illustrations, featuring groups of objects in artful displays, might have been advertisements for stores whose notices appeared at the end of the volume. The author described two Turkish tables as "specimens of the eating-tables used by the wealthy. They are superbly inlaid with mother-of-pearl, a kind of decoration in which the Turks and Arabs excel." A "profusely decorated" metal bowl, pictured leaning against one of the tables, was "of the kind which, filled with water, is passed around by slaves, at an Oriental banquet, for lavatory purposes between the courses." An image of Venetian glass garnered comparable praise (see Figure 5.12). At the end of the volume, readers encountered advertisements from dealers in decorative objects. John Chadwick, for example, "invites attention to his recent Importations of Antiques, Tapestries, Gobelin, Beauvais, Flemish and Spanish; Elegant Antique Embroidered Colchas and Hangings; Antique Silver, Porcelains," while Mitchell, Vance & Co. informs potential customers of their "Gas Fixtures, Clocks, Bronzes, Metal and Porcelain Lamps, and Ornamental Metal-work."[63]

More than half of the volume is devoted to the Cypriot antiquities, and those pages differ markedly from the section on the Turkish tables, Oriental porcelains, Venetian glassware, and so forth. Referring to a vase "having on top the rather crude form of a woman's head," the author observed, "Like all Cypriot work, where the Art-sense was dull, the handle is wanting in grace of curve." For comparison the "student" is urged to "look at a vase almost beside it, which embodies the same idea and has truer Greek feeling in it." Similarly, the author informs the reader, "the Phoenician sculptor desired not to create beauty, but to produce a likeness. He was interested only in the face, and it did not disturb him that he made the hair and the beard fall like folds of cloth."[64] If Phoenician objects were to educate public taste, they could do so only as negative examples.

use. The finest example of Roman glass is the Barberini or Portland vase, in the British Museum, on which is represented in raised figures the marriage of Peleus and Thetis. The specimens of Roman glass in Group XXV. show the forms most in vogue, and indicate that the Romans of the empire were in large measure masters of the subtleties of the glass-making art. Nearly every ornamental device practised by modern skill is here displayed, and even the best Venetian period of glass-blowing has little to offer in the treatment of form and decoration more essentially artistic.

The Jackson Jarves collection of Venetian glass, of which illustrations are given in Group XXVI., furnishes a good opportunity for comparison. The designs are more fragile and fantastic, more inventive and original, perhaps, but not better in form. The genius of the Venetian artist ran riot in a thousand quaint shapes, and we find in his work something of the same wonderful feeling for colour which made the canvasses of Titian, Tintoretto, and Giorgone, such masterpieces. Venetian glass-blowing reached its perfection in the thirteenth century at Murano, one of the islands adjacent to the city, and here for two or three centuries was produced that wonderful glass which is the marvel of modern times. The industry has recently been revived at Murano, but, though the products are beautiful, they do not equal the best results of the medi-

spirit and treatment between the Occident and Orient is immediately perceptible. The Japanese, in all the varieties of their Art, display a richness and sort of grotesque invention very striking. To much of the unrivalled dexterity and finish of detail, so characteristic of the Chinese artists, they added great force of humorous originality and vigour in expressing it. The minor pieces in the lower part of Group XXIV. are good examples of this, while the carving of the elephant may be regarded merely as an illustration of technical fineness of work.

The manufacture of glass, which belongs to both the useful and ornamental arts, is one of the oldest discoveries of human invention, and passes back into the morning of antiquity. Representations of glass-blowers have been found painted on Egyptian tombs, which date three thousand years before Christ. In a previous chapter something has been said of ancient Greek glass, and the perfection which it reached. Let us now take a brief glance at the Roman glass, as shown in the splendid Marquand collection, recently purchased by the Museum. These glass objects were exhumed in different portions of Europe, and bear witness of the old Roman occupation. Group XXV. offers many fine examples of Roman glass, showing the character of its forms and decoration. In many cases this glass, like that of the Greek period excavated at Cyprus, is coloured with a beautiful iridescence, the chemical effect of decay. Though the manufacture of glass was introduced into Rome in the time of Cicero, it was not till the latter years of the first century of our epoch that great skill was attained in making ornamental articles. At this time only articles of luxury were produced, such as vases, wine-jars, and cups for the tables of the wealthy, perfume and other vases for their toilette, and urns and lachrymatories for their tombs. It was not till the third century that articles of glass came into common

Group XXVI.

æval craft. The specimens delineated in Group XXVI. suggest the great variety and delicacy of treatment which the Murano glass-blower was enabled to obtain. Old Venetian glass of the best design is exceptionally rare, not merely on account of the long decadence of the manufacture, but from the excessive fragility of these precious objects.

Figure 5.12. Examples of Venetian glass from the Jarves collection: "The specimens delineated in Group XXVI suggest the great variety and delicacy of treatment which the Murano glass-blower was enabled to obtain. Old Venetian glass of the best design is exceptionally rare." From *The Metropolitan Museum of Art*, edited by L. P. di Cesnola, illustrated by George Gibson (New York: D. Appleton, 1882). The Huntington Library, San Marino, California.

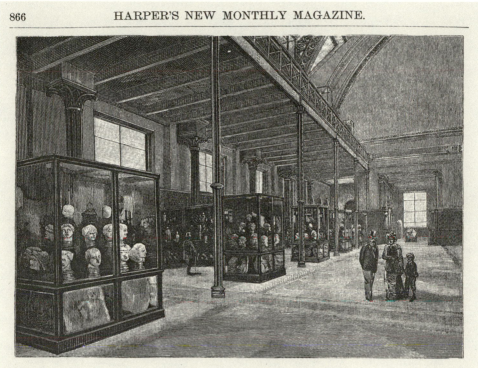

THE CESNOLA COLLECTION UNDER NORTH GALLERY.

Figure 5.13. A part of the Cesnola collection. From "The Metropolitan Museum of Art," *Harper's New Monthly Magazine* 60 (May 1880). University of California Libraries, Annex.

The Metropolitan emphasized the historical, archaeological, and scholarly significance of the Cypriot collection by presenting it in a manner that was characteristic of ethnographic displays. Rather than exhibiting pieces so as to foreground the singular aesthetic merits of individual objects, the Cesnola collection featured repetition and duplication (see Figure 5.13). It could be argued that Cesnola was making a virtue of necessity since he was committed to keeping the enormous collection together. However, exhibits that emphasized repetition were common to nineteenth-century museums of natural history and ethnology and such displays expressed a distinctive theory of knowledge. Steven Conn points out that an "object-based epistemology" bespoke the widespread belief that objects themselves, properly organized and labeled, would convey knowledge to the viewer. Cesnola articulated this outlook when he described the museum's purpose as being "to furnish such an object-library and lecture room as can be had in no other way. It is to be the silent but sure instructor of the casual visitor, while it entertains and delights him."[65] One critic, who reviewed the museum for the *Art Amateur* prior to the publication of Feuardent's charges, thought that the presentation of Cypriot objects was insufficiently entertaining and delightful. He observed that "the present classification [of the Cesnola collection] . . . is . . . serviceable to the scholar and antiquarian," but he wondered whether Cesnola's "horror of charlatanry" had prevented him from creating a more enticing, popular display.[66]

Scholars, Experts, and Archaeologists

Cesnola did his best to gain credibility at a time when the field of archaeology had not yet been professionalized—a period when standards and even goals of excavation were in a state of flux. The founding in 1879 of the Archaeological Institute of America (AIA) signaled not only the United States' entry into the international competition for antiquities, but also its engagement in a wide-ranging discussion about the practice and purposes of archaeology. Unfortunately for Cesnola, the Cypriot collection became a template upon which those discussions played out.

From the outset, scholarly affirmation was more important to Cesnola than popular approval, and he was eager for a connection to the most prominent American intellectual of his time—Charles Eliot Norton. The well-to-do scion of a Boston family, Norton was widely known in scholarly circles not only as the editor of the *North American Review* and translator of Dante, but also for his friendship with European men of letters, notably John Ruskin and Matthew Arnold. In fact, as other Ruskinians, including Stillman and Cook, diverged from the master's teachings, Norton remained loyal. He was Harvard's first professor of fine arts (appointed in 1875), though he did not hold a higher university degree. Although he lacked experience in the field, he was the first president of Boston's Archaeological Institute of America.[67] Norton met Cesnola in London in 1872 and was impressed by the Cypriot collection, which he declared to be "an extraordinary and interesting collection, of great value in the illustration it affords of both ancient history and art."[68] The two men corresponded during the

1870s, and Norton read a chapter of Cesnola's book prior to publication.[69] He also celebrated the importance of the Cypriot collection in a published article for the *Nation*. And Cesnola conveyed something of his own aspirations when he informed his friend, "I will give *facts*, *facts* and *facts*; I will describe some of the tombs found in each ancient city; and the position of the objects, etc. etc. I intend my work to serve as the material for students and lovers of art to write upon, and study."[70]

The Metropolitan hired young men with university credentials, thereby indicating the director's confidence in the merit of the Cypriot collection and his wish to make a lasting impact on the scholarship of antiquity. A. Duncan Savage, appointed as Cesnola's assistant in 1879, had a degree from the University of Virginia and a fellowship at Johns Hopkins University, where he studied with Basil L. Gildersleeve, the preeminent American professor of Greek. (Gildersleeve himself had welcomed Cesnola's collection to the United States.) Savage wrote the Metropolitan's handbook to the Cypriot sculptures. Waldo Pratt, hired as an assistant curator in 1880, had a fellowship from Johns Hopkins in "aesthetic & archaeological studies" and was a protégé of Norton. William Goodyear became the Metropolitan's first curator of paintings in 1882. He had a degree in history from Yale and studied at the University of Heidelberg. And Isaac Hollister Hall, who collaborated with Cesnola on the extensive atlas to the Cypriot collection, became a curator at the Metropolitan in 1885, having earlier been a lecturer in New Testament Greek at Johns Hopkins.[71]

Nonetheless, archaeology in the United States was still the province of amateurs and that fact contributed to the heat and confusion of the controversy. The Archaeological Institute of America played a role in professionalizing the field, but at the time of its founding graduate training was not an established, much less required, pathway into the field.[72] The position of consul was still a relatively common route to archaeological exploration. In fact, in 1881 Norton, on behalf of the AIA, urged the U.S. secretary of state to make fitness for archaeological exploration a criterion in the appointment of consuls. He recommended "men of superior education and of a training that shall have fitted them to appreciate the interest and importance of archaeological inquiries."[73] Norton did not specify the sort of education he had in mind.

Among the men Norton mentioned as positive examples was his friend William Stillman, former editor of the *Crayon*, who later became one of Cesnola's more formidable critics. When the Civil War began Stillman tried to join the Union army, but failed due to bad health. Instead, he served as American consul in Rome and for several years thereafter held the same position in Crete. He would develop a reputation for his photographs of the Acropolis. By the 1870s he was writing on archaeological matters for the *Nation* and other American journals. Stillman's background, rooted in the study of art and art criticism, was sufficient for the AIA, which in 1880 actively supported his leadership in an ultimately unsuccessful bid for an American-led excavation at Knossos.[74]

At a time when archaeology was not yet organized, even in Germany, as an independent field involving the scientific study of ancient objects, Americans understood it to be an adjunct of classical studies (including art history) or, in the case of American antiquities, as an appendage to the emerging field of anthropology. These perspectives were represented within the AIA and tensions between them briefly threatened to split the organization and oust Norton from leadership. The dispute, which erupted a few months before Feuardent leveled his first charges against Cesnola, foreshadowed the conflict that would soon bedevil the Metropolitan. The central mission of the AIA was to lend support to independent excavations and to sponsor expeditions of its own, but where these expeditions would be located was not initially clear. For Norton and others who saw classical Greece as the foundation of art and civilization, archaeology was inseparable from the study of classical antiquity. According to Norton, the AIA's "first objects" were "to increase the interest in Classical Studies by enabling competent persons to make investigations in Greece, Egypt and other countries and to stimulate interest in antiquity and the arts, which proceeded from it."[75] From this perspective, archaeology was inextricably linked to the history of art. It was no coincidence that the vice president of the AIA, Martin Brimmer, was president of the new Boston Museum of Fine Arts.

But some members of the AIA, including the zoologist Alexander Agassiz, Frederick Putnam, curator of Harvard's Peabody Museum (devoted to the emerging field of anthropology), and the historian Francis Parkman were more interested in supporting studies of the indigenous peoples of North and Central America. No one took the position that indigenous objects had value as art. Parkman made the case for New World excavation by noting "the object of the Society . . . [is] the acquisition of Knowledge and not the acquisition of objects or works of art." Members were more sympathetic to the argument articulated by one Mr. Parker, who responded to Parkman by saying that "the Knowledge which was useful to us was not

that of barbarians but that of the cultivated races which had preceded us."
It would, he continued, be "absurd" to "form here in Boston a Society of
ladies and gentlemen to learn about the red Indians." Another speaker
agreed, seeing "no reason for beginning the work of the Institute at a point
where the civilization was inferior to our own instead of superior." As Norton observed, "what we might obtain from the old world is what will tend
to increase the standard of our civilization and culture—if we are ever to
have a collection of European Classical Antiquities in this country we must
make it now." He pointed out that the Metropolitan's Cypriot antiquities
constituted the only "original" collection on exhibit in the United States.[76]

Yet a collection of objects that looked distinctly non-Greek—objects
identified as products of inferior people—was not what they had in mind
when it came to the funding of expeditions. No doubt Norton and other
members of the AIA believed that the Cypriot objects contributed to "useful" knowledge by helping to illuminate the prehistory and early development of Greek art and civilization, but what most of them valued more
were exemplars of classical and Hellenic Greece. As its primary project, the
AIA would soon choose to sponsor an excavation at the ancient and (in
their view) unimpeachably Greek site at Assos.[77]

As the Cesnola controversy escalated, Norton's response was notably
indecisive, and one can easily understand the sense of confusion. He
offended his friend when, on behalf of the AIA, he remained silent after
Feuardent issued the initial charges. When a representative from the
Archaeological Institute canceled an order for the expensive atlas to the
Cypriot collection, Cesnola all but exploded with rage at what he saw as a
sign of Norton's betrayal. In response to an apparently conciliatory letter,
Cesnola was mollified, but he must have been hurt when Norton refused
(or ignored) his request to testify at the trial. And yet, in 1884 Norton was
among a number of luminaries, including the president of Cornell University and the British Museum's specialist in Greek and Roman antiquities,
who sent notes of congratulation following Cesnola's acquittal.[78]

When, several years earlier, Cesnola had decided to subject selected statues to aggressive public scrutiny he was trying to secure his reputation with
Norton and other scholars whose respect he desperately wanted. Given the
state of the field of archaeology, it was not unreasonable to have turned to
sculptors and stonemasons for vindication. As Cesnola wrote to the
Nation's editor and AIA member E. L. Godkin in May of 1881, "I absolutely
care nothing for what the Times and such papers as the Advertiser & Art

Amateur have published . . . but I do care not to lose the esteem of honorable men like yourself." He offered Godkin the following proposal: "I will obtain from the Trustees permission to place at your disposal and that of your friend Prof⁻ Chas Eliot Norton . . . the statue represented in card n 2 by Mr. Feuardent and give you the fullest authority to have said statue N 39 examined by all the professional Sculptors and Stone workers of this city and Boston or such number of them as you and Mr. Norton may think fit to select for that purpose. I will give you full authority to have said statue represented in card N 2 taken apart, and each piece most critically examined by them, Norton and yourself."[79] Unfortunately, Godkin's response to this offer is unknown, but the following March, with support from the trustees, Cesnola did almost precisely what he had proposed. He placed two statues in the main hall of the museum, exposing them to examination by sculptors, stonemasons, scholars, editors, journalists, and the public at large. The proceedings offended Cook, who on this issue appears more modern than his antagonists, but from Cesnola's perspective sculptors and stonemasons were the experts most likely to convince members of the AIA among others. As the trustees hoped and no doubt expected, the result was another vindication for the museum and its director. As newspapers and periodicals took sides following the episode, James Jackson Jarves, living in Florence, wrote an article for the *New York World* in which he declared himself wholly convinced by "conclusive reports of the eminent sculptors and other competent judges, who after thorough investigation of the charges of M. Feuardent and Mr. Cook, pronounce them entirely baseless, confirming the universal European judgment as to the genuineness of the objects and their great value."[80]

By contrast, the writer of a lengthy, carefully reasoned article in the *Century* (probably the magazine's new editor Richard Watson Gilder) was damningly critical of Cesnola even though he tentatively accepted the judgment of "others more competent" with respect to the integrity of statues 32 and 39. The writer recognized the expertise of stonecutters and sculptors, though he doubted the question would be fully settled without "a more thorough use of chemicals and baths than has yet been made." He relied heavily on devastating published statements by Duncan Savage, who initially defended Cesnola but, after conducting his own investigation, resigned from the Metropolitan in 1882. Savage had compared sculptures to photographs taken earlier, and he spoke with janitors (promptly fired by Cesnola) who claimed to have witnessed restorations in progress. The author of the *Century* piece cited testimonials to Savage's good character and concluded that Cesnola had simply lied. For this writer, the issue was not the scraping and hacking per se. In fact, Gilder had participated in the public investigation, making a few cuts with his own penknife. Rather the problem lay with the lies and incompetence that made such an investigation "necessary":

> The recent spectacle of a museum finding it necessary to endeavor to regain public confidence by inviting and permitting editors, stone-cutters, and sculptors to gather around two of its costly antiquities, and to scratch, scrape, hack at, and chisel these unlucky objects, in order to have it proved that they are genuine antiquities, and not fraudulent patchworks of unrelated parts—such a spectacle never was seen before by men or angels. We do not know how it could ever have been made necessary had the Museum's affairs been managed with perfect frankness.[81]

For this writer, the status of statues 32 and 39 was not at the heart of the case. Rather, camouflaged repairs, the likelihood of illegitimate restorations, and contradictory statements with respect to provenance rendered the collection as a whole, unreliable.[82]

Without rejecting the testimony of sculptors and stonemasons, the *Century* turned to another standard against which Cesnola and the trustees could be judged—namely, common practice at Europe's most formidable museums. There, suggested the author, repairs and restorations were made visible to the public and acknowledged on labels. (This was a point made by Feuardent when he issued his initial charges.) For expert opinion on this matter, the author turned to Lucy Wright Mitchell, graduate of Mount Holyoke Seminary and sister of the Harvard classicist Henry Wright. Given Mitchell's gender, her stature as an acknowledged expert was unusual, to say the least, but she was about to publish a two-volume work titled *A History of Ancient Sculpture*—the first general American work on that subject. She had spent years in Europe studying in museums and was familiar with the Metropolitan's Cypriot sculptures.[83] Mitchell was troubled by the cleaning of the sculptures and, even more so, by the sloppy and contradictory recording of provenance. Responding to a query from the *Century*'s author, she declared her hope "that Cesnola will be made to feel the great wrong he has done to science and the American people in imposing upon them patched-up restorations of homeless figures."[84]

The Trial: Expertise, Aesthetic Taste, and Race

Cesnola's trial, which began on October 31, 1883, brought questions of expertise and museum practice to a head without coming to a clear resolution. Cesnola admitted that his workmen had repaired pieces by joining broken parts of the same object, but he never acceded to the charge of having created wholly new parts based on guesswork. He acknowledged that mistakes had been made while he was out of town or in the rush of preparing pieces for exhibition, but he generally blamed others for the errors. He claimed that the most egregious alterations had occurred when the trustee Russell Sturgis was left in charge of the workmen. The "wash" that whitened the stone and camouflaged points of juncture was simply part of the cleansing process. With respect to the mirror in the hand of the small statue deemed by him to be a Venus, Cesnola claimed that "the evident under-cutting which brought out the shape of the mirror" had been created in the process of cleaning layers of encrusted dirt.[85] Witnesses on Cesnola's behalf (the trustee William Prime; and the president of Columbia College, Francis Barnard) argued that it was legitimate to cover repairs under certain circumstances. Cesnola also benefited from the testimony of prominent sculptors who had participated in the investigation of March 1882. Benjamin Braman, a "microscopist and expert in regard to the surfaces of Cypriote Stone," testified that the "surface of the statuette of Venus was wholly that of an ancient hand."[86]

Cesnola's definition of "repairs" was notably broad. For example, he declared that Statue 39 (the priest holding the cow's head) "was badly broken up when found. To permanently repair it and place it in such a condition that the bits of the leg remaining should be able to support the body, a block of Cypriote stone was inserted into the base to supply supports, heels, and ankles." The plan was for the sculpture to be placed on the pedestal containing two feet, but "the ankles wouldn't fit the feet." He called in a stonecutter who "sawed the feet off the block and moved them back to a point where they would fit." These "repairs" had been made with the advice of the sculptor and museum trustee John Q. A. Ward.[87]

Feuardent's lead attorney, Francis Nash Bangs, ridiculed Cesnola for his slippery definition of "repairs" and called on an array of witnesses including Feuardent, former museum workmen, janitors, and others whose testimony was based on claims to expertise. Richard Gilder, who allegedly described himself as an "expert on experts," was among the early witnesses for the plaintiff. (Cook was in Europe during the months of the trial.) Indeed, the prosecution followed lines of argument established by the *Century*. Duncan Savage was a key witness, as was Lucy Mitchell, who testified to practices at the British and Berlin Museums as well as the Louvre.[88]

Bangs, a prominent corporate lawyer, deployed an antielitist argument on behalf of his client, thereby aligning himself with the position Cook had taken before the trial began. The museum, insisted Bangs, was funded at taxpayer expense upon public land, yet an interested visitor risked libelous attacks for exercising "the freedom of speech and liberty of criticism." William Prime all but invited this line of attack by insisting, as he did on other occasions, that the museum was essentially a "private corporation." While scholars and teachers might require information on repairs of objects, Prime "didn't think it necessary that the general public" should be provided with such knowledge by "hand-books or ocular proof."[89]

Both sides deployed humor, as did the papers that reported on the trial, and the jokes highlight the antiforeign, racial assumptions that suffused the controversy (see Figures 5.14 and 5.15). The testimony of the German-born cabinetmaker Feodor Gehlen was a high point in the trial, at least with respect to the laughter that it generated. Gehlen, who had been employed by the museum from 1873 through 1875, told of having reconstructed many of the Cypriot objects. It was difficult to tell whether the court was more amused by Gehlen's accent or by the account of his creations. He and the statues became humorous stand-ins for one another. As the *New York Times* reported, "Mr. Gehans [*sic*] explanations as to the character of work that he had done, given in broken English, were a constant source of amusement to everyone but Mr. Cesnola and his friends." To one statue Gehlen recalled having "added to a face of stone, a head, hair and ears so that when his work was done, the face was converted into a female head, which was mounted on a pedestal and exhibited with others as a genuine Cypriote antiquity." Into "the hand of the so-called Bearded Venus he had placed a dove" that he reconstructed with wood and plaster. And plaster had been used "in the construction of heads of hair, beards, lips, noses, and ears in a great number of cases."[90] At various points the ugliness of objects

THE WORK-ROOM.

Figure 5.14. This illustration of the Metropolitan's workroom accompanied a laudatory article, published in 1879. At that time, no one questioned what the workmen were doing. From "Metropolitan Museum of Art," *Harper's New Monthly Magazine*, December 1, 1879. University of California Libraries, Annex.

THE DEVELOPMENT OF ARCHÆOLOGY.—HOW MODERN MUSEUMS ARE SUPPLIED WITH GENUINE ANTIQUITIES.
SEE PAGE 215.

Figure 5.15. By the time the trial began, the museum's workroom was fodder for jokes. From "The Development of Archaeology: How Modern Museums Are Supplied with Genuine Antiquities," *Frank Leslie's Illustrated Newspaper*, November 24, 1883. Author's collection.

became the subject of jokes. In describing statues "introduced in court for the inspection of the jury," the *New York Times* referred contemptuously to "the life-size figure of the priest holding a cow's head in one hand . . . the mirror-laden Venus, and several smaller figures of grotesque objects." One three-inch statuette was "ugly enough in design to be the *chef d'oeuvre* of the Cypriote antiquities."[91]

But it was Bangs who completely unmasked the subtext of the humor and of the controversy as a whole. Bursts of laughter accompanied his concluding reflection upon the statue of the "little Venus." He found her "not as good looking as many a young American woman I know. She is not as well built as any ordinary ship of war. Her color is bad. She looks something like a fifteenth amendment." And if that was not clear enough, he ridiculed "the manufacture that Mr.—the General—Cesnola calls Venus, and the concern which most of you who have been down South would call a half-dressed mulatto." Bangs evoked political corruption—associated, in many minds, with immigrants as well as railroads—when he described the statue's "Chicago feet, with six toes, the product only of a Chicago graft upon a St. Louis trunk." Then he targeted the statue's uncertain provenance: "What is it, where did it spring from, who made it, and what he made it for, is going to be an unsolved problem." It would be difficult not to read Bangs's account of the Venus metaphorically—as a signifier of immigrants and African Americans who were changing politics and culture in New York City and the nation at large.[92]

In a conflict that had much to do with racist ideas and antiforeign sentiment, it is not surprising that the ethnic background of leading protagonists became part of the narrative. From the outset, Cesnola and his supporters cast Feuardent as a "dealer" and a Jew motivated by greed and financial disappointment. Choate rested a good bit of his case on a not-so-coded demonization of the plaintiff. Meanwhile, Cesnola's aristocratic and military background more or less inoculated him against anti-Italian commentary. As a writer for the *Tribune* observed several years before the trial began, Cesnola was "known to New-York as an Italian nobleman, who had abandoned his brilliant position at home to seek the distinction of an American citizen, who had the uniform of his adopted country and periled his life in her defense." By contrast, Feuardent "was known as the enterprising son of a Hebrew dealer in antiquities."[93] Choate's summary argument provided a subtler rendition of the same point. Referring to Feuardent's attack on Cesnola and Prime, he queried, "What is the use of living, of eating the bread of carefulness, and being good citizens, if men whose characters are the treasures of the city can be struck down by a man like this."[94]

Yet, occasional published comments prior to the trial suggest that Cesnola's ethnic background was a liability, even though Choate's clever defense minimized the damage. The *Century*'s writer noted that Cesnola was "quite unhampered by Anglo-Saxon scrupulosity—he was just the man to extract this antique loot from the Sultan's domain." He was "undoubtedly the man to *get* the collection" but "not the man to take care of it." Also in 1882, an article in the *Critic* drew a connection between Cesnola's faulty archaeological practices and Italian background. The author saw "a fund of naiveté in all this which is eminently Italian. . . . He [the Italian] detests old things. Hence his abnormal haste to reconstruct, renovate and paint up the things in Italy most dear to the traveller. . . . At the bottom of the quarrel about the Cesnola antiquities lies this trait from which the manager can no more escape than from his Italian accent." In the midst of the trial the *Police Gazette* published a long article on the controversy in which Cesnola appeared as "the wily Italian."[95]

After more than three months at trial, the jury vindicated Cesnola on the key charge of defamation. It helped that Bangs had a cold during the last week of the proceedings, while Choate was entirely on his game. Conflicting accounts by experts likely canceled each other out in the minds of jurors, who had to sort through an abundance of confusing testimony. In the end it must have been difficult to determine who or where the most reliable experts were. The *Times* reporter, displeased by the verdict, refused to blame the jurors, who appeared "muddled in a case which has muddled eminent counsel and bewildered everybody who has tried to follow it." This writer believed that "there is no body of expert evidence upon such a subject to be had in this country." As a result, the jurors were "entertained by the opinions and conjectures of some unquestioned experts in sculpture and some possible experts in archaeology, together with the views of persons who were considered by the counsel on either side or even by themselves to be good enough experts in a case where there was so much excited feeling and so little exact knowledge."[96]

In any case, controversy persisted almost as if the trial had never taken place (see Figure 5.16). In 1883 Cook assumed editorship of the *Studio*, an inexpensive art journal published by Feuardent. He did his best to keep the accusations afloat. Assisting in this effort was a new spate of criticism from European archaeologists. Most notable was Max Ohnefalsch-Richter, who

AN ARCHÆOLOGICAL TRIUMPH.

Cesnola: I AM ALL RIGHT AS LONG AS THE TEAM IS WILLING, AND THEY CAN'T KICK.

Figure 5.16. This cartoon suggests that the Cesnola controversy cast a shadow over the museum well into the mid-1880s, despite the verdict of the court. *An Archaeological Triumph*, in *Life*, December 24, 1885. Author's collection.

was working in Cyprus on behalf of the British Museum and disputed the existence of the Curium tomb. He claimed that many objects in the so-called "Curium Treasure" had been purchased "from the natives." Newspapers, including the popular *New York World*, took up the story and Cook promoted it with apparent relish.[97] The *Times* demanded an investigation to which Cesnola, under the cover of the trustees, responded by challenging Ohnefalsch-Richter's character and threatening to sue.[98] Equally damaging for Cesnola was William J. Stillman's report of March 1885, written at the request of New York's American Numismatic and Archaeological Society. At the close of the trial the society had issued a public note of thanks to Feuardent for his sacrifice in the cause of "truth and justice." Stillman's lengthy report validated all of the charges against Cesnola including those by Ohnefalsch-Richter.[99]

Without acknowledging any doubts about the collection, the trustees moved tentatively in the direction pressed by their critics. In 1885 they quietly sold five thousand "duplicate" pieces from the Cesnola collection to Leland Stanford for $9,200—a surprisingly high price given recent history. Also in 1885, a $10,000 donation from Henry Marquand enabled the museum to acquire a "collection of casts representing the masterpieces of sculpture of ancient Greece" from museums throughout Europe.[100]

In 1914, the Metropolitan's new director and board of trustees attempted to clear the air once again. They hired John Linton Myres, professor of ancient history at Oxford, to investigate the objects and to organize a new exhibition. Myres, who had worked in Cyprus and collaborated with Ohnefalsch-Richter, gave Cesnola a qualified vindication. A thorough cleaning of the statues convinced him that charges made by Feuardent and Cook regarding specific objects were greatly overblown. Far more serious, in his view, was the sloppy and ill-recorded processes of excavation, but that was understandable given Cesnola's lack of experience and training. Myres reminded readers that "archaeological research was in its infancy" when Cesnola arrived in Cyprus: "With Cesnola's opportunities, an archaeological genius had the chance to anticipate modern work by a generation; it was a pity—but no fault of Cesnola—that the United States Consul in Cyprus was not an archaeological genius." On the matter of the "Curium Treasure," he was less forgiving. It was, he observed with notable understatement, "easier to excuse neglect of scientific precautions than exaggeration or misstatement."[101]

But the deeper problem for Myres was the narrative that accompanied the collection. He was committed to a new Hellenized account of ancient

Cyprus, claiming that Minoans from Crete had colonized the island during
the late Bronze Age, "about 1400 BC." For several hundred years, according
to this story, "not Cyprus only but all this end of the Mediterranean became
. . . a strong outpost of Western civilization." Only later did Phoenicians
replace Minoans as the dominant trading people of the Mediterranean and
not until "the beginning of the historic age in Greece and Italy" would
"western influences once more reassert themselves in Cyprus."[102] Cesnola
had situated Cyprus within the Orient, emphasizing Eastern influences in
the development of Greek culture; Myres gave priority to "western influences" on the island delivered through the medium of an archaic Minoan
incursion. The latter point of view opened the way for a more respectful
treatment of some Cypriot pieces as art.

Myres told his historical story in the catalog's introduction, but when it
came to the exhibition itself he adopted practices that fell in line with the
museum's aestheticizing orientation. He deemed it best to narrow the historical treatment and to "base the new arrangement solely on considera-
tions of workmanship and style." (In Myres's view, Cesnola's practices of
excavation made it impossible to cull an accurate historical story from the
objects themselves.) At the same time, the reorganization of 1914 relegated
more than half of the collection to the basement. These pieces constituted
"purely archaeological material which could never be expected to appeal
to the general public." Only the "finest specimens of each kind"—still an
enormous collection including almost 1,100 vases and more than 400
sculptures—would occupy the Cesnola Room and adjoining spaces. As
Myres put it, the need for a more spacious display of fewer pieces "becomes
more apparent in proportion as its artistic value is appreciated."[103]

Significance

The duration and intensity of the Cesnola controversy suggests that it
touched more than one cultural nerve. In part it was a matter of timing.
Britain's occupation of Cyprus in 1878 stimulated archaeological interest in
the island on the eve of the Metropolitan's big move to Central Park. The
very attention that helped to make Cesnola a celebrity also invited criticism.
Meanwhile, the founding of the Archaeological Institute of America in the
same year signaled growing interest in the establishment of methodological
standards not only in archaeology but also in the area of museum display.

Cesnola's practices were sloppy even for their own time, but his misfortune was to present his collection to the world at the very moment when archaeological practices were undergoing scrutiny. The controversy can be seen as an episode within an international conversation concerning standards of excavation and presentation.

The Cesnola controversy was also about race and the historical narrative that bolstered the late nineteenth-century notion of "Western civilization." Stories that gave meaning to the collection raised difficult questions not only by presenting ancient Cyprus as a place of cultural mixing but also by emphasizing Hellenism's Oriental roots. In Cesnola's account, the Occident and Orient seemed to merge. Indeed Cyprus itself—located at the periphery of the Levant—threatened to disrupt East-West cultural and racial distinctions. At a time when European and American scholars were deeply invested in classical Greece as the apex of art and foundation of European of civilization, Cesnola's Orientalizing narrative devalued most of the Cypriot objects.

Finally, the conflict that engulfed the museum during the 1880s highlights tensions between archaeological or historical and aestheticizing modes of display. Was the art museum to be a beacon of beauty for the education of taste, the improvement of manufactures, and the uplift of American homes? Or would it present objects as windows onto the peoples that used and produced them? The Metropolitan incorporated both of those perspectives, but Cesnola's collection, due in part to its very enormity, made it difficult to maintain the balance. In a world that measured artistic and moral quality along racial axes, attention to producers had the potential to undermine aesthetic appreciation.

CHAPTER 6

The Battle for Sundays at the Museum

As controversy over the Cypriot collection began to recede during the mid-1880s another battle heated up—the battle for Sunday openings, not only at the Metropolitan Museum but also at Central Park's American Museum of Natural History. This second and more protracted controversy began in 1881, less than a year after Feuardent issued his initial charges against Cesnola. It escalated in 1884, pitting the majority of the museums' trustees against a broad coalition that included much of the city government, most of the New York press, liberal Protestant denominations, business owners, reformers, and New York's increasingly non-Protestant immigrant working class.[1] The *New York Times* published more than sixty articles on the Sunday campaign, but the more popular papers—the *Herald* and the *World*—also drove the story and helped to create a broader social movement. The museum's battles of the 1880s stoked each other, fueling anger at Cesnola and the board of trustees, while keeping them in the news. The Metropolitan was an elite institution, but a much wider public claimed it for themselves and came to appreciate the museum's contents in their own ways.

The Sunday controversy cannot be understood apart from the massive influx of immigrants that transformed New York's cultural and political landscape. Immigration had waned through the Civil War and the depression of 1873, but the numbers of newcomers surged during the 1880s and continued to grow throughout the first decade of the twentieth century. Between 1880 and 1914 more than twenty million immigrants came to the United States, and most of them arrived at New York Harbor. Irish peasants, beset by agricultural depression, joined their Irish American countrymen. In 1890, the Irish population in New York and Brooklyn was 275,156—up about 15,000 from what it had been in 1860. During the same thirty-year period, the city's German-speaking population rose from 119,064 to 210,723, and the number grew further during the 1890s. Unlike the Irish, many of the Germans who settled in New York City were artisans and some were socialist political refugees from the revolutions of 1848 and the Franco-Prussian War. By the last decade of the nineteenth century, according to the most comprehensive history of the city, New York "stood third behind Berlin and Vienna as a German-speaking metropolis."[2] In 1880, one-third of New York City's population had been born in Germany or Ireland.[3]

The very scale of immigration in the late nineteenth probably accentuated the sense that "new immigrants" were radically different from earlier arrivals. As Hasia Diner points out, Eastern European Jewish immigrants shared much with the Central European Jews who came in earlier decades. Like their predecessors, they had fled deepening poverty, anti-Semitism, and political instability. In 1870 some of New York's sixty thousand Jewish residents spoke Yiddish rather than German. But by the early 1890s, Jews in the city numbered more than 170,000, and most, having come from Russia and Poland, were Yiddish speakers. Immigration from Italy also grew dramatically. Environmental disasters and competition born of global capitalist transformation made life increasingly difficult for peasants in Italy's already impoverished southern provinces. When Cesnola arrived in New York fewer than nine hundred Italians lived in the city. By 1880 New York's population included twenty thousand people of Italian descent; twenty years later the mostly Catholic, Italian American population numbered approximately 250,000. The city's Chinese population may have reached 10,000 by 1890, though the census registered the number at only 2,048. Mostly male, the Chinese who arrived in New York during the late 1870s and 1880s had fled the anti-Chinese violence that engulfed much of California and the West. Meanwhile, immigrants were arriving in the United States from Greece, while Arabs (mostly Christians) came from the Ottoman province of Syria.[4]

For native-born urbanites the transformation was impossible to miss. Wealthy families moved farther uptown, creating distance from the working-class tenements that clustered on the lower east side of Manhattan, but the polyglot city was inescapable. William Dean Howells's 1889 novel *A Hazard of New Fortunes* evoked these changes from the perspective of one prosperous American-born Protestant. The protagonist—and barely disguised authorial stand-in—Basil March is a liberal magazine editor, recently arrived in New York from Boston. During a ride on the elevated train he looks out at Lower East Side:

> March noticed what must strike every observer returning to the city after a prolonged absence: the numerical subordination of the dominant race. If they do not out-vote them, the people of Germanic, of Slavonic, of Pelasgic, of Mongolian stock outnumber the prepotent Celts. . . . The small eyes, the high cheeks, the broad noses, the puff lips, the bare, cue-filleted skulls, of Russians, Poles, Czechs, Chinese; the furtive glitter of Italians; the blonde dullness of Germans; the cold quiet of Scandinavians—fire under ice—were aspects that he identified, and that gave him abundant suggestion for the personal histories he constructed.[5]

Howells recognized that this newly "heterogeneous commonwealth" was pressing "public spirited" men to think in new ways about the public culture of the city. The museums at Central Park were part of that conversation.

The Growing Campaign

By the time the Metropolitan Museum opened at its permanent location on Eighty-First Street, Central Park itself was under mounting popular pressure. Designers Frederick Olmsted and Calvert Vaux had envisioned it as a restful retreat from the tensions of urban life and an antidote to the expanding world of commercial amusements. Owners of real estate surrounding the park had been emphatic in their efforts to make the area inviting to upper-class residents. Insofar as working people had a place in this picture it was as students of bourgeois decorum and recipients of nature's calming influence. But working-class visitors found ways to make their own claims on the park, particularly after changes in administration made the park's board more receptive to popular political pressure. In 1870 the Democrat-controlled state legislature vested the mayor with power to appoint park commissioners. It thereby transferred the park from state to local control. The new administrative framework inevitably sensitized commissioners to popular opinion and, over time, shifted control to Democrats. No longer could museum trustees count on the park's administration to be dominated by sympathetic Republicans. Meanwhile, the Sixth Avenue elevated train, which opened in 1878, eased transportation from the downtown tenements, as did the opening of new carriage lines.[6]

The first major push in the battle for Sunday openings came in the form of a petition initiated by a small group of German Americans who were affiliated with America's preeminent German-language daily, the *New Yorker Staats-Zeitung*. Their outlook reflected German traditions that made Sunday a day of recreation not only for Jews, whose Sabbath was Saturday, but also for Protestants and Catholics. The "Continental Sabbath" was a point of pride for German Americans whose beer gardens remained open on Sundays as places for club meetings and family recreation.[7] The petition contained about ten thousand signatures, but the impetus came from the prosperous men who promoted it. The *Staats-Zeitung*, unlike the German-language socialist weekly *New Yorker Volkszeitung*, was liberal in its politics and oriented more to middle-class than working-class readers. The editor, Oswald Ottendorfer, was a native of Moravia who had fled his country following the revolution of 1848. He began working for *Staats-Zeitung* in 1851 and eventually married its owner.[8] The paper did not express the radicalism of the editor's youth. Ottendorfer was a Republican, though he spoke out against nativist currents within that party. When, in 1872, German American workers at William Steinway's piano factory went on strike for an eight-hour workday, *Staats-Zeitung* sided with Steinway even to the point of pushing for police intervention. In addition to Ottendorfer, leading signers of the petition for Sunday opening included Steinway, along with August Belmont, the wealthy German Jewish banker, and Sigismund Kaufman, a German-born attorney who wrote for *Staats-Zeitung* and, like Ottendorfer, was a refugee of 1848.[9] A letter to John Taylor Johnston from the owner of a carriage factory confirms that the petition had the support of some employers and may have been circulated by them: "This petition herewith has been signed by three hundred and twenty-six men in our employ out of a total of 575, and they have asked us to forward it to you. We heartily endorse the petition of our hands, believing that if it is granted its influence will be *good*."[10]

The German-born Felix Adler, who actually presented the petition to the Parks Department in April 1881, was among a group of young urban reformers who were turning their attention to the problem of poverty and the conditions of working-class life. Adler was the son of New York's leading Reform rabbi, but religious skepticism prevented him from following in his father's footsteps. Following three years of study in Germany, he accepted a nonresident faculty position at the newly founded Cornell University. By the late 1870s, he had founded the Ethical Culture movement—a secular religion that focused on social improvement and ethical behavior in the world. After helping to create the first free kindergarten on the East Coast of the United States, he turned his attention to the reform of elementary education. By the early 1880s, he was deeply involved in the growing movement to improve conditions in New York's tenements.[11] The Open Sunday petition linked many of the causes that absorbed Adler's attention: it represented an attack on Christian orthodoxy and privilege as well as commitment to working-class education.

Clarence Cook, backed by the *Art Amateur*, gave full support to the petitioners. In fact, the magazine anticipated the petition by a year. Montague Marks, the magazine's editor, was Jewish—the son of a prominent London rabbi. As the brother-in-law of Emma Lazarus, the labor radical whose 1883 poem "The New Colossus" would later grace the Statue of Liberty, Marks had ties to the intellectual community that promoted the first campaign for Sunday openings. Support for the petitioners was also consistent with the magazine's broader vision of the museum's social role. Marks and Cook wanted the Metropolitan to become an educator of taste for artisans and consumers. To perform that role it would have to be widely accessible. An editorial published in May 1880, probably written by Marks, declared that the trustees should not receive one dollar of the city's contribution until the museum was "opened on Sunday afternoons . . . the only one on which the working public can visit it."[12] The following year, several months after the presentation of the German American petition, Cook attacked "the illiberal policy of the museum in refusing to open it on Sundays." He claimed to know "many workmen who have never been inside the Museum for this reason."[13]

Most of the trustees dug in their heels, but the petitioners had one staunch ally in Joseph Choate, who was also a trustee at the Museum of Natural History. Choate voiced his support for Sunday openings a full year before the German American petition made the case. In a private note to Cesnola he expressed his hope "that the Trustees will at an early day consider the expediency of having the museum open on Sunday which will immediately double its usefulness and interest. . . . Imagine the Louvre closed on Sunday!"[14] Instead, the trustees, led by William Johnston, ignored Choate's request and refused to respond publicly to the petition. They also worked behind the scenes to crush the proposal. Morris Jesup, the banker, devout Presbyterian, and president of the board at the Museum of Natural History, began hosting meetings at his home of a committee consisting of trustees from both museums. His primary purpose was to deal with the Sunday issue. In 1882, when William T. Walters, a wealthy Baltimore art collector, offered ten thousand dollars to defray the cost of Sunday openings for a period of five years, Johnston quietly returned the check.[15] That year, according to one newspaper report, the trustees also deflected a legislative bill that would have forced Sunday openings. They allegedly did so by privately pledging to make the change voluntarily and then reneging on the promise.[16] Meanwhile, Cesnola and his allies were hoping that Cornelius Vanderbilt, a museum trustee, would follow through on a tentative offer to donate funds for a new building and endowment that would entirely exempt the trustees from obligations to taxpayers.[17] The offer never came through, but it is telling that by the winter of 1882 the embattled trustees were looking for ways to free themselves of public pressure.

A critical juncture in the campaign for Sunday openings was the successful movement, spearheaded by German immigrants, to institute Sunday concerts in Central Park. The first of these concerts, described by the *New York Times* as "a great big labor-union picnic," took place in July of 1884, and their widely acknowledged success not only weakened the position of outspoken Sabbatarians, but also provoked the Park Commission and other arms of the city government to pressure the museums. When, in January 1885, trustees of the Museum of Natural History requested funds for a new extension, the Park Commission threatened to make financial support contingent on Sunday openings. Several months later the Board of Aldermen and the mayor raised the possibility that the annual $30,000 appropriation might be withheld if the trustees of both museums continued to resist Sunday openings. Through 1885 pressure mounted in the press.[18]

The trustees did their best to delay and prevaricate by postponing meetings, pointing to the cost of keeping the museums open an extra day, lobbying the state legislature, and worrying publicly about the reaction of staunchly Sabbatarian donors.

Jesup laid out their arguments in October 1885 at a meeting of the Board of Estimate and Apportionment held in the office of the mayor. Daniel Huntington, vice president of the Metropolitan's board, was also present along with other unnamed trustees. Jesup began by insisting that the museums were already fulfilling their contracts with the city by opening their doors to the public free of charge on Wednesday, Thursday, Friday, and Saturday of each week. He reiterated the claim that that donors had made their gifts on the assumption that Sunday would be a day of rest, and minimized the museums' financial obligation to taxpayers, observing that the city had "given scarcely more than one quarter" of the operating costs. He also emphasized the expense of Sunday openings, insisting that "a force of men tried and trained for the work, would have to be employed permanently, at a greatly increased expense." Finally, he insisted that the strict Sabbath was in the best interest of the workers. If "popular reverence for the day as a non-secular day" were compromised, it would become another workday.[19] Instead he recommended that employers provide a half holiday on Saturdays. Jesup pointed to the example of England "where the laws and customs protect the right to rest on Sunday."[20] He did not acknowledge Boston's Museum of Fine Arts, which had been open on Sundays since 1876. Nor did he reference newer American museums that were following Boston's lead.[21] At the end of the year, when John Taylor Johnston addressed the board, he made his own position clear by rejecting the "erroneous idea" that "your Museum is a public institution." William Prime was even more emphatic in denouncing "the foolish notion . . . that the public has a say in the management of this museum. We want it understood that we're running our own machine here and don't propose to be interfered with." Rather than opening on Sunday, he suggested that the museum might move to a new building outside of the park.[22]

Resistance from the trustees provoked the creation of a second petition that circulated in late 1885 and early 1886. Samuel P. Putnam, who spearheaded the campaign, was secretary of the American Secular Union, an organization dedicated to the separation of church and state. With about nine thousand signatures, the petition represented a wide swath of the population. It garnered support from manufacturers, judges, policemen, politicians, liberal clergymen, and 120 unions, or "almost all the labor organizations of the city."[23] This time labor moved closer to the forefront of the battle. New York's Central Labor Union (CLU), representing about 50,000 working people, attached its own resolution to the general petition:

> *Whereas.* It being a standing complaint that the working population do not show sufficient interest in matters of refinement and culture; and
> *Whereas,* It being impossible for working men and women to visit the public places established for the purpose of furnishing all

with the means by which their knowledge and appreciation of such things may be increased, largely because on the only days when the working people have the opportunity for such diversion and improvement the libraries, museums and art galleries are closed; and

Whereas, working people have to contribute the larger share toward the maintenance of these public institutions; therefore, be it

Resolved, That we, as representatives of many thousands of these unprivileged men and women, hereby demand that all public libraries, museums, and art galleries be kept open on Sundays and holidays.[24]

The CLU, known for orchestrating the nation's first Labor Day parade, represented skilled and unskilled workers including retail clerks. It was closely allied with the Knights of Labor calling for an eight-hour workday, equal pay for equal work, and an end to child labor. For the city's restive working class, the Sunday campaign was part and parcel of the CLU's broader struggle against "all class privilege."[25]

A reporter for the *Herald*, who interviewed labor leaders on the Sunday question, presented further evidence of working-class interest in the museums. The prolabor activist and editor John Swinton believed that at least 75 percent of working people "would be extremely delighted" if the museum was open on Sundays. The reason, he continued, "is very plain. Workingmen feel that they have a right to some measures of enjoyment in this world, and that as they cannot have it on week days, they ought certainly not to be deprived of it on Sundays." Swinton reminded the reporter that the city's growing immigrant population was used to Sunday recreation: "To a Frenchman, a German, a Spaniard, an Italian, a Hungarian, or even an Englishman, a Sunday in New York is the dullest day imaginable." The president of the Progressive Cigarmakers' Union agreed. He observed, "There are five hundred thousand workingmen and workingwomen in this city . . . of whom probably not more than one in a thousand ever thinks of going to church." And yet "on holidays and occasional Saturdays they go to museums and for days afterward you can hear them talking about what they have seen." A self-described "workingman" who belonged to the Central Labor Union insisted that workers "have as much right as any other class to whatever amusement and instruction can be obtained from museums and art galleries, and that as they cannot visit such places on week days, they should be enabled to visit them on Sundays."[26]

The second petition campaign tracked escalating labor struggles in New York and throughout the nation. The year 1886 saw a rise in strike activity that reached a crescendo in March of that year when 200,000 workers, under the auspices of the Knights of Labor, joined a strike against the Union Pacific Railroad. On May 1, 1886, 340,000 workers across the country took to the streets to demand an eight-hour day. Three days later, in Chicago's Haymarket Square, a bomb disrupted a labor rally, killed seven policemen, and provoked a frenzy of antilabor and nativist hostility. Meanwhile, tensions mounted in New York. Beginning in March, streetcar workers organized three strikes that threatened to paralyze the city. The conflict began with demands for a two-dollar wage and twelve-hour day. Although strikers enjoyed some initial success, the police played a pivotal role in their eventual defeat. Labor leaders also mounted boycotts against offending businesses, including bakeries and a music hall. The full force of municipal authority pushed back. By May 1, when 45,000 New York workers turned out for the nationwide one-day strike, one hundred labor activists were already in jail. The district attorney selected five boycotters—all immigrants—for prosecution on the grounds of "extortion," and in July a judge meted out harsh sentences ranging from eighteen months to nearly four years. John Swinton, a prescient commentator on the events of 1886, declared, "Class lines are being closely drawn. There is a determination among bosses to stamp out labor organizations and suppress speech and press to the furthest possible limit. This determination is shared by officers of the law."[27]

In the wake of the crackdown on boycotts, the CLU turned to its offshoot, the United Labor Party (ULP), and focused attention on the forthcoming mayoral election. The ULP's nominee was the radical journalist and printer Henry George, widely known for his book *Progress and Poverty*, which probed the roots of economic inequality in the age of industrialization. George, who was a member of the Knights of Labor, located the central problem of industrial society in the ownership of land by speculators (including railroads and banks) and urban landlords. His message resonated in New York, where laboring people lived in crowded tenements and wealthy men, who owned prime real estate, used municipal authorities to control the streets. George's campaign called for structural changes designed to foster democratic control of the city. He spoke out against the owners of tenements and denounced the various means by which wealthy New Yorkers gained undue influence over the police and other aspects of municipal government. Significantly, Felix Adler supported George even though none of the major dailies endorsed the campaign. Only some weeklies—*John Swinton's Paper*, the *New Yorker Volkszeitung*, and the *Irish World*—along with a reform daily called *Truth* backed the United Labor Party. It came as no surprise that George lost the election, but his close second-place finish, ahead of the Republican Theodore Roosevelt, worried the city's elite.[28]

The activism and political mobilization of laboring people gave establishment political leaders good reason to support the call for open Sundays. Mayor Abram Hewitt, the Democrat and iron manufacturer who defeated George, backed the petitioners, as did the Park Board, the Board of Estimate, the Board of Aldermen, and most of the city's press. If the majority of trustees initially favored a policy that amounted to excluding working-class visitors, many prosperous and powerful New Yorkers saw support for Sunday openings as a way to win votes and assuage the anger of laboring people. John D. Crimmins, appointed as a park commissioner in 1884, is a case in point. He inherited a building company from his Irish father and remained a Democrat throughout his career. His attitude toward park workers was paternalistic, even to the point of supporting Henry George's call for worker pensions. Crimmins was also a determined advocate of Sunday openings. At one point he baited recalcitrant trustees by offering to cover the cost on his own until the museums received sufficient compensation from the city.[29] But Crimmins was no radical. As he informed the *Herald*'s reporter, "No means should be overlooked to make the mass of the people contented with their lot. That is the only cure for anarchy and socialism, and I tell you that in the present state of society the wealthy people of New York cannot afford to neglect any opportunity to quell discontent in the masses."[30] Similarly, Mayor Hewitt declared that "the establishment of free museums is a necessity which every day becomes more apparent and without them we should become a city of rich men and savages."[31] Clearly, the Sunday issue attracted large and diverse constituencies acting from a range of motives. Among reformers and politicians, visions of working-class uplift and appeasement were intertwined.

Meanwhile, clergymen and other interested parties weighed in. A number of religious leaders, including the powerful Catholic archbishop Michael Corrigan and Albany's Episcopalian bishop William Cresswell Doane, spoke out in favor of a strict Sabbath. They presented their argument before a meeting organized by the New York Sabbath Committee, while several museum trustees sat on the podium.[32] The New Methodist Conference was also alarmed by the proposed relaxation of the Sabbath. That body voted unanimously to call upon the state legislature to "defeat this attempt to secularize and desecrate the Sabbath." Conservative trustees must have been pleased to learn of a letter to the park commissioners from a group of ministers and teachers of uptown Sabbath schools who feared that Sunday openings "would tempt many young people from the afternoon Sabbath schools, which afford many of them the only moral instruction they receive." They reminded the trustees that many taxpayers and museum donors were staunch Sabbatarians and insisted, without citing evidence, that European experiments with Sunday openings had failed.[33]

But liberal religious leaders were more widely quoted in the press. They ran the gamut of denominations. "Let our museums be open on Sunday," declared the Reverend N. B. Thompson of the Free Baptist Church. "In this proposed act . . . I see the introduction of a system by which the advantages of the rich are extended to the poor. . . . May God smile upon this effort to open the museums."[34] Unitarians were friendly to the proposal, as were Episcopalians, who took the lead in New York's Social Gospel movement. The eminent Episcopalian R. Heber Newton believed that there was "more fear to religion from our insisting upon an obsolete and arbitrary notion of Sunday and from cramming it down the throats of the mass of men who do not really believe in it than from any such relaxation of the Blue laws as is now proposed." There was, he added, "already too much talk about Christianity being a rich man's religion." Newton urged members of his congregation to sign the petition. William S. Rainsford, rector of St. George's Episcopal Church on the Lower East Side of Manhattan, became a leader in the urban church ministry. He too was a signer.[35] For Jews the Sunday question carried special significance. As Rabbi J. Silverman, of Temple Emanu-El, observed, "a 'Sacred Sunday' was an institution unworthy of the Government of this free country."[36]

For a core group of trustees in both museums the prospect of liberalizing the Sabbath was anathema. As the *New York Times* reported, Morris Jesup was "the most strenuous of any of the Trustees of the Museum of Natural History against Sunday opening."[37] William Prime, vice president of the Metropolitan's board, would prove to be even more intransigent. He wrote to his friend Cesnola, "I am no Puritan, but I *will* have one day in seven for rest . . . I *will* have that day as the immovable centre of Christian faith, Christian intelligence, Christian civilization . . . I will not employ fifty men on Sunday to make a show for ten thousand."[38] In a letter to Johnston, he presented a more pragmatic argument, insisting that "the adoption of Sunday exhibitions" would "drive from the Museum some at least of its supporters." It would, he believed, turn the religious press against the museum and lead them to see it "as a duty to do all in their power to destroy the institution which they regard as desecrating Sunday."[39] Prime's ally William E. Dodge, who was active in various Presbyterian missionary efforts and, along with Jesup, a founder of the Young Men's Christian Association, let Cesnola know his thoughts on Sunday openings when he wrote, "with the whirl & rush of life we need rest." The Presbyterian John Taylor Johnston was also committed to the strict Sabbath, as was the artist Daniel Huntington, who was one of the longest serving trustees.[40]

But the majority of the trustees were not concerned with the Sabbath as a matter of principle. It is telling that the Metropolitan's trustees made a habit of admitting special guests on Sundays, without objection from the conservatives.[41] For Cesnola, the key issue was loyalty to Prime, his close friend and most loyal supporter on the board. As he informed another board member, "I am against opening the Museum on Sunday, for no other reason except that if we do, we lose Prime; otherwise I have not only always been in favor of the measure, but I believe it will do *good*—I have been brought up in the old country in the city of Turin, and I don't remember ever having visited the Museums of Italy, except on Sunday."[42] Other trustees, including Henry Marquand, who would become president of the board in 1889, expressed concern that potential donors would withdraw their bequests if the Metropolitan compromised on the issue of the Sabbath. He also feared that Sunday visitors would damage works of art.[43] Robert Hoe, an active member of the board, told a *New York Times* reporter that he favored "testing the matter" by opening on several Sundays "to draw a satisfactory conclusion as to the possible good it may do." Nonetheless, he worried along with others that some of the "best donors" would withdraw support if the museum capitulated to the "popular clamor."[44]

Conservative trustees held sway with their less orthodox colleagues because the majority of the board was hostile to popular democracy and resistant to the reformist outlook that was already making inroads among influential New Yorkers. By the 1880s, staunch Sabbatarianism was sometimes difficult to disentangle from general suspicion of working-class immigrants. Marquand and others expressed concern that Sunday visitors would pose a danger to the museum's holdings, yet he showed no concern when

Cesnola invited stonemasons and others to inspect controversial Cypriot statues by cutting, scraping, and pouring acid. In January 1886, when a reporter for the *Herald* asked about the mounting petition campaign, Marquand gave a revealing answer. He did "not think the petition would do much good. . . . But a petition signed by a few prominent heads of families whose interest in the city is well known, would, I confess, have much more weight with me."[45] Cesnola might privately declare the Sunday openings would "do good," but he was contemptuous of the working-class visitors that Sunday openings were designed to attract. When the *Herald* interviewed him in January 1887, he declared that the sort of people likely to visit the museum on Sunday "are not the respectable laboring-class. They are the loafers; the scum." Cook quoted an unnamed trustee who allegedly declared: "We don't care to have people come to the Museum who have to think twice about spending twenty-five cents."[46] As the Sunday campaign escalated at the end of the decade, the *New York Times* speculated that the growing number of foreign-born workers contributed to the trustees' intransigence: "The great foreign population, largely uneducated, has so upset municipal politics that it is hard for an American of education to be firmly friendly to the civic majority."[47]

Nonetheless as 1886 came to an end, supporters of Sunday openings were hopeful. That year the House of Lords finally joined the House of Commons in voting to open London's national museums to Sunday visitors.[48] In so doing, it deprived Jesup and his allies of a valuable argument. Meanwhile, as spokesmen for both museums worried openly about the potential for added costs, the New York City Board of Estimate appropriated an additional ten thousand dollars annually to each museum conditional on Sunday openings. (Several months later the city dangled an additional five thousand dollars to each museum with the same stipulation.) On January 1, 1887, the *New York Times* could report that "there is every prospect that the Trustees of the Metropolitan Museum of Art and the American Museum of Natural History will in the near future yield to the demand of the people to open those institutions on Sunday." Two days later the *Tribune* made a similar prediction. The reporter observed that "Many of the trustees of both museums have been in favor of this action since it was first agitated. . . . Others, who were strongly opposed to it at first, are now inclined to favor a trial as an experiment."[49]

Such predictions were premature. In the Metropolitan's annual report of 1886, John Taylor Johnston responded aggressively to the Sunday advocates without mentioning the controversy directly. He complained that public funding for the Metropolitan was stingy in comparison to parliamentary support for London's museums, and he pointed to the trustees' generous investment of time and money. Johnston evoked the board's sense of ownership by recalling recent history: "When the Museum was removed from 14th Street to the Park in 1879, every one of the many thousand fragile objects in your collections was packed and handled . . . by Trustees, and received and unpacked in the Park Building by other Trustees." Referring to the Metropolitan as "your museum," he reminded the board of having contributed $25,696.21 to the cost of running the museum over the preceding twelve months while the city had contributed $14,839.61—slightly less than the promised $15,000 annual allotment. Another $7,780 had come from returns on investments and $2,177 from admissions fees. Johnston charged that the Parks Department had reneged on its contract to maintain the building, thereby forcing the trustees to spend $12,000 for repairs between 1880 and 1886. He urged the trustees to create an endowment in order to reduce the museum's dependence on taxpayer funds. If the annual support of the Metropolitan became entirely "dependent on bargains with politicians," Johnston warned, "it would be very certain to pass into the hands and management of city officials . . . a fate which all intelligent men would look upon as deplorable."[50] In March 1887, barely three months after Johnston presented the annual report, the conference committee of the two Central Park museums met to discuss the Sunday question. Only two members—Joseph Choate and Robert Hoe—voted for the change.[51]

Although the trustees stonewalled, they still managed to extricate funds from the city. They received their annual allotments ($15,000 annually to each museum) and used their influence with the state legislature to gain authorization for the release of city funds to cover the cost of a second proposed expansion for the Metropolitan. They initially refused an additional $10,000 offered to each museum because the allocation was conditional on Sunday openings, but in 1888 they acceded to a compromise. The trustees would accept the additional money in return for opening the museum on two evenings each week, including Saturday. (Problems with the electrical system would delay evening openings until 1890.) Despite the efforts of Mayor Hewitt's successor and opposition at various stages of the process, the Museum of Natural History received funding for its own projected expansion without compromising on the Sunday question.[52]

When the Metropolitan opened its first new wing in December 1888, Prime took the opportunity to minimize the city's financial contribution along with the museum's public debt, but he also signaled the trustees' growing emphasis on funding as the primary obstacle to Sunday openings: "The Museum is our property, bought with our money, managed by our Trustees, its current expenses paid by us out of our private treasury, its purchases all private purchases by ourselves. The City is chargeable with no responsibility for our work in the institution. It has not paid and does not pay a dollar toward the formation and never-ending increase of the Museum, nor does it pay the current expenses of keeping it open free to the public."[53] Trustees were quick to claim that the new wing had itself added to the museum's financial burdens and by 1890 they were insisting that open Sundays would cost an additional $12,000 annually.

Meanwhile, the press aggressively maintained pressure on the trustees of both Central Park museums and inflamed public opinion (see Figure 6.1). In January 1889 the *New York Dispatch* let it be known that seven years earlier the museum's management had ignored William Walters's offer of $10,000 to defray the cost of Sunday openings. That information prompted a new outburst of bad publicity, particularly after Cesnola denied the report and Walters responded with a copy of his original letter.[54] A writer for the *New York Times* drew the obvious conclusion by noting that "the Trustees can no longer resist the opening upon the ground of its expense."[55]

Resistance on religious grounds also began to lose credibility after Cesnola inadvertently revealed his habit of admitting specially approved Sunday visitors. As early as 1882, a German American named Alwin R. Buechner wrote directly to Cesnola, having heard that the museum provided Sunday tickets to the trustees' friends and acquaintances. He requested a comparable favor. "I have," he wrote "been trying to go to the museum since a long time, but have not succeeded in finding time."[56] Clearly, there were whispers about the private guests, but Cesnola's revelatory interview with the *Herald* in the winter of 1887 invited charges of hypocrisy. In response to the news, Crimmins made his own Sunday visit in order to see what was going on. He told a reporter that he "saw a lot of Di Cesnola's friends" at the museum, but when he walked inside with his children, the doorkeeper turned them away. Cesnola defiantly told the *Herald* that he had Crimmins "put out."[57] The *World* revived the controversy in February 1891 when it sent a reporter to observe special Sunday guests visiting the Metropolitan through a side door. The report on these findings prompted a writer for the *Herald* to attack the trustees' hypocrisy as a "morsel that can't go down the New York esophagus without causing a fit

Figure 6.1. *Puck* mocks Marquand for saying that the museum was "intended as much for the humblest artisan as for the most refined lover of the fine arts." Yet "this is how the workingman enjoys the Museum on his only day of liberty." Samuel Ehrhart, *The Metropolitan Museum,* cover illustration, *Puck,* January 2, 1889. New-York Historical Society.

of coughing and profanity."[58] The *World* and a competing daily, the *Continent*, kept up the pressure with ostentatious offers of $2,500 and $10,000 respectively in support of Sunday openings.

Toward the Progressive Museum

The third and largest petition campaign for Sunday openings began in March 1891; initiated by well-to-do reformers, it rapidly extended to the immigrant working class. The barrage of reportage led by the *World* was likely a catalyst, but the issue also tapped growing reformist concern over conditions in tenement housing. Prosperous women seem to have started the first of several petitions.[59] They won support from a group of prominent men, including the retired judge Henry L. Howland; J. Hampden Robb, president of the Parks Department; Charles C. Beaman, Joseph Choate's law partner; Richard Watson Gilder, editor of the *Century Magazine;* and Rev. William Rainsford. Ultimately the petition generated by this contingent garnered about thirty thousand signatures. Theodore Roosevelt, William Vanderbilt, and Louis Tiffany were among the signers.[60]

Several weeks later the campaign moved to another part of the city under the auspices of Charles B. Stover, director of the Neighborhood Guild, a settlement house on the Lower East Side that provided classes, youth clubs, and a kindergarten for tenement dwellers. Stover had been trained for the Presbyterian ministry, but his religious doubts came to a head while studying in Germany and traveling abroad. In England he had met Moncure Conway, the American expatriate abolitionist who was active in England's secular movement and Sunday opening campaign. When Stover returned to New York, he became involved in the Ethical Culture Society and the growing crusade to reform tenement housing. Beginning in April 1891 he deployed an "army of small boys" to distribute petitions in working-class neighborhoods. The *New York Times* reported that the labor unions "rallied behind" Stover and passed resolutions of their own. According to one report, the campaign received endorsements not only from the Central Labor Union, but also from "the Board of Delegates of Building Trades, the Knights of Labor, the Federation of Labor, and the Working Women's Society." In the end the petition carried about 50,000 signatures, or about 80,000 when joined with petitions that circulated in more prosperous parts of the city. Stover pressed his point by pledging to raise $4,000—

enough to maintain Sunday openings through the summer. As he informed an interviewer from the *Times*, the experiment would "prove whether the working people want to go to a place where they can be educated as well as entertained on Sunday. It will prove whether the charge of the anti-Sunday-opening contingent, that the Sunday crowd would deface the art treasures, is true or false." More broadly, he insisted that supporters of Sunday openings wanted the museum to "become a more universal and more available means of 'public education' than it can be now . . . so that the 'industrial classes' can have a chance to go there and be instructed and 'the poor' to go and be happy"[61] (see Figure 6.2).

Like Stover, leaders in the campaign for Sunday openings generally de-emphasized the discourse of moral and spiritual uplift that had predominated among art promoters of the mid-nineteenth century. Rather, in celebrating the value of the museum to the "industrial classes" Stover was alluding to the claim that aesthetic education, among consumers and producers, would improve the quality of American products, while offering wholesome entertainment to working people. An article in the *World* was more explicit. The writer acknowledged the museum's power to inspire the "imagination" and "high impulses" but was equally interested in its practical impact. "This opening of the means of culture to the masses" would result "in better workmanship, more tasteful material forms and an enlarged market value for goods of American make." "There is," concluded the article, "money value in beauty, and the capacity to produce beauty is the result of culture."[62]

By the time the Metropolitan's board received the final petition, the balance of power had shifted. The trustees met on May 18, 1891, at the home of Robert Hoe to decide the Sunday question, and when it came to a vote, Choate finally held sway. Twelve trustees supported the policy of open Sundays. There were four dissenters, including Prime, Huntington, and Dodge. The trustees proudly refused to acknowledge offers of money from Stover or the newspapers. Nor did they hold out for funding from the city. Instead they indicated that the maintenance of open Sundays would be contingent on additional public support in the next funding cycle.[63] Prime resigned from the board, and several donors retracted their bequests, but the press generally celebrated the new policy.[64] The trustees' decision signaled the beginning of a fundamental shift within the museum away from defensive insularity and toward an alignment with the reform-oriented ideas that suffused the petition campaigns.

LIFE'S SUNDAY VISIT TO THE METROPOLITAN MUSEUM.
SUGGESTED AS A GOOD DESIGN FOR A TAPESTRY TO BE HUNG IN THAT PROGRESSIVE INSTITUTION.

Figure 6.2. *Life's Sunday Visit to the Metropolitan Museum* depicts working men charging the museum and the trustees. Innocence and virtue, in the form of a young child on a horse, lead the way with a banner that reads, "For the Public Good." Through the tunnel a crowd can be seen following behind. The caption reads, "Suggested as a good design for a tapestry to be hung in that progressive institution." From *Life*, November 13, 1890. Author's collection.

Notably, the *World* now endorsed the trustees' request for compensation from the city. The paper changed its tone, but not its basic argument. Observing that the Metropolitan "exists and is managed for the people—for all the people, not just for those who are able to pay $10 a year or go in at a side door on Sunday," the writer declared it reasonable for the city "to pay for the support of the Museum, and not depend either upon the generosity of the Trustees, which has been very great, or upon private contributions to maintain it."[65] As a public institution that finally fulfilled its obligations, the museum deserved public support.

The Sunday Visitors

When, in May of 1891, New York's Metropolitan Museum finally opened to the public free of charge on Sunday, reporters were out in force. The high level of interest testified to the intensity of conflict that preceded the event. In fact, published observations of the Sunday visitors provide an exceedingly rare opportunity to glimpse the reactions of nineteenth-century working-class museumgoers (see Figure 6.3). To a casual observer the Metropolitan might have seemed like a grand reinvention of the Art-Union's Free Gallery. More than 14,000 people were in attendance. About half that number came a week later, but on the third Sunday, attendance was back up to nearly 9,000. Reporters drew attention to the size and diversity of the crowd. Among the visitors were members of the Central Labor Union who "hurried through their business and adopted a resolution to proceed [to the museum] in a body." Whereas women composed most of the museum's weekday visitors, men were conspicuously present among the Sunday crowd.[66] Some came in all-male groups, as did the off-duty soldiers and the sailors from William Vanderbilt's yacht. Others came with their wives and children. A reporter for the *World* saw "family groups innumerable with father, mother and an indefinite number of children, cousins, aunts and uncles." This writer exuberantly concluded that the crowd represented "every grade and shade of life in the manifold variety to be seen in New York's streets." The *Tribune*'s reporter witnessed "carpenters, blacksmiths, machinists, farmers, tailors, day laborers and clerks," and a writer for the *Washington Post* who attended later in the summer found that "fully two-thirds of the visitors are of foreign birth—German, French, Spanish, Italian,

Figure 6.3. *The People at the Art Museum Yesterday*, illustration in the *New York World*, June 8, 1891. Note the sailors ("Six of Kind) in the upper left corner; "Mechanic and Family," upper right; a "fiend" poking a picture with his umbrella, lower right; Chinese man, lower left. The image of the crowd is a far cry from common portrayals of the museum as an elegant space sparsely populated by sedate visitors. Library of Congress microfilm.

and Russian." He also saw "several well-dressed, attractive Japanese—men and women—in American garb."[67]

Whether critical or supportive, press reports made it clear that working-class visitors were an incongruous presence with much to learn about the art museum. Accounts generally declared the Sunday experiment to have been a great success, but assessments of the crowd's behavior ran the gamut. The *Tribune*'s reporter observed that visitors "for the most part, walked leisurely and studiously from room to room and gallery to gallery," but also noted the "people whose dazed expression showed that they had never looked upon a work of art before." He imagined that some of these people "expected to find canvas-covered curiosities and the freaks which are the drawing cards of the dime museums." A writer for the *New York Post* concurred, suggesting that the first Sunday visitors derived their "conception of a 'museum' from the specimens which flourish in the Bowery and . . . came fully expecting to see the 'woolly horse,' the fat woman, the living skeleton and perhaps other 'freaks' unrivaled elsewhere." He proceeded to enumerate the "repulsive" habits displayed by too many of the Sunday visitors. In addition the "habit of plentiful expectoration deduced from an incessant addiction to tobacco-chewing" and disregard of the prohibition against smoking, he noted that visitors also disobeyed rules against eating within the confines of the galleries. Though "eatables were denied entry . . . and the men at the gates confiscated whatever of the kind they saw . . . this merely excited an ingenuity of smuggling and did not cut off the crowd's refreshment." Especially annoying to this reporter was "the insidious and peripatetic luncheon of peanuts. The shells fell to the . . . littered floor, or into the sarcophagi of Egyptian dynasties." Worst of all was the "alarming habit possessed by the undesirable element . . . of laying hands on everything." People were so fascinated by "the mighty paw and unsheathed claws of Barye's Lion" that they "could not forebear to shake hands with him to feel its claws, to test the sharpness, and strength of them, and—to pull them off." Meanwhile, "several cups and saucers in one of the Dutch cabinets were broken and one saucer was filched."[68] Henry Marquand, in his annual report to the trustees, confirmed his own predictions by noting the "many visitors [who] took the liberty of handling every object within reach" even to the point of "marring, scratching and breaking articles unprotected by glass." And some visitors "brought with them peculiar habits which were repulsive and unclean."[69]

Yet, other accounts suggested that Sunday visitors practiced their own forms of discrimination. They appeared to show special interest in objects that related to their native countries or that exemplified familiar crafts. Thus "some soft-stepping Chinamen . . . took deep interest in . . . the exquisite ceramics from their native land," while sailors "looked at the model of a Spanish galleon." Women clustered around the collection of rare laces, "commenting upon the minute details of stitch and needlework and pattern."[70] The laces also attracted special attention from a group of Italians who "examined every case minutely" and, according to the *Sun's* reporter, "were evidently from the lace-making country." Men "with traces of oil on their figures that spoke of the engine, the lathe, or the forge" seemed to find a small collection of medieval ironwork "particularly fascinating."[71]

There was a striking convergence in the observation that the Sunday crowds gravitated to the picture galleries where they were particularly impressed by narrative, historical paintings. The *World*'s reporter noted that visitors "gathered as if by instinct in front of the notable paintings by great masters." Popular favorites were Václav Brožik's *Columbus at the Court of Ferdinand and Isabella,* Rosa Bonheur's *Horse Fair,* and Ernest Meissonier's *1807.* The *New York Continent* reported that "there was always a crowd in front of *The Horse Fair* while the big picture of *Columbus before Ferdinand and Isabella* came in for a large share of popular admiration." The *Washington Post*'s reporter noticed that "historical pictures were eagerly inspected and explained to the small fry of the family." He overheard one man giving a spontaneous "oration" in front of the painting of *Columbus at the Court.* Women, according to several observers, liked the portraits, especially "the pictures that tell a story or have a touch of sentiment." A reporter observed that spectators like to compare the images to people whom they knew: "the most frequent remarks I heard were 'Now doesn't——look just like that!' or, 'That would pass for a picture of so and so.' And 'Mercy, what styles; I'm glad we don't wear such things now.' "[72]

These accounts testify to the Metropolitan Museum's engagement with a public that extended far beyond the confines of its wealthy board of trustees, but they also hint at the distance between the Metropolitan and its antebellum predecessor. The presence of ten or eleven park policeman stationed to assist the attendants bespoke the trustees' uneasiness about the Sunday visitors and, in some cases, outright hostility.[73] That the Sunday visitors were the objects of such intense scrutiny was itself an indication of their unfamiliarity within the walls of the museum. The *Sun* reported, "There were two classes of visitors. Those who came to see the Museum and those who came to see the people." Among the observers were several trustees and park commissioners, as well as the critic Clarence Cook. Moncure Conway was also in attendance, along with his daughter who had collected signatures for the women's petition. They arrived in the late afternoon, "when the crowd they wanted to see was largest. Then they came in little companies of three or four and took seats in the main hall where they could see the real crowd as it swept past them." As if to accentuate the gulf between observer and observed, the reporter took the opportunity to note that the larger group "had the real fun."[74]

Such descriptions of the Sunday visitors reveal a significant shift away from the sensibility that had shaped the Art-Union. Art enthusiasts of the antebellum era assumed that artistic taste involved the ability to comprehend moral messages carried by paintings, and they believed that stories embedded in artworks were an appropriate subject of conversation among tasteful viewers. Because they thought that pictures could operate "like speeches," managers of the Art-Union devoted their gallery to paintings, featured narrative pictures, and, through the pages of the *Bulletin*, sought to facilitate the processes of comprehension and moral uplift. Sunday visitors appeared to follow that script without prompting. Not only did they gravitate to the paintings; they also discussed the stories that they saw in the images. Yet, by the end of the nineteenth-century, this way of looking seemed naive to more experienced museumgoers. In line with a much wider cultural movement, artists and critics increasingly blurred distinctions between paintings and other art objects, and they assumed that tasteful spectatorship involved the ability to glean ineffable spiritual satisfaction through appreciation of the decorative, formal, or surface elements in painting. From this perspective, the affinity of Sunday visitors for pictures that told stories seemed off the mark. A writer for the *Herald* got to the nub of the matter. Visiting the museum on a November Sunday in 1894, he found it especially interesting to see what working-class men chose to look at. "Invariably," he observed, "it is the historical pictures. Art for art's sake means little to a man who drives a truck, but he can thrill over the spiritual rendering of a scene that he knows took place. He tells the stories to the children, and he shows them what a great man is, and they feel it as the artist meant they should." In fact, few critics—much less trustees—would have gone so far as to wholly embrace the notion of "art for art's sake." The imagined link between artistic beauty and morality died hard. Yet, by the time the museum opened to Sunday crowds, there was a distinct gap between this allegedly unsophisticated interest in narrative meaning and modern, educated ways of looking at art.[75]

By the end of the year, even Marquand had to admit that "judging from the number of Sunday visitors" the experiment had been a "pronounced success." The element of turbulence and disorder" that had initially disturbed him and other trustees seemed to dissipate, and by August he believed he saw a change in the character of Sunday crowds. The "laboring classes" were still well represented, but in his view they were now "respectable, law-abiding, and intelligent." He also noticed that young people were visiting the museum on Sunday more than on any other day. At least on the matter of attendance, the numbers bear out Marquand's observation. The first open Sunday saw the largest attendance, but from June 7 through September 27, 1891, the day's visitor count averaged 6,403.[76] The following year Sunday attendance totaled 405,411, with an average of 5,869 Sunday visitors. The Metropolitan could hardly be classified among the most popular working-class amusements, but through the turn of the century it attracted a remarkably steady stream of Sunday visitors. From 1893 through 1904 turnstiles registered nearly 12,831,555 visitors to the museum in total, with attendance at its highest on Saturdays and Sundays.[77]

One thoughtful critic anticipated the direction in which the museum would move in the early twentieth century and some lessons it would take from the Sunday crowds. Mariana Griswold Van Rensselaer was a member of New York's old mercantile elite, but she embraced the idea of art education for the masses, writing not only for the short-lived, highbrow *Art Review* but also for the *World* and *Harper's Weekly*. She had been a signer of the 1891 petition for Sunday openings. Her special interest was landscape design, but like Clarence Cook, she published widely on art-related topics. Also like him, she took her role as a critic seriously. She welcomed Sunday openings at the museums, noting that the invitation to "delight your eyes with things of beauty" is "gladly accepted by scores of thousands whose opportunities for pleasure and self-instruction are very scant." But she worried that popular audiences might not be ready for what they saw. Van Rensselaer undoubtedly had the Cesnola collection in mind when she observed that the insufficiently educated visitor was likely to be "confused by his ignorance of the fact that . . . the value of some works of art is historical rather than intrinsic, that the purpose is to show not only forms of pure and finished beauty, but also the mile-stones that have marked the different roads along which men have struggled towards these forms." She supported the museum's attention to historically significant objects, but she also hoped that large collections of lesser works would be weeded out in favor of the best exemplars of each type. Likewise, she insisted that visitors needed more and better handbooks to explain what they were seeing and to emphasize objects deserving of most attention. In sum, while Van Rensselaer supported Sunday openings and educational outreach, she also believed that popularizing initiatives required the display of masterworks as defined by experts such as herself.[78]

Not until the first decade of the twentieth century did the Metropolitan move aggressively in the direction once advocated by Cook, Van Rensselaer, and others. The death of the railway magnate Jacob S. Rodgers brought what was then a massive and unanticipated bequest worth nearly five million dollars. Interest on those funds would help to initiate a new era in acquisitions. After Cesnola's death in 1904, J. P Morgan, the millionaire art collector who replaced Marquand as president of the board, was free to begin the process of hiring a professional staff. Sir Caspar Purdon Clarke took the position of director after a long career at the South Kensington Museum. For the new position of assistant director, the museum hired Edward Robinson, scholar of classical antiquities and former director of Boston's Museum of Fine Arts. Several years later, when ill-health forced Clarke to retire, Robinson took his place. The new regime pledged to set new standards for acquisitions, turning away unwanted gifts, selling off duplicates, and relegating other objects to the basement.

Clarke made his commitment to the decorative and industrial arts clear from the outset. He wanted the Metropolitan to be "a museum of fine arts in which all the arts shall be represented." Significantly, the Metropolitan's annual report for 1905 reaffirmed the trustees' commitment to the areas of "Classical Antiquities, Painting and Sculpture . . . as the base from which the other Decorative Arts are evolved." But they also emphasized the importance of carved woodwork, textiles, ceramics, and metalwork, among other things. And they signaled the director's interest not only in building a collection of furniture but also in the exhibition of "entire rooms of different countries and periods."[79] A writer for the New York Post celebrated the museum's new management with the observation that "any policy that makes us realize that the standards for the so-called fine and for the industrial arts are identical is a wholesome policy. . . . In any normally creative period, the difference between decorating a spoon-handle and a cathedral is chiefly quantitative. . . . The important thing is quality."[80] In fact, within the context of the museum the term "industrial art" came to signify antique objects that could inspire or inform modern manufactured products and not necessarily modern industrially made goods themselves. It is telling that the retail magnate Benjamin Altman, whose 1913 bequest included thirteen Rembrandts among other masterworks, also bequeathed tapestries, enamels, porcelains, gold and crystal objects, and antique furniture.[81] Altman's

Figure 6.4. Compared to the image of the museum published in *Harper's Weekly* in 1880 (Figure 5.1), this illustration, marking the opening of the new wing, places the Cesnola collection at the margins in the upper left corner. The focus is on the collection of casts, increasingly emphasized for its role in the education of taste. *The New Home of the Metropolitan Museum of Art*, drawing by C. D. Weldon, in *Harper's Weekly*, December 29, 1888. Author's collection.

department store was widely known and appreciated in New York for its furniture, rugs, and other housewares.

The new administration was committed not only to what Clarke referred to alternately as the "arts and crafts" and "industrial arts" but also to maintaining a balance between history and beauty—between chronological exhibits depicting the history of civilizations and displays of distinctively beautiful objects. (Robinson had resigned from his position at the Boston Museum of Fine Arts in opposition to the radical aestheticism that became dominant at that institution. He too favored balance.) However, the type of history presented by the Metropolitan in the early twentieth century would be firmly anchored in the class and racial outlook of the professional staff and trustees. It is notable that the museum's extensive cast collection—created in the aftermath of the Cesnola controversy—focused almost entirely on Greek and Roman antiquity, while the growing collection of decorative art comprised rarefied objects owned (or formerly owned) by the well-to-do[82] (see Figure 6.4).

Under the new regime, connoisseurship would be wedded to an emphasis on education. The board phased out the industrial art schools in the 1890s, but the administration worked to bring the educational mission into the museum itself through lecture programs, coordination with schools and settlement houses, and the publication of handbooks. Average yearly attendance during the first decade of the new administration increased, with proportionate growth in the numbers of visitors who came on Sundays. The high point was 1909, when the Metropolitan put on the Hudson-Fulton Exhibition, which showcased American and Dutch painting and American furniture, silver, and other objects.[83] Of the nearly 938,000 people who visited the museum in 1909, 332,954 came on Sundays. How working-class visitors understood the exhibit (and the intended lessons in taste, civic pride, and patriotism) remains as elusive as the reactions of the earlier generation of Sunday visitors. What seems clear is that the Metropolitan's leadership had absorbed the perspective of its harshest nineteenth-century critics. In 1914, the year in which John Linton Myres curated the reconstituted Cesnola collection, the museum also sponsored six lectures in Yiddish.[84]

Edith Wharton's Museum

Edith Wharton, among the most astute literary observers of New York's late nineteenth-century elite, set a critical scene of her novel *The Age of Innocence* among the Metropolitan Museum's enormous collection of Cypriot antiquities. The deserted gallery was a meeting place for her characters—furtive would-be lovers—Newland Archer and Countess Ellen Olenska. As she described the encounter, Ellen and Newland avoid "the popular 'Wolfe collection,' whose anecdotic canvases filled one of the main galleries." Instead they wander "down a passage to the room where the 'Cesnola antiquities' moldered in unvisited loneliness. They had this melancholy retreat to themselves."

As the seated Newland gazes at Ellen, she peruses the cases that "were crowded with small broken objects—hardly recognizable domestic utensils, ornaments and personal trifles—made of glass, of clay, of discolored bronze and other time-blurred substances."

"It seems cruel," she says, "that after a while nothing matters . . . any more than these little things, that used to be necessary and important to forgotten people, and now have to be guessed at under a magnifying glass and labeled: 'Use unknown.'"[1]

There are many intriguing things about this interaction, not least that the setting is an anachronism: The scene purportedly takes place at the Central Park building during the 1870s, before the Metropolitan had actually moved to that site. But for purposes here the most striking feature of the passage is the reference to the Cesnola antiquities. Wharton, who was born in 1867, published her novel six years after Myres recataloged the collection. She undoubtedly knew that it had been the center of a furious controversy.[2] From one perspective, the antiquities signify the upper-class New York world that was the subject of Wharton's work. But the reference also points obliquely to the emergence of an aestheticizing orientation to art and museum display associated with the burgeoning global market in domestic decoration.

Through the character of Ellen and the novel as a whole, Wharton displayed archaeological, historical, and anthropological inclinations—a tendency to look at objects for what they could (or could not) tell her about the peoples that lived among them. Yet, in many ways Wharton was also Clarence Cook's intellectual descendant. It is notable that small broken relics rather than the larger controversial sculptures are the objects of Ellen's reflections. Equally significant is the suggestion that the original use of those objects was "domestic," "personal," and "ornamental." Wharton believed that the things with which one chose to live were expressions of *personal* character and quality. She informed her readers that Ellen's "skillful use of a few properties" turned her New York drawing room "into something intimate, 'foreign,' subtly suggestive of old romantic scenes and sentiments."[3] Not coincidentally Wharton's first book, published in 1897, was *The Decoration of Houses*, an instructional guide, oriented to wealthy readers.[4] Unlike Cook, she took no interest in the project of middle- or working-class uplift, yet her aesthetic orientation, like his, was personal and domestic, suffused with an interest in the subject of interior design and inextricably linked to new patterns of household decor. Wharton's condescending allusion to the "anecdotic canvases" of the "popular 'Wolfe collection'" referenced the antiquated taste for didactic, narrative pictures rejected by sophisticated turn-of-the-century connoisseurs. *The Age of Innocence* gestured toward an outlook that gave importance to grand historical, ethnographic narratives, but it also evoked Wharton's more aestheticizing point of view.

Wharton's references to the Metropolitan Museum may well have contributed to its reputation as a mausoleum of turn-of-the-century elite culture. In her fictional writing, she portrayed art museums as sites of uplifted reflection or conversation—places that naturally attracted people of high character and class. Thus Mrs. Quentin, the refined maternal character in the short story "Quicksand," regularly went to the Metropolitan "to seek in the enjoyment of the beautiful the distraction that many of her acquaintances appeared to find in each other's company." As in *The Age of Innocence*, a consequential, high-minded conversation takes place within one of the museum's galleries.[5] Similarly, in *The Custom of the Country*, the cultivated and ultimately tragic character of Ralph "fled for solace to museums and galleries" as an escape from his beautiful but entirely materialistic wife. For Wharton, art museums in general, and the Metropolitan in particular, were cherished retreats from America's "gros public," which she found sorely lacking "on the aesthetic side."[6] From that perspective, her dismissive reference to the Wolfe collection alluded to a dissonant popular presence within the museum's rarefied setting.

Yet the Metropolitan was a culturally ambivalent institution, considerably more inclusive than Wharton was able to acknowledge. From the outset it was deeply embedded in the world of New York's upper crust, and in this sense it was (and remains) well within the tradition of New York's earlier institutions of fine art. But like its predecessors it was subject to intense popular pressure and enmeshed within the social and political movements of its times. Nineteenth-century urbanites engaged passionately with centers of art exhibition. Institutions founded and directed by the city's male elite sparked resentment but also widespread popular fascination. The controversies that they engendered charted broader urban transformations—from the era when merchant amateurs shaped elite institutions to the rise of industrial capital and incipient professionalization; from the age of artisanal production to the rise of factories, department stores, and international consumer emporiums; from the time when the Irish, African Americans, and native-born whites predominated among the urban working class to the age of mass immigration; from the period when political conflict revolved around the slavery question to the class warfare of the late nineteenth century; from the era when art promoters could liken paintings to speeches to a time when painting itself took its place among the decorative arts.

Fueling the controversies that roiled the American Art-Union and its successor was the conviction that the taste for art was a signifier of humanity. That belief gave urgency to disputes about access to art institutions and to controversies about the definition of art itself. The sense that taste mattered deeply—that it had a role to play in the social and political fabric of the nation—transformed ephemeral disputes into culture wars and made art institutions battlegrounds in the great struggles of the nineteenth century.

NOTES

Introduction

Note to epigraphs: *Oswego (NY) Commercial Times*, December 1, 1848, in Newspaper Clippings, vol. 1, American Art-Union Papers, New-York Historical Society; [Elizabeth A. Tompkins], "Going to Grant's Tomb," *Washington Post*, July 26, 1891.

1. On the American Art-Union, see Chapter 1, n. 1.

2. On the Metropolitan Museum's history see Chapter 4, n. 1.

3. Dan Schiller, *Objectivity and the News: The Public and the Rise of Commercial Journalism* (Philadelphia: University of Pennsylvania Press, 1981), 14.

4. "A Book That Is Always Open," *New York World*, May 10, 1891, p. 18. Sales increased over the course of the 1890s. See Frank Luther Mott, *American Journalism: A History of Newspapers in the United States through 260 Years, 1690–1950* (New York: Macmillan, 1950), 507. By the middle of the decade, according to one estimate, circulation had nearly doubled. See Michael Schudson, *Discovering the News: A Social History of American Newspapers* (New York: Basic Books, 1978), 111. See also Steven L. Vaughn, ed., *Encyclopedia of American Journalism* (New York: Routledge, 2008), 345–346.

5. Carol Duncan, *Civilizing Rituals: Inside Public Art Museums* (New York: Routledge, 1995), 65 and passim.

6. Lawrence W. Levine, *Highbrow/Lowbrow: The Emergence of Cultural Hierarchy in America* (Cambridge, MA: Harvard University Press, 1988); Paul DiMaggio, "Cultural Entrepreneurship in Nineteenth-Century Boston: The Creation of an Organizational Base for High Culture in America" and "Cultural Entrepreneurship in Nineteenth-Century Boston, Part II: The Classification and Framing of American Art," *Media, Culture and Society* 4 (1982): 33–50, 303–322.

7. Pierre Bourdieu, *Distinction: A Social Critique of the Judgement of Taste*, trans. Richard Nice (Cambridge, MA: Harvard University Press, 1984); Pierre Bourdieu and Alain Darbel, *The Love of Art: European Art Museums and Their Public*, trans. Caroline Beattie and Nick Merriman (Stanford, CA: Stanford University Press, 1990), 1–4, 37–70.

8. Neil Harris, *Cultural Excursions: Marketing Appetites and Cultural Tastes in Modern America* (Chicago: University of Chicago Press, 1990), 56–81; William Leach, *Land of Desire: Merchants, Power, and the Rise of a New American Culture* (New York: Pantheon, 1993), 164–173, 313–314, 318; J. M. Mancini, *Pre-Modernism: Art-World Change and American Culture from the Civil War to the Armory Show* (Princeton, NJ: Princeton University Press, 2005); Jeffrey Trask, *Things American: Art Museums and Civic Culture in the Progressive Era* (Philadelphia: University of Pennsylvania Press, 2012); Steven Conn, *Museums and American Intellectual Life,*

1876–1926 (Chicago: University of Chicago Press, 1998), 192–262; Carol G. Duncan, *A Matter of Class: John Cotton Dana, Progressive Reform, and the Newark Museum* (Pittsburgh, PA: Periscope, 2009). Tony Bennett explores the history of museums in relation to other sites, notably fairs and amusement parks, as places of reform and regulation; see Bennett, *The Birth of the Museum: History, Theory, Politics* (London: Routledge, 1995).

9. Neil Harris, *The Artist in American Society: The Formative Years, 1790–1860* (Chicago: University of Chicago Press, 1982).

10. Sir Joshua Reynolds, *Discourses on Art*, ed. Robert R. Wark (New Haven, CT: Yale University Press, 1988), xviii, 171.

11. John Barrell, *The Political Theory of Painting from Reynolds to Hazlitt: "The Body of the Public"* (New Haven, CT: Yale University Press, 1986), 69–162. On Reynolds in America, see also Lillian B. Miller, *Patrons and Patriotism: The Encouragement of the Fine Arts in the United States, 1790–1860* (Chicago: University of Chicago Press, 1966), 17–19; Reynolds, *Discourses*, 90.

12. Ian Pears, *The Discovery of Painting: The Growth of Interest in the Arts in England, 1680–1768* (New Haven, CT: Yale University Press, 1988), 1–50 and passim.

13. Janice G. Schimmelman, *American Imprints on Art through 1865: Books and Pamphlets on Drawing, Painting, Sculpture, Aesthetics, Art Criticism, and Instruction; An Annotated Bibliography* (Boston: G. K. Hall, 1990), 5–7, 158–165. On the impact of Scottish Enlightenment thinkers in the United States, see Lori Merish, *Sentimental Materialism: Gender, Commodity Culture, and Nineteenth-Century American Literature* (Durham, NC: Duke University Press, 2000); William Palmer Hudson, "Archibald Alison and William Cullen Bryant," *American Literature* 12, no. 1 (March 1940): 59–68.

14. On the aesthetic theory of the Scottish Enlightenment, see Alexander Broadie, ed., *The Cambridge Companion to the Scottish Enlightenment* (Cambridge: Cambridge University Press, 2003), 280–297, 316–337; Harold Osborne, *Aesthetics and Art Theory: An Historical Introduction* (New York: E. P. Dutton, 1970), 150–170. See also William Walker, "Ideology and Addison's Essays on the Pleasures of the Imagination," *Eighteenth-Century Life* 24, no. 2 (2000): 65–84. For accounts that locate the British aesthetic philosophers in a wider continental conversation, see Terry Eagleton, *The Ideology of the Aesthetic* (Oxford: Blackwell, 1990); Preben Mortensen, *Art in the Social Order: The Making of the Modern Conception of Art* (Albany: State University of New York Press, 1997); Nick Prior, *Museums and Modernity: Art Galleries and the Making of Modern Culture* (Oxford: Berg, 2002), 99–138.

15. Henry Home, Lord Kames, *Elements of Criticism* (New York: Collins & Hannay, 1830), [vi], xiii.

16. Archibald Alison, *Essays on the Nature and Principles of Taste* (Edinburgh, 1790), viii.

17. Alexander Gerard, *An Essay on Taste: To which is now added part fourth, Of the Standard of Taste*, 3rd ed. (Edinburgh, 1780), 191.

18. Kames, *Elements of Criticism*, 103.

19. Edmund Burke, *A Philosophical Enquiry into the Origin of Our Ideas of the Sublime and Beautiful*, ed. James T. Boulton (Oxford: Basil Blackwell, 1987), 23; David Hume, *Selected Essays*, ed. Stephen Copley and Andrew Edgar (New York: Oxford University Press, 1993), 133–154.

20. Hume, *Selected Essays*, 12, 173.

21. Gerard, *An Essay on Taste*, 11, 15, 18, 37.

22. Alison, *Essays*, 23.

23. Hume, *Selected Essays*, 150–151.

24. Adam Ferguson, *Principles of Moral and Political Science, 1792* (New York: Garland, 1978), 1:298.

25. Kames, *Elements of Criticism*, 444.

26. Ibid., 445.

27. Alison, *Essays*, 25, 28.

28. Hume, *Selected Essays*, 149.

29. John Brewer, *The Pleasures of the Imagination: English Culture in the Eighteenth Century* (New York: Farrar, Straus and Giroux, 1997); Sarah Knott and Barbara Taylor, eds., *Women, Gender and Enlightenment* (Basingstoke, UK: Palgrave, 2005), 297–305, 224–242.

30. Ann Bermingham and John Brewer, eds., *The Consumption of Culture, 1600–1800: Image, Object, Text* (London: Routledge, 1995), 489–513; Sylvana Tomaselli, "The Enlightenment Debate on Women," *History Workshop Journal* 20 (Autumn 1985): 101–123; Knott and Taylor, *Women, Gender and Enlightenment*, 8–29, 70–96; Elizabeth Eger, *Bluestockings: Women of Reason from Enlightenment to Romanticism* (London: Palgrave Macmillan, 2010), 32–58.

31. David Hume, *Essays and Treatises on Several Subjects* (Basil, 1793), 1:213.

32. Ibid., 140.

33. On aesthetic theory, visual culture, and political ideas in the early national United States, see Wendy Bellion, *Citizen Spectator: Art, Illusion, and Visual Perception in Early National America* (Chapel Hill: University of North Carolina Press, 2011); Edward Cahill, *Liberty of the Imagination: Aesthetic Theory, Literary Form, and Politics in the Early United States* (Philadelphia: University of Pennsylvania Press, 2012); Catherine E. Kelly, *Republic of Taste: Art, Politics, and Everyday Life in Early America* (Philadelphia: University of Pennsylvania Press, 2016). On notions of aesthetic taste later in the nineteenth century, see Roger B. Stein, *John Ruskin and Aesthetic Thought in America, 1840–1900* (Cambridge, MA: Harvard University Press, 1967); Richard Lyman Bushman, *The Refinement of America: Persons, Houses, Cities* (New York: Vintage Books, 1992); Merish, *Sentimental Materialism*; Barbara Dayer Gallati, ed., *Making American Taste: Narrative Art for a New Democracy* (London: New-York Historical Society in association with D. Giles, 2011).

Chapter 1

1. For standard accounts of the American Art-Union, see Mary Bartlett Cowdrey, ed., *American Academy of Fine Arts and American Art-Union: Introduction, 1816–1852* (New York: New-York Historical Society, 1953); Lillian B. Miller, *Patrons and Patriotism: The Encouragement of the Fine Arts in the United States, 1790–1860* (Chicago: University of Chicago Press, 1966), 160–172; Maybelle Mann, *The American Art-Union* (Otisville, NY: ALM Associates, 1977). For brief but valuable references, see Neil Harris, *The Artist in American Society: The Formative Years, 1790–1860* (Chicago: University of Chicago Press, 1982), 183, 228, 231–232, 246, 257, 271–272, 275, 281. This chapter draws from my prior work on the Art-Union while also benefiting from more recent research. See Rachel N. Klein, "Art and Authority in Antebellum New York City: The Rise and Fall of the American Art-Union" *Journal of American History* 81, no. 4 (March 1995): 1534–1561. For an analysis of the American Art-Union (AAU) art and ideology, see Patricia Hills, "The American Art-Union as Patron for Expansionist Ideology in the 1840s," in *Art in Bourgeois Society, 1790–1850*, ed. Andrew Hemingway and William Vaughan (Cambridge: Cambridge University Press, 1998), 314–339. An alternate

but compatible perspective on landscape art favored by the AAU is Carol Troyon, "Retreat to Arcadia: American Landscape in the American Art-Union," *American Art Journal* 23, no. 1 (1991): 20–37. For a prosopography of Art-Union managers and officers as well as the fullest account of the organization's early years, see Arlene Katz Nichols, "Merchants and Artists: The Apollo Association and the American Art-Union" (Ph.D. diss., City University of New York, 2003). For a study that emphasizes the contribution of the Young America Democrats, see Edward L. Widmer, *Young America: The Flowering of Democracy in New York City* (New York: Oxford University Press, 1999), 141–154 and passim. For a catalog to an exhibition of Art-Union material that includes valuable essays on the organization, see Amanda Lett, Patricia Hills, Peter John Brownlee, and Randy Ramer, *Perfectly American: The Art-Union and Its Artists* (Tulsa, OK: Gilcrease Museum, 2011). For a comparative perspective, see Joy Sperling, " 'Art, Cheap and Good': The Art Union in England and the United States, 1840–60," *Nineteenth Century Art Worldwide* 1, no. 1 (2002), http://www.19thc-artworldwide.org/spring02/196—qart-cheap-and-goodq-the-art-union-in-england-and-the-united-states-184 060. See also David Shapiro, "William Cullen Bryant and the American Art-Union," in *William Cullen Bryant and His America*, ed. Stanley Brodwin and Michael D'Innocenzo (New York: AMS Press, 1983), 85–95.

2. David B. Dearinger, ed., *Rave Reviews: American Art and Its Critics, 1826–1925* (New York: National Academy of Design, 2000), 32–33.

3. Rita Susswein Gottesman, *The Arts and Crafts in New York, 1800–1804: Advertisements and News Items from New York City Newspapers* (New York: New-York Historical Society, 1965), 43–44; Sean Wilentz, "Artisan Republican Festivals and the Rise of Class Conflict in New York City, 1788–1837," in *Working-Class America: Essays on Labor, Community, and American Society*, ed. Michael H. Frisch and Daniel J. Walkowitz (Urbana: University of Illinois Press, 1983); Jenna M. Gibbs, *Performing the Temple of Liberty: Slavery, Theater, and Popular Culture in London and Philadelphia, 1760–1850* (Baltimore: Johns Hopkins University Press, 2014), 24–25.

4. William Bentley, *The Diary of William Bentley* (Salem, MA: Essex Institute, 1905–1911), 3:96.

5. *Longworth's American Almanac, New-York Register, and City Directory . . .* (New York: D. Longworth, 1801, 1803; Thomas Longworth, 1830); George L. McKay, *A Register of Artists, Engravers, Booksellers, Bookbinders, Printers & Publishers in New York City, 1633–1820* (New York: New York Public Library, 1942); Harold E. Dickson, *John Wesley Jarvis, American Painter, 1780–1840* (New York: New-York Historical Society, 1949), 63–66, 96–106; Christopher Kent Wilson, "The Life and Work of John Quidor" (Ph.D. diss., Yale University, 1982), 26–31; John Durand, *The Life and Times of Asher B. Durand* (New York: Charles Scribner's Sons, 1894), 22–24.

6. The most comprehensive account of New York's academy is Carrie J. Rebora, "The American Academy of the Fine Arts, New York, 1802–1842" (Ph.D. diss., City University of New York, 1990). See also Winifred E. Howe, *A History of the Metropolitan Museum of Art with a Chapter on the Early Institutions of Art in New York* (New York: Metropolitan Museum of Art, 1913), 7–35; Cowdrey, *American Academy of Fine Arts and American Art-Union: Introduction*, 3–94; Miller, *Patrons and Patriotism*, 87–102. Thomas Bender locates the American Academy within the public culture of early New York; see Bender, *New York Intellect: A History of Intellectual Life in New York City, from 1750 to the Beginnings of Our Own Time* (New York: Knopf, 1987), 50–65, 126–128.

7. Rebora, "The American Academy," 36.

8. Dearinger, *Rave Reviews*, 33–36; Bender, *New York Intellect*, 62–66.

9. Bender, *New York Intellect*, 47–88; Evan Cornog, *The Birth of Empire: DeWitt Clinton and the American Experience, 1769–1828*, 62–72.

10. DeWitt Clinton, *A Discourse Delivered Before the American Academy of the Arts by the Honourable De Witt Clinton, LL.D. (President), 23d October, 1816* (New York: T & W Merlein, 1816), 13, 16–17.

11. Minutes of Meetings, 1802–1817, 26–39, Records, 1802–1840, American Academy of the Fine Arts, New-York Historical Society (hereafter cited as NYHS).

12. Bender, *New York Intellect*, 61–62.

13. Rebora, "The American Academy," 57–101, 337–421.

14. Ibid., 37, 344–345, 354.

15. Dorothy C. Barck, ed., *Letters from John Pintard to His Daughter Eliza Noel Pintard Davidson, 1816–1833* (New York: New-York Historical Society, 1940–1941), 4 vols., 1:25–26; Joseph Hopkinson, *Annual Discourse* (Philadelphia, 1810), 24.

16. Andrea Stulman Dennet, *Weird and Wonderful: The Dime Museum in America* (New York: New York University Press, 1997), 18.

17. On Charles Willson Peale's museum, see Laura Rigal, *The American Manufactory: Art, Labor, and the World of Things in the Early Republic* (Princeton, NJ: Princeton University Press, 1998); David R Brigham, *Public Culture in the Early Republic: Peale's Museum and Its Audience* (Washington, DC: Smithsonian Institution Press, 1995); Charles Coleman Sellers, *Mr. Peale's Museum: Charles Willson Peale and the First Popular Museum of Natural Science and Art* (New York: Norton, 1980); Sidney Hart and David C. Ward, "The Waning of an Enlightenment Ideal: Charles Willson Peale's Philadelphia Museum, 1790–1820," *Journal of the Early Republic* 8 (Winter 1988): 389–418. On the wax figures that populated early museums, see Catherine E. Kelly, *Republic of Taste: Art, Politics, and Everyday Life in Early America* (Philadelphia: University of Pennsylvania Press, 2016), 159–194. For a study of illusionary art that explores the cultural outlook underlying Peale's museum, see Wendy Bellion, *Citizen Spectator: Art, Illusion, and Visual Perception in Early National America* (Chapel Hill: University of North Carolina Press, 2011). On Daniel Bowen's Columbian Museum in Boston, modeled on Peale's museum, see Julia Stern, *The Plight of Feeling: Sympathy and Dissent in the Early American Novel* (Chicago: University of Chicago Press, 1997), 126–130, 265–268; Loyd Haberly, "The Long Life of Daniel Bowen," *New England Quarterly* 32 (September 1959): 320–332.

18. Gottesman, *Arts and Crafts in New York, 1800–1804*, 22–23.

19. Bender, *New York Intellect*, 46–47; *The Old Merchants of New York City*, vol. II (New York: Thomas R. Knox & Co., 1885), 224–225.

20. Gottesman, *Arts and Crafts in New York, 1800–1804*, 19, 25.

21. "Amusement and Instruction," *National Advocate* (New York), June 28, 1816; "Oh Fair! The Beautiful Petticoat and the Pretty Petticoats!," *New York Morning Herald*, September 26, 1837; "Fair at Niblo's," *New York Morning Herald*, September 27, 1837.

22. Stephan Oettermann, *The Panorama: History of a Mass Medium* (New York: Zone Books, 1997), 69.

23. Lillian Beresnack Miller, "John Vanderlyn and the Business of Art," *New York History* 32, no. 1 (January 1951): 38 (quoting *Minutes of the Common Council of the City of New York*).

24. Ibid., 33–44.

25. Vanderlyn to John Vanderlyn Jr., April 22, 1820, Vanderlyn Papers, NYHS.

26. Vanderlyn to John Vanderlyn, Jr., October 31, 1821, Vanderlyn Papers, NYHS.

27. Rebora, "The American Academy," 137–138.

28. Catherine Hoover Voorsanger and John K. Howat, eds., *Art and the Empire City: New York, 1825–1861* (New York: Metropolitan Museum of Art; New Haven, CT: Yale University Press, 2000), 3–45; Edwin G. Burrows and Mike Wallace, *Gotham: A History of New York City to 1898* (New York: Oxford University Press, 1999), 452–472; Kenneth T. Jackson, *Crabgrass Frontier: The Suburbanization of the United States* (New York: Oxford University Press, 1985), 14–20.

29. Shane White, *Stories of Freedom in Black New York* (Cambridge, MA: Harvard University Press, 2002), 12.

30. Bayrd Still, *Mirror for Gotham: New York as Seen by Contemporaries from Dutch Days to the Present* (New York: Fordham University Press, 1994), 102–103. On prostitutes and the "third tier," see Timothy J. Gilfoyle, *City of Eros: New York City, Prostitution, and the Commercialization of Sex, 1790–1920* (New York: W. W. Norton, 1992), 67, 108–112; Daniel Walker Howe, ed., *Victorian America* (Philadelphia: University of Pennsylvania Press, 1976), 111–120.

31. Peter George Buckley, "To the Opera House: Culture and Society in New York City, 1820–1860" (Ph.D. diss., State University of New York at Stony Brook, 1984), 84–139; David Grimsted, *Melodrama Unveiled: American Theater and Culture, 1800–1850* (Berkeley: University of California Press, 1968), 46–75.

32. Marvin McAllister, *White People Do Not Know How to Behave at Entertainments Designed for Ladies and Gentlemen of Colour: William Brown's African and American Theater* (Chapel Hill: University of North Carolina Press, 2003); White, *Stories of Freedom*, 68–126; Leslie M. Harris, *In the Shadow of Slavery: African Americans in New York City, 1626–1863* (Chicago: University of Chicago Press, 2003), 78–79, 96–133. See also Leslie M. Alexander, *Black Identity and Political Activism in New York City, 1784–1861* (Urbana: University of Illinois Press, 2008), 24–153.

33. Gottesman, *Arts and Crafts in New York, 1800–1804*, 52–53. On female visitors at Peale's and Bowen's museums, see Brigham, *Public Culture in the Early Republic*, 6–9, 29–30; and Stern, *The Plight of Feeling*, 126–130, 265–268.

34. Hopkinson, *Annual Discourse*, 34–35.

35. "Report of the Committee of Visitors of the American Academy of the Fine Arts for October 1817," Minutes of Meetings, 1817–1830, Records, 1802–1840, American Academy of the Fine Arts, NYHS, 32–33.

36. Minutes of the Proceedings of the American Academy of the Fine Arts Held in the New York Institution from January 1817 (July 1824), Records, 1802–1840, American Academy of the Fine Arts, Records, NYHS.

37. Mrs. [Frances] Trollope, *Domestic Manners of the Americans*, 4th ed. (London: Whittaker, Treacher, 1832), 216–217.

38. For a nuanced account of the founding of the NAD that challenges triumphalist accounts, see Rebora, "The American Academy," 244–317; also see Miller, *Patrons and Patriotism*, 100–102; Bender, *New York Intellect*, 126–130; and Paul J. Staiti, *Samuel F. B. Morse* (Cambridge: Cambridge University Press, 1989), 149–174.

39. Morse to his parents, December 22, 1814, in *Samuel F. B. Morse: His Letters and Journals*, ed. Edward Lind Morse (Boston: Houghton Mifflin, 1914), 1:164; and Morse to Mr. and Mrs. Jarvis, September 17, 1811, in Morse, *Letters and Journals*, 1:46–47.

40. Wilson, "Life and Work of John Quidor," 52–58; Staiti, *Samuel F. B. Morse*; Morse, *Letters and Journals*, 1:164.

41. On the proliferation and expansion of New York theaters, see Buckley, "To the Opera House," 143–144.

42. Bender, *New York Intellect*, 75–78, 126–127; Miller, "John Vanderlyn and the Business of Art," 38. For an account of the venues for the exhibition of art in New York City through the antebellum period, see Voorsanger and Howat, *Art and the Empire City*, 47–81.

43. On P. T. Barnum's American Museum, see P. T. Barnum, *The Life of P. T. Barnum* (New York: Redfield, 1855); Neil Harris, *Humbug: The Art of P. T. Barnum* (Chicago: University of Chicago Press, 1973); Benjamin Reiss, "P. T. Barnum, Joice Heth, and Antebellum Spectacles of Race," *American Quarterly* 51 (March 1999): 78–107; A. H. Saxon, "P. T. Barnum and the American Museum," *Wilson Quarterly* 13 (Autumn 1989): 130–139.

44. "Notice to Persons of Color," *New York Tribune*, February 27, 1849.

45. Buckley, "To the Opera House," 142–143.

46. Ibid., 139–161; Richard Butsch, "Bowery B'hoys and Matinee Ladies: The Re-Gendering of Nineteenth-Century American Theater Audiences," *American Quarterly* 46, no. 3 (September 1994): 377–378, 383–388; Howe, *Victorian America*, 111–120.

47. Buckley, "To the Opera House," 148.

48. For a pioneering discussion that elaborates these themes while providing an account of the era's most popular American exhibition picture, see Ellen Hickey Grayson, "Art, Audiences, and the Aesthetics of Social Order in Antebellum America: Rembrandt Peale's 'Court of Death'" (Ph.D. Diss. Columbia University, 1995).

49. William Dunlap, *History of the Rise and Progress of the Arts of Design in the United States* (New York: George P. Scott, 1834), 1:340–357.

50. "Painting: Mr. Dunlap's Historical Paintings," *New-York Mirror*, March 24, 1832, 299. See also "Dunlap's Historical Paintings," *New-York Mirror*, February 11, 1832, 254.

51. Lee Parry, "Landscape Theater in America," *Art in America* 59 (November–December 1971): 57.

52. "Panorama of Jerusalem," *New York Spectator*, January 21, 1839; "Battle of Waterloo," *Morning Herald*, August 31, 1840. In addition, New Yorkers could attend the stationary panorama of Rome; see "Panorama of Rome," *New York Spectator*, August 13, 1840.

53. *Description of Banvard's Panorama of the Mississippi River, Painted on Three Miles of Canvas: Exhibiting a View of Country 1200 Miles in Length, Extending from the Mouth of the Missouri River to the City of New Orleans; Being by Far the Largest Picture Ever Executed by Man* (Boston: John Putnam, 1847), 48; Oettermann, *The Panorama*, 323–342.

54. Parry, "Landscape Theater in America," 52–61; Barbara Novack, *Nature and Culture: American Landscape and Painting, 1825–1875* (New York: Oxford University Press, 1980), 15–28.

55. This discussion is based on Ethan Robey, "The Utility of Art: Mechanics' Institute Fairs in New York City, 1828–1876" (Ph.D. diss., Columbia University, 2000) and Sven Beckert and Julia B. Rosenbaum, *The American Bourgeoisie: Distinction and Identity in the Nineteenth Century* (New York: Palgrave Macmillan, 2010), 119–134. On the mechanics societies, see also Bender, *New York Intellect*, 78–87.

56. "Fair of the American Institute," *Mechanics' Magazine* 8, no. 6 (December 1836): 289–309.

57. "The American Institute at New York," *Niles Weekly Register* 3, no. 10 (October 30, 1830): 164.

58. "Sixth Annual Fair of the American Institute of New-York," *Mechanics' Magazine* 2, no. 4 (October 1933): 175.

59. "Fair of the American Institute," *Mechanics' Magazine* 8, no. 6 (December 1836): 297–298.

60. On the fairs' places of consumption, see Robey, "The Utility of Art," 78–133; Beckert and Rosenbaum, *American Bourgeoisie*, 119–134.

61. "Mechanics' Fair," *National Advocate, for the Country* (New York), November 14, 1823.

62. "The Fair I," *New York Herald*, September 26, 1837, 2.

63. "Mechanics' Fair," *New York Herald*, October 2, 1837, 2.

64. "The Fair I," *New York Herald*, September 26, 1837, 2.

65. See note 1.

66. Elizabeth Gilmore Holt, ed., *The Triumph of Art for the Public, 1785–1848: The Emerging Role of Exhibitions and Critics* (Princeton, NJ: Princeton University Press, 1983), 415–417; Daniel J. Sherman, *Worthy Monuments: Art Museums and the Politics of Culture in Nineteenth-Century France* (Cambridge, MA: Harvard University Press, 1989), 132–137; Lyndel Saunders King, *The Industrialization of Taste: Victorian England and the Art Union of London* (Ann Arbor: University of Michigan Research Press, 1985); Cowdrey, *American Academy of Fine Arts and American Art-Union: Introduction*, 133–134; Thomas S. Cummings, *Historic Annals of the National Academy of Design* (Philadelphia: George W. Childs, 1865), 148; "Art Enterprise in Europe," *Cosmopolitan Art Journal* 2 (1857–1858); "The American Art-Union," *Knickerbocker; or, New-York Monthly Magazine* 32 (November 1848): 442–443.

67. Widmer, *Young America*, 12 and passim.

68. Ibid., 125–154.

69. Buckley, "To the Opera House," 198–245; Iver Bernstein, *The New York City Draft Riots: Their Significance for American Society and Politics in the Age of the Civil War* (New York: Oxford University Press, 1990), 43–72, 125–161; Edward Pessen, "The Wealthiest New Yorkers of the Jacksonian Era: A New List," *New-York Historical Society Quarterly* 54 (1970): 45–172; Edward Pessen, *Riches, Class, and Power Before the Civil War* (Lexington, MA: D. C. Heath, 1973); Edward Pessen, "Philip Hone's Set: The Social World of the New York City Elite in the 'Age of Egalitarianism,' " *New-York Historical Society Quarterly* 56 (1972): 285–308. For a list of Art-Union managers and officials, see Baker, "The American Art-Union," 105–107.

70. Allan Nevins, ed., *The Diary of Philip Hone, 1828–1851* (New York: Dodd, Mead, 1927), 2:655, 667.

71. Prosper W. Wetmore, "Old New York Revived—Continued," *Historical Magazine and Notes and Queries, Concerning the Antiquities, History and Biography of America*, 2nd ser., 2 (1867): 292; John Wakefield Francis, *Old New York; or, Reminiscences of the Past Sixty Years* (New York: W. J. Widdleton, 1865), 115–140.

72. Arlene Katz Nichols provides a valuable prosopography of Apollo and Art-Union officials and managers. Her dissertation also probes ways in which the organization reflected the outlook of merchants. See Nichols, "Merchants and Artists," 336–439 and passim.

73. Charles Howland Russell, *Memoir of Charles H. Russell, 1796–1884* (New York, 1903), 29–77. On the Pacific Mail Steamship Company, see *In the Circuit Court of the United States, Southern District of New York, in Equity, Marshall O. Roberts, the United States Mail Steamship Company, the Pacific Mail Steamship Company, Edwin Croswell, Prosper M. Wetmore, James Van Nostrand . . . Defendants, ads. Albert G. Sloo and Ellwood Fisher, Complainants* (New York: Wm. C. Bryant, 1856); Alessandro Arseni, "The Panama Route, 1848–1851, *Postal Gazette* 2 (November 2006): 10–11.

74. Pessen, *Riches, Class, and Power Before the Civil War*, 320.

75. Of fourteen Art-Union officials whose church affiliation can be positively identified, eleven were Episcopalian, one Catholic, one Unitarian, and one Dutch Reformed. Samuel M. Showmaker, *Calvary Church: Yesterday and Today* (New York: Fleming H. Revell, 1936), 291–303; "Obituaries," *New York Times*, February 11, 1861, July 8, 1866, February 10, 1869, November 30, 1870, June 20, 1877, March 2, 1878, July 26, 1878, August 21, 1879, September 15, 1880, November 8, 1881, June 8, 1884; Nevins, *Diary of Philip Hone*, 2:xiv; William Allen Butler, *Evert Augustus Duyckinck: A Memorial Sketch Read Before the New York Historical Society, January 7, 1879* (New York: Trow's Printing and Bookbinding, 1879), 12.

76. 71· Francis, *Old New York*, 295.

77. Gilbert H. Muller, *William Cullen Bryant: Author of America* (Albany: State University of New York Press, 2008), 84–85. On the Sketch Club, see James T. Callow, *Kindred Spirits: Knickerbocker Writers and American Artists, 1807–1855* (Chapel Hill: University of North Carolina Press, 1967), 12–29.

78. Bryant to Edmonds, July 2, 1847, Francis W. Edmonds Papers, William L. Clements Library, University of Michigan, Ann Arbor.

79. *The Letters of William Cullen Bryant*, ed. William Cullen Bryant II and Thomas G. Voss (New York: Fordham University Press, 1975–), 2:18.

80. Nevins, *Diary of Philip Hone*, 1:134–35.

81. Philip Hone, manuscript diary (1828–1851, 28 vols.), 13:307, NYHS.

82. Francis, *Old New York*, 294–295.

83. Herring to John P. Ridner (Corresponding Secretary), October [1 or 3] 1840, American Art-Union, Letters Received, April 1838–November 7, 1849, Reel 8, NYHS.

84. Buckley, "To the Opera House," 181–183.

85. "Annual Report," *Transactions of the American Art-Union . . . 1845*, 5. See also "To the Members of the American Art-Union," *Bulletin of the American Art-Union*, August 25, 1848, 15.

86. "Proceedings at the Annual Meeting," *Transactions of the American Art-Union . . . 1846*, 6.

87. "Proceedings at the Annual Meeting," *Transactions of the American Art-Union . . . 1847*, 14.

88. Gourlie to Edmonds, February 9, 1841, Francis W. Edmonds Papers, Clements Library.

89. Widmer, *Young America*, 100.

90. On antebellum theater riots, see Buckley, "To the Opera House," 162–196; Paul A. Gilje, *The Road to Mobocracy: Popular Disorder in New York City, 1763–1834* (Chapel Hill: University of North Carolina Press for the Institute of Early American History and Culture, 1987), 246–253; Grimsted, *Melodrama Unveiled*, 65–74.

91. *Transactions of the American Art-Union . . . 1846*, 26.

92. *Transactions of the American Art-Union . . . 1847*, 15–16.

93. *Transactions of the American Art-Union . . . 1844*, 10.

94. In 1849, the peak year of Art-Union membership, New York State accounted for 53 percent of subscribers; New Jersey and Pennsylvania, 8 percent; Midwest, 9 percent; New England, 17 percent; Southern states (including Maryland), 13 percent. Ministers, doctors, judges, and generals were conspicuously present among the subscribers. Honorary secretaries

are described in "Distribution of the American Art-Union," *Literary World*, December 29, 1849, 566.

95. Cowdrey, *American Academy of Fine Arts and American Art-Union: Introduction*, 110–113.

96. "The Art-Union Prizes for the Present Year," *Courier and Enquirer*, reprinted in the *Bulletin of the American Art-Union*, November 25, 1848, 32. See also "The Art-Union and Its Friends," *Literary World*, November 25, 1848, 852–853.

97. "Annual Report," *Transactions of the American Art-Union . . . 1849*, 38; Baker, "The American Art-Union," 224–225; "American Art-Union Distribution," *Bulletin of the American Art-Union*, December 25, 1848, 7–32; "Annual Distribution of Paintings and Other Works of Art," *Bulletin of the American Art-Union*, December 1849, 49–72.

98. "Annual Report," *Transactions of the American Art-Union . . . 1847*, 21–22.

99. "The Art-Union and Its Friends," *Literary World*, November 25, 1848, 852. The article was quoted in the *Bulletin of the American Art-Union*, November 25, 1848, 43. See also Cummings, *Historic Annals*, 215. On the Art-Union gallery, see, Lett, *Perfectly American*, 101–127.

100. *Diary of George Templeton Strong*, ed. Allan Nevins and Milton Halsey Thomas (New York: Macmillan, 1952), 2:74; George G. Foster, *New York by Gas-Light and Other Urban Sketches*, ed. Stuart M. Blumin (Berkeley: University of California Press, 1990), 72. See also William M. Bobo, *Glimpses of New-York City* (Charleston, SC: J. J. McCarter, 1852), 159.

101. "Annual Report," *Transactions of the American Art-Union . . . 1848*, 46; "Annual Report," *Transactions of the American Art-Union . . . 1849*, 34; Cowdrey, *American Academy of Fine Arts and American Art-Union: Introduction*, 215–216. For New York's population in 1850, see Foster, *New York by Gas-Light*, 3.

102. "The Art-Union and Its Friends," *Literary World*, November 25, 1848, 852–853. See also "The American Art-Union," *Knickerbocker; or, New York Monthly Magazine* 32 (November 1848): 446.

103. *Oswego Commercial Times*, December 1, 1848, Newspaper Clippings, vol. 1, American Art-Union Records, NYHS (hereafter cited as AAU Records).

104. "The Fine Arts," *Literary World*, April 3, 1852, 251. On the inclusivity of the Free Gallery and its purported impact on laboring people, see "Annual Report," *Transactions of the American Art-Union . . . 1847*, 20–22; "Annual Report," *Transactions of the American Art-Union . . . 1848*, 46–47.

105. "Annual Report," *Transactions of the American Art-Union . . . 1845*, 8; "Annual Report," *Transactions of the American Art-Union . . . 1847*, 22–23. See also Cowdrey, *American Academy of Fine Arts and American Art-Union: Introduction*, 172–173.

106. Andrew Warner to William [illegible] Redin, July 17, 1849, Letterpress Books, July 12–November 5, 1849, AAU Records.

107. "Annual Report," *Transactions of the American Art-Union . . . 1845*, 7.

108. Cowdrey, *American Academy of Fine Art and American Art-Union: Introduction*, 161. Paintings purchased by the Art-Union are listed in Mary Bartlett Cowdrey, ed., *American Academy of Fine Art and American Art-Union: Exhibition Record, 1816–1852* (New York: New-York Historical Society, 1953).

109. Lett, *Perfectly American*, 64–79; Hills, "American Art-Union as Patron"; and Angela Miller, "Landscape Taste as an Indicator of Class Identity in Antebellum America," in Hemingway and Vaughan, *Art in Bourgeois Society*, 314–361. For an analysis of gender in western

genre painting, see also Elizabeth Johns, *American Genre Painting: The Politics of Everyday Life* (New Haven, CT: Yale University Press, 1991), 60–99.

110. *Catalogue of Paintings by Daniel Huntington, N.A., Exhibiting at the Art-Union Buildings, 497 Broadway* (New York, 1850), 11.

111. Reproductions of Art-Union etchings and engravings are included in Mann, *The American Art-Union*, 39–75. See also Cowdrey, *American Academy of Fine Arts and the American Art-Union: Introduction*, 286–293; and Lett et al., *Perfectly American*.

112. Nichols, "Merchants and Artists," 311–312; Lett et al., *Perfectly American*, 52–53.

113. Karen M. Adams, "The Black Image in the Paintings of William Sidney Mount," *American Art Journal* 7, no. 2 (November 1975): 42–59. See also Christopher J. Smith, *The Creolization of American Culture: William Sidney Mount and the Roots of Blackface Minstrelsy* (Urbana: University of Illinois Press, 2013); Janice Gray Armstrong, ed., *Catching the Tune: Music and William Sidney Mount* (Stony Brook, NY: Museums at Stony Brook, 1984). Elizabeth Johns sees an anti-abolitionist message in the painting; see Johns, *American Genre Painting*, 33–35.

114. For contradictory readings of *War News from Mexico*, see Hills, "American Art-Union as Patron," 329–331; Patricia Hills, "Picturing Progress in the Era of Westward Expansion," in *The West as America: Reinterpreting Images of the Frontier*, ed. William H. Truettner (Washington, DC: Smithsonian Institution Press, 1991), 104–110; Lett et al., *Perfectly American*, 71–72; Joy Peterson Heyrman, ed., *New Eyes on America: the Genius of Richard Caton Woodville* (New Haven, CT: Walters Art Museum distributed by Yale University Press, 2012), 27–38, 99; Justin Wolff, *Richard Caton Woodville: American Painter, Artful Dodger* (Princeton, NJ: Princeton University Press, 2002), 95–133; Johns, *American Genre Painting*, 121–122.

115. "The Gallery," *Bulletin of the American Art-Union* 2, no. 2 (May 1849): 9–10.

116. Elizabeth Johns suggests ways in which the picture could be differently read by northern and southern viewers; see Johns, *American Genre Painting*, 180. Wolff, *Richard Caton Woodville*, finds politically subversive meanings in the painting while acknowledging the tendency of the New York press to read it as a unifying, even sentimental image. Seth Rockman considers Woodville in relation to the Baltimore political culture in which the artist was raised; he points out that Woodville "like many nineteenth-century Americans . . . could recognize slavery as a troubling contradiction without necessarily embracing emancipation or the civil equality of people of color"; Seth Rockman, "An Artist of Baltimore," in Heyrman, *New Eyes on America*, 37.

117. "New Works by American Artists Abroad," *Bulletin of the American Art-Union*, no. 3 (June 1850): 46.

118. "To the Members of 1850," *Bulletin of the American Art-Union*, December 31, 1850, 189.

119. "Affairs of the Association," *Bulletin of the American Art-Union*, November 1, 1851, 135.

120. "Affairs of the Association," *Bulletin of the American Art-Union*, April 1, 1850, 2.

121. Only three Art-Union engravings (Francis Edmonds's *Sparking* and *The New Scholar*, and Woodville's *Old '76 and Young '48*) depicted contemporary domestic scenes. The latter two focus on male figures and none portray the theme of maternal influence. Johns points out that the Art-Union, in selecting *The New Scholar*, revealed the managers' belief that "the only point at which the domestic sphere would be of interest to the broad American public was the point at which the boy left it." See Johns, *American Genre Painting*, 137–156.

122. *Catalogue of Paintings by Daniel Huntington*, 37.

123. See chapter 3.

124. "Annual Report," *Transactions of the American Art-Union . . . 1844*, 6.

125. "Annual Address," *Transactions of the American Art-Union . . . 1849*, 34.

126. The dinner celebrating the opening of the new gallery is described in "American Art-Union," *New York Daily Tribune*, December 21, 1849; "The Opening of the New Gallery," *Bulletin of the American Art-Union* 2, no. 7 (October 1849): 6–7; "The Art-Union—Opening of the New Gallery," *Literary World*, September 22, 1849, 253–254. On changing domestic relationships and the passing world of elite male sociability and control, see Elizabeth Blackmar, *Manhattan for Rent, 1785–1850* (Ithaca, NY: Cornell University Press, 1989), 72–148; Buckley, "To the Opera House," 221–237.

127. Honorary secretaries and subscribers are listed in the *Transactions of the Apollo Association* (1839–1843) and *Transactions of the American Art-Union* (1844–1851).

128. John A. Dix to F. W. Edmonds, December 15, 1845, Box 2, Francis W. Edmonds Papers, Clements Library, University of Michigan.

129. Advertisement, *Bulletin of the American Art-Union* 2, no. 1 (April 1849): 32; "Names of Members," *Transactions of the American Art-Union . . . 1849*, 68; Hone, manuscript diary, NYHS, 28:367; Cowdrey, *American Academy of Fine Arts and American Art-Union: Exhibition Record*, 335–336.

Chapter 2

1. J. Sullivan to Robert F. Fraser, June 10, 1845, American Art-Union (AAU) Records, New-York Historical Society (NYHS), Letters Received, February 17–December 11, 1845. Reel 10.

2. D. McConaughy to Fraser, December 4, 1847, AAU Records, Letters Received, Reel 14, November 27–December 31, 1847, Reel. 14.

3. Thomas B. White to Fraser, January 13, 1848, AAU Records, Letters Received, January 1–February 29, 1848, Reel 15.

4. Homer Foot to Andrew Warner, January 12, 1848, AAU Records, Letters Received, January 1–February 29, 1848, Reel 15.

5. E. N. Fairchild to Warner, January 3, 1848, AAU Records, Letters Received, January 1–February 29, 1848, Reel 15.

6. Clarendon Harris to Fraser, December 6, 1847, and Alexander G. Stephens to R. Fraser, November 27, 1847, AAU Records, Letters Received, November 27–December 31, 1847, Reel 14.

7. O. S. Roat to Fraser, January 17, 1847, AAU Records, Letters Received, December 13, 1846–June 30, 1847, Reel 12. See also "Proceedings at the Annual Meeting," in *Transactions of the American Art-Union . . . 1846*, 30; "Proceedings at the Annual Meeting, 1848," *Transactions of the American Art-Union . . . 1848*.

8. Thomas B. White to Fraser, January 13, 1848, AAU Records, Letters Received, January 1, 1848–November 7, 1849, Reel 15.

9. W. S. Solomon to the Committee of Management, January 8, 1844, AAU Records, Letters Received, February 2, 1843–March 20, 1844, Reel No. 9.

10. J. C. Partridge to Fraser, January 12, 1847, AAU Records, Letters Received, December 13 1846–June 30, 1847, Reel 12; "Names of Members with Their Places of Residence," *Transactions of the American Art-Union . . . 1846*, 62.

11. S. H. Clark to Warner, December 4, 1851, AAU Records, Letters Received, December 1–31, 1851, Reel 38.

12. [William] Baldwin to Warner, December 13, 1851, AAU Records, Letters Received, December 1–31, 1851, Reel 38.

13. E. H. Rice to Warner, December 12, 1851, AAU Records, Letters Received, December 1–31, 1851, Reel 38.

14. See, e.g., "Art-Union Lottery and Its Movements," *New York Herald*, January 4, 1852; "Curious Doings of the Recent Grand Jury," *Herald*, January 26, 1852; "The American Art-Union and the Fine Arts," *Herald*, January 27, 1852; "The Art-Union in Trouble," *Herald*, January 29, 1852; "The Art-Union Drawing," *Herald*, February 2, 1852. See also Mary Bartlett Cowdrey, ed., *American Academy of Fine Art and American Art-Union: Introduction, 1816–1852* (New York: New-York Historical Society, 1953), 225–240.

15. "A Subscriber" to Fraser, July 25, 1846, and J. Sullivan to Fraser, July 9, 1846, AAU Records, Letters Received, June 22–December 12, 1846, Reel 10.

16. Joshua Francis to the AAU, January 4, 1848, and John Viall to the President and Directors of the AAU, February 7, 1848, AAU Records, Letters Received, January 1–February 29, 1848, Reel 15.

17. Daniel Remick to Warner, December 9, 1851, AAU Records, Letters Received, December 1–31, 1851, Reel 38.

18. John Hooker to Warner, December 15, 1851, AAU Records, Letters Received, December 1–31, 1851, Reel 38.

19. A. McNair Cunningham to Warner, December 29, 1851, AAU Records, Letters Received, December 1–31, 1851, Reel 38.

20. H. R. Gaylord to Warner, December 15, 1851, AAU Records, Letters Received, December 1–31, 1851, Reel 38.

21. Henry I. Haw[illegible] to Fraser, December 16, 1846, AAU Records, Letters Received, December 13 1846–June 30, 1847, Reel 12.

22. Herman Wendell, M.D., to Durand, October 1850, Asher Brown Durand Papers, New York Public Library (NYPL), microfilmed by Smithsonian Institution Archives of American Art (hereafter cited as AAA).

23. [Unsigned] to the AAU, December 8 [1851], AAU Records, Letters Received, December 1–31, 1851, Reel 38.

24. Herring to John P. Ridner, August 27, 1840, AAU Records, Letters Received, April 1837–March 1842, Reel 8

25. James O. Brayman to [unidentified], November 27, 1850, AAU Records, Letters Received, November 22–December 16, 1850, Reel 32.

26. W. Whitman to Warner, December 18, 1851, AAU Records, Letters Received, December 1–31, 1851, Reel 38.

27. Allan Nevins, ed., *The Diary of Philip Hone, 1828–1851* (New York: Dodd, Mead, 1927), 2:866.

28. This account is based on Peter George Buckley, "To the Opera House: Culture and Society in New York City, 1820–1860" (Ph.D. diss., State University of New York at Stony Brook, 1984).

29. William Rounseville Alger, *Life of Edwin Forrest, the American Tragedian* (Philadelphia: J. B. Lippincott, 1877), 1:416–417. On Bryant's relationship with Forrest, see William

Cullen Bryant II and Thomas G. Voss, eds., *The Letters of William Cullen Bryant* (New York: Fordham University Press, 1975–), 2:257, 281, 288, 290, 320, 323, 472–473.

30. Buckley, "To the Opera House," 25.

31. Bryant, *Letters*, 3:117, 122. On the formation of the card, see Buckley, "To the Opera House," 62–75, 198–293. Duyckinck lived at 20 Clinton Place for forty years until his death in 1878. See James Grant Wilson, *Bryant and His Friends: Some Reminiscences of the Knickerbocker Writers* (New York: Fords, Howard & Hulbert, 1886), 419; William Allen Butler, *Evert Augustus Duyckinck: A Memorial Sketch Read Before the New-York Historical Society, January 7, 1879* (New York: Trow's Printing and Bookbinding, 1879), 7.

32. "Books of the Week," *Literary World*, August 18, 1849, 129.

33. "The Progress of Brutality," *Literary World*, July 6, 1850, 1.

34. Item in the *Evening Mirror*, September 21, 1849, "Newspaper Clippings," 2:25, AAU Records.

35. "The International Art-Union," *Bulletin of the American Art-Union*, November 1849, 13. For a discussion of the Dusseldorf gallery, see "The School of Art at Dusseldorf," *Bulletin of the American Art-Union*, April 1, 1850, 5–7.

36. [Illegible], *Albany* [illegible], October 13, 1849, "Newspaper Clippings," 2:55, AAU Records.

37. "International Art-Union New Gallery," *New York Daily Tribune*, November 1, 1849.

38. The author was referencing the artists Claude Joseph Vernet, Paul Delaroche, and Ary Sheffer.

39. "The International Art-Union," *Bulletin*, November 1849, 12–13; *New York Daily Tribune*, October 30, 1849. See also "Opening of the Pictorial Show Rooms of the American Branch of the French House of Messrs. Goupil, Vibert & Co.," *Evening Mirror*, November 1, 1849, "Newspaper Clippings," 2:97, AAU Records; For a discussion of the relationship of Scheffer, Vernet, and Delaroche to the Orléanist regime, see Michael Marrinan, *Painting Politics for Louis-Philippe: Art and Ideology in Orléanist France, 1830–1848* (New Haven, CT: Yale University Press, 1988).

40. "The Art-Union," *Morning Courier and Enquirer*, October 1, 1849, reprinted in *Bulletin*, October 1849, 2.

41. "The American Art-Union and Messrs. Goupil, Vibert & Co," *Literary World*, October 20, 1849, 337.

42. Ibid.

43. See, for example, "Mr. Willis and the Art Unions," *New York Scorpion*, November 3, 1849, in "Newspaper Clippings," 2:101, AAU Records. At the end of 1849 Bryant was still a proponent of Goupil, Vibert & Co., though he never deviated in his support for the AAU. "The Art-Union Controversy," *Evening Post*, October [illegible] 1849, "Newspaper Clippings," 2:49, AAU Records.

44. On Willis's involvement in the Forrest divorce case, see Thomas N. Baker, *Sentiment and Celebrity: Nathaniel Parker Willis and the Trials of Literary Fame* (New York: Oxford University Press, 1999), 115–157; Nevins, *Diary of Philip Hone*, 2:898. Mrs. N. P. Willis was repeatedly mentioned as Catherine Forrest's companion at the divorce trial; see, for example, "The Forrest Divorce Case," *Herald*, December 24, 1851, 4.

45. *The Diary of George Templeton Strong*, ed. Allan Nevins and Milton Halsey Thomas (New York: Macmillan, 1952), 2:122; James Grant Wilson, *The Memorial History of the City of*

New York (New York, 1893), 4:72–73; Nevins, *Diary of Philip Hone*, 2:909. For an account that locates Willis as representing a "layer of gentility" just below the rank of Hone and Strong, see Buckley, "To the Opera House," 238–245.

46. *The Works of William Makepeace Thackeray* (New York: Charles Scribner's Sons, 1904), 31:435.

47. Baker, *Sentiment and Celebrity*, 10.

48. Frank Luther Mott, *A History of American Magazines*, vol. 2, *1850–1865* (Cambridge, MA: Harvard University Press, 1938), 57, 349–355.

49. Charles H. Brown, *William Cullen Bryant* (New York: Charles Scribner's Sons, 1971), 294.

50. "Women and Literature," *Home Journal*, August 5, 1848, 2.

51. Frank Luther Mott, *A History of American Magazines, 1747–1850* (New York: D. Appleton, 1930), 325; N. P. Willis, *Lecture on Fashion: Delivered Before the New York Lyceum*, Mirror Library, no. 32 (New York: Morris & Willis, 1844), 10; see, for example, "Paris Fashions for the New-Year," *Home Journal*, January 27, 1849, 3; and "Parisian Gossip," *Home Journal*, February 28, 1850, 2. Willis's only novel offers further evidence of the author's fascination with aristocratic women. See N. Parker Willis, *Paul Fane; or, Parts of a Life Else Untold* (New York: Scribner, 1857). On Willis's British connections, see Baker, *Sentiment and Celebrity*, 61–85.

52. Wetmore to Duyckinck, March 25 [1849], Duyckinck Papers, NYPL, AAA microfilm, Reel N9.

53. Willis, *Lecture on Fashion*, 2, 3, 12.

54. Ibid., 2, 10.

55. "Business Position of Artists," *Home Journal*, November 10, 1849, 2. See also "International Art-Union," *Home Journal*, April 21, 1849, 2; "The International Art-Union," *Home Journal*, April 28, 1849, 2; and "The Two Art-Unions," *Home Journal*, October 13, 1849, 2.

56. "Crushing of the National Academy of Design and True Art by the Amateur Merchants of the Art-Union," *Home Journal*, October 27, 1849, 2. Willis's critique was echoed in "Art-Unions: Their True Character Considered," *International Magazine of Science and Art* 2 (1850–1851): 191–195.

57. "The Two Art-Unions," *Home Journal*, October 13, 1849, 2.

58. "The American Art-Union," *Knickerbocker* 32 (November 1848): 447; "Has the Art-Union Increased the Taste and Knowledge of the People in Matters of Art?," *Bulletin of the American Art-Union*, October 1849, 18.

59. "Art-Union Critics," *Bulletin of the American Art-Union*, December 1850, 144. See also "The Enemies of the American Art-Union," *Bulletin of the American Art-Union*, December 1849, 6–13.

60. "Fine Art," *Home Journal*, January 5, 1850, 2; defacement of Art-Union paintings mentioned in "City Items," *New York Tribune*, December 24, 1849, and January 4, 1850.

61. *New York Scorpion*, April 28, 1849, "Newspaper Clippings," vol. 1, AAU Records.

62. On the decorous behavior of visitors to the Free Gallery, see Prosper Wetmore, "Address," *Transactions of the American Art-Union . . . 1847*, 16; "Annual Report," *Transactions of the American Art-Union . . . 1847*, 20–22; "Annual Report," *Transactions of the American Art-Union . . . 1848*, 47; "Annual Report," *Transactions of the American Art-Union . . . 1849*, 34.

63. "The Friends of the Art-Union," *Bulletin of the American Art-Union*, April 1850, 2; "Art-Union Critics," *Bulletin*, December 1850, 144.

64. "A New Art-Union," *Home Journal*, May 11, 1850, 4; Willis was not alone in pointing favorably to the London plan. See "American Art and Art Unions," *Christian Examiner* 48 (March 1850), 218. In advocating that prize winners be allowed to deal directly with artists, Willis was calling for an adaptation of the London plan. The latter required prize winners to purchase artworks from specified galleries or exhibitions. See "Our Art Unions," *Irish Quarterly Review* 3 (1853): 994–995; and "Art-Unions," *North British Review* 26 (1857): 512–513.

65. "Public Art Galleries," *Home Journal*, August 31, 1850, 2; see also "Private Galleries of Art," *Home Journal*, August 17, 1850, 2.

66. Thomas S. Cummings, *Historic Annals of the National Academy of Design* (Philadelphia: George W. Childs, 1865), 166–167, 215–216, 218. On the relationship between the Art-Union and the National Academy, see Cowdrey, ed., *American Academy of Fine Art and American Art-Union: Introduction*, 176–201. See also John Durand, *The Life and Times of A. B. Durand* (New York: Charles Scribner's Sons, 1894), 168–174. William Sidney Mount more than once felt insulted by the Art-Union and articulated the common complaint. See Mount to George Pope Morris, December 3, 1848, and Charles Lanman to Mount, April 25, 1850, in Alfred Frankenstein, *William Sidney Mount* (New York: Harry N. Abrams, 1975), 234; 124.

67. J. F. Kensett to his uncle, May 20, 1849, John F. Kensett Miscellaneous Notes and Drafts of Letters, box 31, folder 4, New York State Library, Albany, AAA, Microfilm, Reel 1533.

68. Cowdrey, ed., *American Academy of Fine Art and American Art-Union: Introduction*, 176–200; Samuel F. B. Morse to AAU, December 5, 1840, American Art-Union, Letters Received, April 1838–March 1842, Reel 8. See also Cummings, *Historic Annals*, 165–167.

69. John H. Gourlie to Francis William Edmonds, February 9, 1841, Francis W. Edmonds Papers, William L. Clements Library, University of Michigan, Ann Arbor.

70. Cowdrey, ed., *American Academy of Fine Art and American Art-Union: Introduction*, 182–183.

71. Ibid., 184–185.

72. Kensett to his uncle, May 20, 1849, Kensett Miscellaneous Notes, see note 67.

73. Mount to Morris, December 3, 1848, and Lanman to Mount, April 25, 1840, in Frankenstein, *William Sidney Mount*, 234; 124.

74. Huntington to Edmonds, January 30, 1841, Francis W. Edmonds Papers.

75. Thomas Cole to Edmonds, November 7, 1840, Francis W. Edmonds Papers.

76. Worthington Whittredge, "The American Art Union," *Magazine of History* 7, no. 2 (February 1908): 65; "To the Friends of the American Art-Union," *Bulletin of the American Art-Union*, October 1849, 5; "The Huntington Exhibition," *Bulletin of the American Art-Union*, April 1850, 4; Baker, "The American Art-Union," 176.

77. "The Art-Union: A Card," *New York Tribune*, December 25, 1851. The number grew to twenty-two. See "The Art-Union Lottery Again," *New York Herald*, December 30, 1851, 4.

78. Francis Gerry Fairfield, *The Clubs of New York* (1873; repr., New York: Arno Press, 1975), 29–56; John H. Gourlie, *Origin and History of "The Century"* (New York: W. C. Bryant, 1856), 31.

79. Gourlie, *Origin and History of "The Century*," 7–8.

80. "The American Art-Union," *New York Herald*, November 27, 1851. Doughty had earlier objected that prices offered by the Art-Union were too low. See Doughty to James Herring, December 9, 1839, Letters Addressed to the American Art-Union, vol. 1, no. 65, AAU Papers.

81. John Kendrick Fisher to Augustus Greele, Chairman of the Committee of Management, March 1, 1841, AAU Records, "Letters Received," April 1838 to March 1842, Reel 8.

82. Ibid.

83. J. K. Fisher, "Fine Arts, Galleries, Exhibitions, etc. [nos. 1–3]," *Literary World*, February 9, 1850, 132–133 (no. 1), February 23, 1850, 182 (no. 2), and March 2, 1850, 206–207 (no. 3).

84. Ibid., February 23, 1850, 182.

85. "City Items," *New York Tribune*, September 13 and October 16, 1850.

86. "The Art-Union and Its Assailants," *New York Tribune*, November 30, 1850. An account of the "Artists' Art Union" by George Foster suggests that the organization was already underway in 1849. Foster, *New York in Slices: By an Experienced Carver* (New York: W. F. Burgess, 1849), 118–119; see also "The American Artists' Association, *New York Herald*, January 16, 1852.

87. For a detailed account of Whitley's involvement in the Art-Union controversy that overstates the artist's role, see E. Maurice Bloch, "The American Art-Union's Downfall," *New-York Historical Society Quarterly* 37 (October 1953): 331–359. Letters by Doughty and Fisher are published in "The American Art-Union," *New York Herald*, November 25, 1851; and "Art-Union," *Herald*, December 18, 1851.

88. Dan Schiller, *Objectivity and the News: The Public and the Rise of Commercial Journalism* (Philadelphia: University of Pennsylvania Press, 1981), 47–75 and passim; Buckley, "To the Opera House," 358–365; Alexander Saxton, *The Rise and Fall of the White Republic: Class Politics and Mass Culture in Nineteenth-Century America* (London: Verso, 1990), 95–108.

89. William Wells Brown, *Clotel & Other Writings*, ed. Ezra Greenspan (New York: Library of America, 2014), 298–299.

90. Saxton, *Rise and Fall of the White Republic*, 98–99, 103–104.

91. "The Forrest and Willis Case—Queer Developments," *New York Herald*, September 30, 1850, 4.

92. On the relationship between the *Herald* and the National Academy, see "The New York Herald vs. the National Academy of Fine Arts," *Broadway Journal*, July 26, 1845, 44–45.

93. John Smith the Younger, "Rambling Epistles from New York," *National Era* (Washington, DC), November 2, 1848, 173.

94. "Letters from Grace Greenwood," *National Era*, December 13, 1849, 198.

95. Bloch, "American Art-Union's Downfall," 350–352.

96. "The American Art-Union," *New York Herald*, December 15, 1851; "The American Art-Union Again," *Herald*, December 22, 1851; "The Art-Union Lottery Again," *Herald*, December 30, 1851; "The Art-Union Lottery and Its Movements," *Herald*, January 4, 1852; "Curious Doings of the Recent Grand Jury," *Herald*, January 26, 1852; "The Art-Union in Trouble," *Herald*, January 29, 1852; "The Art-Union Drawing," *Herald*, February 2, 1852; "The Art-Union and Its Apologist," *Herald*, February 19, 1852.

97. Mott, *History of American Magazines*, 2:190; *Police Gazette* [January 13, 1848; handwritten], Newspaper Clippings, vol. 1, AAU Records.

98. Ann Fabian, *Card Sharps, Dream Books, & Bucket Shops: Gambling in 19th-Century America* (Ithaca, NY: Cornell University Press, 1990), 113–128.

99. "Lotteries—Art-Unions," *New York Herald*, February 14, 1852; "Art-Union Still in Trouble," *Herald*, March 28, 1852. See also "Injunction on the Art-Union," *Herald*, March 17, 1852. Willis and his supporters saw the lottery as evidence that the Art-Union was debasing

artistic standards. See "Crushing of the National Academy of Design and True Art by the Amateur Merchants of the Art-Union," *Home Journal*, October 27, 1849, 2; "Art-Unions: Their True Character Considered," *International Magazine of Science and Art* 2 (1850–1851): 191–195.

100. "The Art Union in Court," *New York Herald*, March 10, 1852, 2. See also "The Art Union Drawing," *Herald*, February 2, 1852, 2; "Quashing of the Art-Union Indictment," *Herald*, March 10, 1852, 4.

101. On the auction, see Amanda Lett, Patricia Hills, Peter John Brownlee, and Randy Ramer, *Perfectly American: The Art-Union and Its Artists* (Tulsa, OK: Gilcrease Museum, 2011), 40–43. The *New York Herald* reported extensively on the legal proceedings by and against the Art-Union: "Libels and Libel Suits," January 6, 1852; "Curious Doings of the Recent Grand Jury," "Indictment of the Art Union Lottery Against the Herald," January 26, 1852; "The Art Union in Trouble," January 29, 1852; "Indictment of the Art Union Lottery Against the Herald," February 14, 1852; "The Art Union Indictment against the Herald," February 16, 1852; "Quashing of the Art-Union Indictment" and "The Art Union in Court—Defeat of Its Indictment Against the Herald," March 10, 1852; "Injunction on the Art Union Lottery," March 13, 1852; "Injunction on the Art Union," March 17, 1852; "The Art-Union Injunction," March 23, 1852; "James Gordon Bennett vs. the American Art-Union," March 23, 1852; "The Art Union Lottery in Court," March 24, 1852; "Art-Union Still in Trouble," March 28, 1852; "American Art-Union Lottery Indicted," April 1, 1852; "The Art-Union Lottery," April 4, 1852; "Art-Union—The Long Agony Protracted," April 17, 1852. See also Bloch, "American Art-Union's Downfall," 331–359.

102. For Whitley's attack on the Western Art-Union, see T. W. Whitley, *Reflections on the Government of the Western Art Union and Review of the Works of Art on Its Walls* (Cincinnati: Printed at the Herald Office, 1848).

103. Thomas B. Read to Cyrus Garrett, October 17, 1852, Read Family Papers, Private Lender, AAA microfilm.

104. Lilly Martin Spencer to her parents, December 8, 1851, Lilly Martin Spencer Papers, Private Lender, AAA microfilm, Reel 131. For a sympathetic evaluation of the Art-Union by an artist, see Whittredge, "The American Art Union," 63–68.

105. "The Children's Art-Union," *Nursery: A Monthly Magazine for Youngest Readers* 12 (1872): 112.

Chapter 3

1. Edwin G. Burrows and Mike Wallace, *Gotham: A History of New York City to 1898* (New York: Oxford University Press, 1999), 659–666. Population results from the United States Census are summarized in https://en.wikipedia.org/wiki/List_of_most_populous_cities_in_the_United_States_by_decade (July 28, 2017); Catherine Hoover Voorsanger and John K. Howat, eds., *Art and the Empire City: New York, 1825–1861* (New York: Metropolitan Museum of Art; New Haven, CT: Yale University Press, 2000), 3–45; Eugene Moehring, "Space, Economic Growth, and the Public Works Revolution in New York," in Ann Durkin Keating, Eugene P. Moehring, and Joel A. Tarr, *Infrastructure and Urban Growth in the Nineteenth Century* (Chicago: Public Works Historical Society, 1985), 29–45. See also Sean Wilentz, *Chants Democratic: New York City and the Rise of the American Working Class, 1788–1850* (New York: Oxford, 1984), 107–140.

2. "New-York Daguerreotyped: Business-Streets, Mercantile Blocks, Stores, and Banks," *Putnam's Monthly Magazine of American Literature, Science, and Art*, April 1853, 357–358.

3. Voorsanger and Howat, *Art and the Empire City*, 364.

4. Burrows and Wallace, *Gotham*, 666–667; Christopher Gray, "Streetscapes/The A. T. Stewart Department Store; A City Plan to Revitalize the 1846 'Marble Palace," *New York Times*, March 20, 1994; Jay E. Cantor, "A Monument of Trade: A. T. Stewart and the Rise of the Millionaire's Mansion in New York," *Winterthur Portfolio* 10 (1975): 165–168; Harry E. Resseguie, "Alexander Turney Stewart and the Development of the Department Store, 1823–1876," *Business History Review* 39, no. 3 (Autumn 1965): 301–322. On the transformation of retail and expansion of manufactures, see Voorsanger and Howat, *Art and the Empire City*, 3–45, 243–375.

5. For the most thorough survey and discussion of New York's art venues during the antebellum decades, see Voorsanger and Howat, *Art and the Empire City*, 46–81.

6. *Trow's New-York City Directory for 1853–1854* (New York: John F. Trow, 1853), 21–764, HathiTrust Digital Library.

7. Ibid.; Neil Harris, *The Artist in American Society, The Formative Years, 1790–1860* (Chicago: University of Chicago Press, 1982), 254–282.

8. Voorsanger and Howat, *Art and the Empire City*, 58–59, 103–104.

9. Malcolm Goldstein, *Landscape with Figures: A History of Art Dealing in the United States* (New York: Oxford University Press, 2000), 26–44.

10. April F. Masten, *Art Work: Women Artists and Democracy in Mid-Nineteenth-Century New York* (Philadelphia: University of Pennsylvania Press, 2008), 12–21, 39–73. On nineteenth-century American women artists and art education, see also Laura R. Prieto, *At Home in the Studio: The Professionalization of Women Artists in America* (Cambridge, MA: Harvard University Press, 2001).

11. Horace Greeley, rev. and ed., *Art and Industry: As Represented in the Exhibition at the Crystal Palace, New York—1853–4 . . . From the New York Tribune* (New York: Redfield, 1853), xxiii–xxiv; Charles Hirschfeld, "America on Exhibition: The New York Crystal Palace," *American Quarterly* 9 (Summer 1957): 101–116; Ivan D. Steen, "America's First World's Fair: The Exhibition of the Industry of All Nations at New York's Crystal Palace," *New-York Historical Society Quarterly* 47 (1963): 257–287; Thomas Gordon Jayne, "The New York Crystal Palace: An International of Exhibition of Goods and Ideas" (master's thesis, University of Delaware, 1990); Charlotte Emans Moore, "Art as Text, War as Context: The Art Gallery of the Metropolitan Fair, New York City's Artistic Community, and the Civil War" (Ph.D. diss., Boston University, 2009), 19–35; P. T. Barnum, *Life of P. T. Barnum* (New York: Redfield, 1855), 386–388.

12. William C. Richards, *A Day in the New York Crystal Palace and How to Make the Most of It: Being a Popular Companion to the "Official Catalogue," and a Guide to All the Objects of Special Interest in the New York Exhibition of the Industry of All Nations* (New York: G. P. Putnam, 1853), 9–25, 163–167.

13. "The Crystal Palace; Rev. Mr. Chapin's Sermon on the Moral Significance of the Crystal Palace," *New-York Daily Times*, July 18, 1853, 1.

14. Greeley, *Art and Industry*, ix.

15. Horace Greeley, *The Crystal Palace and Its Lessons: A Lecture* (New York: Dewitt and Davenport, 1851), 29. See also Wilentz, *Chants Democratic*, 369–370.

16. Greeley, *Crystal Palace and Its Lessons*, 30.

17. Greeley, *Art and Industry*, 50, 52, 119.

18. Ibid., 50.

19. Moore, "Art as Text, War as Context," 51–55; Thomas S. Cummings, *Historic Annals of the National Academy of Design* (Philadelphia: George W. Childs, 1865), 238.

20. "The Crystal Palace: Rev. Mr. Chapin's Sermon."

21. "Greeley, *Art and Industry,* 28.

22. Benjamin Silliman Jr., *The World of Science, Art and Industry: Illustrated from Examples in the New York Exhibition, 1853–54* (New York: G. P. Putnam, 1854), xi, 64.

23. Lori Merrish, *Sentimental Materialism: Gender, Commodity Culture, and Nineteenth-Century American Literature* (Durham, NC: Duke University Press, 2000); Richard L. Bushman, *The Refinement of America: Persons, Houses, Cities* (New York: Random House, 1992).

24. "Notices of the Fine Arts: The Life School," *Godey's* 34 (May 1847): 264.

25. Beaumont, "The Arts of Design, and Their Influence on the Mechanic Arts of This Country," *Godey's* 36 (March 1848): 185.

26. "Notices of the Fine Arts: The Artist—His Mission—His Life," *Godey's* 38 (February 1849): 147–148.

27. "The Cosmopolitan Art Association: Its Past—Its Present—Its Future," *Cosmopolitan Art Journal* 2, supp. (December 1857): 54; Wendy Jean Katz, *Regionalism and Reform: Art and Class Formation in Antebellum Cincinnati* (Columbus: Ohio State University Press, 2002), 22, 28, 69, 76–77, 180; Mary Sayre Haverstock, Jeanette Mahoney Vance, and Brian L. Meggitt, eds., *Artists in Ohio, 1787–1900: A Biographical Directory* (Kent, OH: Kent State University Press, 2000), 985; Walter Sutton, "The Derby Brothers: 19th Century Bookmen," *University of Rochester Library Bulletin* 3, no. 2 (Winter 1948), available at River Campus Libraries, Online Projects and Publications, rbscp.lib.rochester.edu/2444.

28. "List of Honorary Secretaries in the Principal Cities," *Cosmopolitan Art Journal* 3 (December 1859): 258; "Expressly for the Ladies," *Cosmopolitan Art Journal* 1 (November 1856): 68. See also C. L. Derby, "To Our Lady Friends," *Cosmopolitan Art Journal* 1 (November 1856): 74.

29. "'The Women of America' and the 'Cosmopolitan," *Cosmopolitan Art Journal* 2 (December 1857): 44–45.

30. "Academy of Design Exhibition," *Cosmopolitan Art Journal* 4, no. 2 (June 1860): 81.

31. "Manifest Destiny," *Cosmopolitan Art Journal* 2, no. 1 (December 1857): 45–46. See also Sutton, "The Derby Brothers: 19th Century Bookmen"; Bushman, *Refinement of America,* 223, 300, 435.

32. "Department of Useful Art: First Article; The Haughwout Establishment," *Cosmopolitan Art Journal* 3, no. 3 (June 1859): 141–147.

33. "Palissy the Potter: An Art Romance," *Cosmopolitan Art Journal* 2 (1857–1858): 8–14, nos. 2 and 3 (double number) (March, June 1858): 73–78; Marilyn G. Karmason with Joan B. Stacke, *Majolica: A Complete History and Illustrated Survey* (New York: Harry N. Abrams, 1989), 9, 19–20.

34. "Palissy the Potter," *Cosmopolitan Art Journal* 2, nos. 2 and 3 (March, June 1858): 74.

35. "The Dollars and Cents of Art," *Cosmopolitan Art Journal* 4 (March 1860): 30.

36. "Ruskin on Economy in Art," *Cosmopolitan Art Journal* 2 (December 1857): 31.

37. "Mrs. Lilly M. Spencer's Paintings," "Shake Hands," *Cosmopolitan Art Journal* 1 (September 1857): 165 [unnumbered, 169]; "Cosmopolitan Items," *Cosmopolitan Art Journal* 1 (June 1857): 137. For discussions of "Shake Hands," see Robin Bolton-Smith, *Lilly Martin Spencer 1822–1902: The Joys of Sentiment* (Washington, DC: Smithsonian Institution Press, 1973), 166–

167; Elizabeth Johns, *American Genre Painting: The Politics of Everyday Life* (New Haven, CT: Yale University Press, 1991), 162–164; David M. Lubin, *Picturing a Nation: Art and Social Change in Nineteenth Century America* (New Haven, CT: Yale University Press, 1994), 159–204, 170–74, 180–82, 193; Katz, *Regionalism and Reform*, 35–37. For a reading that places the painting in the context of political democracy and points to painting as a depiction of labor, see April F. Masten, "Shake Hands? Lilly Martin Spencer and the Politics of Art," *American Quarterly* (June 2004): 348–394.

38. "Wood Engraving," *Cosmopolitan Art Journal* 1 (November 1856): 53.

39. "Engraving and Portraiture," *Cosmopolitan Art Journal* 3 (March 1859): 83.

40. "Photography," *Cosmopolitan Art Journal* 2 (September 1858): 180–182.

41. Janice Simon, "*The Crayon*, 1855–1861: The Voice of Nature in Criticism, Poetry, and the Fine Arts" (Ph.D. diss., University of Michigan, 1990), 41 and passim. See also Roger B. Stein, *John Ruskin and Aesthetic Thought in America, 1840–1900* (Cambridge, MA: Harvard University Press, 1967), 101–123; Masten, *Art Work*, 13, 37–38, 42.

42. William James Stillman, *The Autobiography of a Journalist* (Boston: Houghton, Mifflin, 1901), 1:7–28; Stephen L. Dyson, *The Last Amateur: The Life of William J. Stillman* (Albany: State University of New York Press, 2014), 5–21.

43. Stillman, *Autobiography*, 1:109–118, 128–129; Dyson, *The Last Amateur*, 23–50.

44. Dyson, *The Last Amateur*, 45, 75–98.

45. Stillman, *Autobiography*, 1:109–118, 128–29; Dyson, *The Last Amateur*, 23–50.

46. Stillman, *Autobiography*, 1:129, 222.

47. Ibid., 129

48. John Ruskin, *The Two Paths: Being Lectures on Art, and Its Application to Decoration and Manufacture Delivered in 1858–9* (London: Smith, Elder, 1859), 50–51.

49. On Ruskin's art criticism, see Robert L. Herbert, ed., *The Art Criticism of John Ruskin* (New York: Doubleday, 1964), vii–xxx; Roger B. Stein, *John Ruskin and Aesthetic Thought in America, 1840–1900* (Cambridge, MA: Harvard University Press, 1967).

50. Herbert, *Art Criticism of John Ruskin*, 97, 153.

51. Ibid., 93–108.

52. Ibid., 158.

53. John Ruskin, *The Opening of the Crystal Palace: Considered in Some of Its Relations to the Prospects of Art* (London: Smith, Elder, 1854), 7.

54. Herbert, *Art Criticism of John Ruskin*, 99.

55. Ruskin, *The Two Paths*, 129, 130–32.

56. Simon, "*The Crayon*, 1855–1861," 1–18.

57. For an analysis that emphasizes Ruskin's influence on the *Crayon*, see Stein, *John Ruskin and Aesthetic Thought*, 101–123.

58. "Introductory," *Crayon* (January 3, 1855): 1.

59. "Sketchings . . . Our Commercial Explosion," *Crayon* 4 (November 1857): 344.

60. "Introductory," *Crayon* (January 3, 1855): 1. On the *Crayon*'s attack on materialism and the editors' vision of redemption, see Simon, "*The Crayon*, 1855–1861," 55–128.

61. "Sketchings," *Crayon* 3 (November 1856): 343–344.

62. "The Basis of Criticism," *Crayon* 1 (March 21, 1855): 177.

63. "Amateur Criticism," *Crayon* 1 (May 2, 1855): 273; Ruskin, *The Two Paths*, 56.

64. "The Position of the Artist," *Crayon* 1 (March 28, 1855): 193; Cornelius Bellows to Editors, May 22, 1855, John Durand Papers, New York Public Library, Archives of American Art.

65. William S. Steere to Durand, August 19, 1857, Durand Papers.

66. Simon, "*The Crayon*," 45.

67. "Exhibition at the National Academy. Second Article," *Crayon* (3 May 1856): 146. For the Cosmopolitan's first celebration of Spencer, see "Masters of Art and Literature," *Cosmopolitan Art Journal* 1 (November 1856): 49–50.

68. P. Green, "Sketchings," *Crayon* 2 (December 1855): 37. On the *Crayon*'s critique of the art unions and the Cosmopolitan Art Association, see Simon, "*The Crayon*," 68–74.

69. "Sketchings," *Crayon* 4 (August 1857): 252–253.

70. William M. Rossetti, "Correspondence," *Crayon* 1 (April 25, 1855): 264.

71. Ernest Renan, "The Poetry of the Crystal Palace," *Crayon* 6 (October 1859): 297.

72. "Sociology: The Family as a Work of Art; No. IV," *Crayon* 3 (November 1856): 337; Stillman to Durand, October 23, 1856, Durand Papers. On efforts to attract female readers, see Simon, "*The Crayon*, 1855–1861," 45.

73. Clarence Cook, "Home Arts," *Crayon* 3 (July 18, 1856): 38–39.

74. "Woman's Position in Art," *Crayon* 8 (February 1861): 28.

75. "The Position of the Artist," *Crayon* 1 (March 28, 1855): 193.

76. "Hints to American Artists," *Crayon* 6 (May 1859): 145–146.

77. [Durand], "Sketchings: Annual Address to Our Readers and Friends," *Crayon* 8 (January 1861): 20.

78. "Klopstock," *Crayon* 4 (January 1857): 8.

79. Renan, "Poetry of the Crystal Palace," 295.

80. Ernest Renan, "The Canticle of Canticles," *Crayon* 7 (December 1860): 344.

81. "General History of the Semitic Languages," *Crayon* 5 (January 1858): 14.

82. Adolf Stahr, "The Torso," *Crayon* 5 (August 8, 1857): 225–226.

83. "A Novel View of Shakespeare's Genius," *Crayon* 8 (January 1861): 6.

84. Janice Simon, "Imaging a New Heaven on a New Earth: *The Crayon* and Nineteenth-Century American Periodical Covers," *American Periodicals* 1 (Fall 1991): 11–24, quotation at 17.

Chapter 4

1. Michael Steven Shapiro, ed., *The Museum: A Reference Guide* (New York: Greenwood Press, 1990), 31–35. On the Metropolitan Museum, see also Winifred E. Howe, *A History of the Metropolitan Museum of Art with a Chapter on the Early Institutions of Art in New York* (New York: Metropolitan Museum, 1913); Leo Lerman, *The Museum: One Hundred Years and the Metropolitan Museum of Art* (New York: Viking, 1969); Debora Silverman, *Selling Culture: Bloomingdale's, Diana Vreeland, and the New Aristocracy of Taste in Reagan's America* (New York: Pantheon, 1986); Calvin Tomkins, *Merchants and Masterpieces: The Story of the Metropolitan Museum of Art*, rev. ed. (New York: Henry Holt, 1989); Michael Gross, *Rogues' Gallery: The Secret History of the Moguls and the Money That Made the Metropolitan Museum* (New York: Broadway Books, 2009). For significant discussions of the Metropolitan's history, see Roy Rosenzweig and Elizabeth Blackmar, *The Park and the People: A History of Central Park* (Ithaca, NY: Cornell University Press, 1992), 340–341, 357–365, 387–388; Carol Duncan, *Civilizing Rituals: Inside Public Art Museums* (London: Routledge, 1995), 48–71; Alan Wallach, *Exhibiting Contradiction: Essays on the Art Museum in the United States* (Amherst: University of Massachusetts Press, 1998); Steven Conn, *Museums and American Intellectual Life, 1876–1926* (Chicago: University of Chicago Press, 1998), 9–10, 195–220; J. M. Mancini, *Pre-Modernism:*

Art-World Change and American Culture from the Civil War to the Armory Show (Princeton, NJ: Princeton University Press, 2005), 48, 125–131; Andrew McClellan, *The Art Museum from Boullee to Bilbau* (Berkeley: University of California Press, 2008); Jeffrey Trask, *Things American: Art Museums and Civic Culture in the Progressive Era* (Philadelphia: University of Pennsylvania Press, 2012). For valuable historiographical overviews, see Michael Steven Shapiro, ed., *The Museum: A Reference Guide*. On the history of the Chicago Art Institute and the transformation of turn-of-the-century culture, see Helen Horowitz, *Culture and the City: Cultural Philanthropy in Chicago from the 1880s to 1917* (Chicago: University of Chicago Press, 1989). For a study of turn-of-the-century British municipal museums that explores the transformation of museum culture in that context, see Amy Woodson-Boulton, "Temples of Art in Cities of Industry: Municipal Art Museums in Birmingham, Liverpool, and Manchester, c. 1870–1914" (Ph.D. diss., University of California, Los Angeles, 2003).

2. Anthony Burton, *Vision & Accident: The Story of the Victoria and Albert Museum* (London: V&A Publications, 1999), 41–92.

3. Charles C. Perkins, "American Art Museums," *North American Review* 3, no. 228 (July 1870): 1–29.

4. [James Jackson Jarves], "Can We Have an Art-Gallery?," *Christian Examiner* 72, no. 2 (March 1862): 207, 209.

5. Ibid., 207, 213.

6. Ibid., 214–215.

7. Jarves described the narrative that Carol Duncan identified as the "the ritual task of the Louvre" in which the "visitor was to reenact that history of genius, re-live its progress step by step and, thus enlightened, know himself as a citizen of history's most advanced nation-state." See also Duncan, *Civilizing Rituals: Inside Public Art Museums* (London: Routledge, 1995), 27; Carol Duncan and Alan Wallach, "The Universal Survey Museum," *Art History* 3, no. 4 (December 1980): 448–469. On Jarves's personal experience at the Louvre, see Francis Steegmuller, *The Two Lives of James Jackson Jarves* (New Haven, CT: Yale University Press, 1951), 105–111.

8. James Jackson Jarves, *The Art-Idea: Sculpture, Painting, and Architecture in America*, 2nd ed. (New York: Hurd and Houghton, 1865), 335.

9. Ibid., 342–344, 347–48.

10. Steegmuller, *Two Lives of James Jackson Jarves*, 181–182, 195, 209–214; New-York Historical Society, Committee on the Fine Arts, Minutes, 1856–1880, 9, 11, 19, 39–40, 158–159, 260–261, NYHS; New-York Historical Society, Executive Committee Minutes, September 1852–January 2, 1861, 283, 318–320, NYHS; Robert Hendre Kelby, *The New York Historical Society, 1804–1904* (New York: Published for the Society, 1905).

11. New-York Historical Society Executive Committee, Minutes, 1852–1861, 283 NYHS; New-York Historical Society, Committee on the Fine Arts, Minutes, 1856–1880, 427–429 NYHS. See further Charlotte Emans Moore, "Art as Text, War as Context: The Art Gallery of the Metropolitan Fair, New York City's Artistic Community, and the Civil War" (Ph.D. diss., Boston University, 2009), 52–57.

12. Roy Rosenzweig and Elizabeth Blackmar, *The Park and the People: A History of Central Park* (Ithaca, NY: Cornell University Press, 1992), 350.

13. New-York Historical Society, Minutes, 4:1, 93, 363 NYHS; New-York Historical Society, Committee on the Fine Arts Minutes, 1856–1880, 1–2.

14. "The Abbott Collection of Egyptian Antiquities," *Catalogue of the Museum and Gallery of Art of the New-York Historical Society, 1862* (New York: Printed for the Society, 1862), 5–72; see also New-York Historical Society, Minutes, 4:260–261.

15. "Abbott Collection of Egyptian Antiquities," 5, 72.

16. Rosenzweig and Blackmar, *The Park and the People*, 349–351; New-York Historical Society, Executive Committee Minutes, September 1852–January 7, 1861, 283, 318–320; January 28, 1862–September 1866, 84–89, 98–99, 101–109, 273, 318–319, 326–328; October 1866–January 1873, 122–123; Kelby, *New York Historical Society*, 52–58.

17. Ethan Robey, "The Utility of Art: Mechanics' Institute Fairs in New York City, 1828–1876" (Ph.D. diss., Columbia University, 2000), 315.

18. On New York's wartime economy, see Beckert, *Monied Metropolis*, 111–144. On the city's wartime art scene, see Neil Harris, *The Artist in American Society: The Formative Years, 1790–1860* (Chicago: University of Chicago Press, 1982), 313–316; Moore, "Art as Text, War as Context," 101–167.

19. *Metropolitan Fair in the Aid of the United States Sanitary Commission* (New York: Charles O. Jones, 1864); "The Metropolitan Fair," *Harper's Weekly*, April 16, 1864, 244, 246; Jeanie Attie, *Patriotic Toil: Northern Women and the American Civil War* (Ithaca, NY: Cornell University Press, 1998), 198–219; Evdokia Savidou-Terrono, "For 'The Boys in Blue': The Art Galleries of the Sanitary Fairs" (Ph.D. diss., City University of New York, 2002); "The Metropolitan Fair," *New York Daily Tribune*, April 6, 1864.

20. *Catalogue of the Art Exhibition at the Metropolitan Fair, in Aid of the U.S. Sanitary Commission* (New York: J. F. Trow, 1864); Moore, "Art as Text, War as Context," 302–465. For an analysis of differences between the art gallery of the Metropolitan Fair and displays of art at the Mechanics Institute fairs that has a direct bearing on my discussion, see Robey, "The Utility of Art," 337–339.

21. Henry W. Bellows, *Historical Sketch of the Union League Club of New York: Its Origin, Organization, and Work, 1863–1879* (New York: Club House, 1879), 11–12, 60, 66, quotation at 57; Beckert, *Monied Metropolis*, 130–140, 246.

22. Winifred E. Howe, *A History of the Metropolitan Museum of Art with a Chapter on the Early Institutions of Art in New York* (New York: Metropolitan Museum of Art, 1913), 107–108.

23. On the founding and early history of the Metropolitan Museum, see ibid., 99–140; Calvin Tomkins, *Merchants and Masterpieces: The Story of the Metropolitan Museum of Art*, rev. ed. (New York: Henry Holt, 1989), 15–48; Rosenzweig and Blackmar, *The Park and the People*, 341, 349–365; Conn, *Museums and American Intellectual Life*, 192–262; Nathaniel Burt, *Palaces for the People: A Social History of the American Art Museum* (Boston: Little, Brown, 1977), 3–128.

24. Tomkins, *Merchants and Masterpieces*, 15–48; Howe, *History of the Metropolitan Museum of Art*, 99–140.

25. A list of the Metropolitan's trustees can be found in Tomkins, *Merchants and Masterpieces*, 395–399.

26. Beckert, *Monied Metropolis*, 268; on Marquand, see Cynthia Saltzman, *Old Masters, New World: America's Raid on Europe's Great Pictures* (New York: Viking, 2008), 12–13.

27. Kenneth T. Jackson, ed., *Encyclopedia of New York City* (New Haven, CT: Yale University Press, 1995), 219; Tomkins, *Merchants and Masterpieces*, 15–16, 69, 73–75; Edward Sanford

Martin, *The Life of Joseph Hodges Choate*, vol. 1 (London: Constable, 1920), 427, 452; and vol. 2 (New York: Charles Scribner's Sons, 1920), 1–4, 46–49; "Marshall O. Roberts Dead," *New York Times*, September 12, 1880, 5.

28. William Cullen Bryant, *Letters from the East* (New York: Putnam & Son, 1869), 55–214; Tomkins, *Merchants and Masterpieces*, 32.

29. Brian Yothers, *The Romance of the Holy Land in American Travel* (Surrey: Ashgate, 2007), 21.

30. Metropolitan Museum of Art (MMA), *Annual Reports of the Trustees of the Association, 1871–1902* (New York: Metropolitan Museum of Art, [1903]), 23–24; Conn, *Museums and American Intellectual Life*, 29, 195–198.

31. Tomkins, *Merchants and Masterpieces*, 36–59. On the controversy surrounding the Cesnola Collection, see Chapter 5.

32. MMA, *Annual Reports . . . 1871–1902*, 145–147, 166–172, 176.

33. Beckert, *Monied Metropolis*, 145–236, quotation at 179; Edwin G. Burrows and Mike Wallace, *Gotham: A History of New York City to 1898* (New York: Oxford University Press, 1999), 978–980.

34. "The Metropolitan Museum of Art," *Daily Tribune* [date penciled in as December 14, 1874], MMA Newspaper Clippings, 1870–1873, Thomas J. Watson Library, Metropolitan Museum, New York.

35. Letter from William J. Hoppin, in *A Metropolitan Art-Museum in the City of New York: Proceedings of a Meeting Held at the Theater of the Union League Club, Tuesday Evening, November 23, 1969* (New York: Printed for the Committee, 1869), 26, 28; "National Museum of Art: Report to the Executive Committee, February 14th, 1870," [n.d.], p. 7, Metropolitan Museum of Art (MMA) Business Archives.

36. *A Metropolitan Art-Museum in the City of New York*, 5; MMA, *Annual Reports . . . 1871–1902*, 24.

37. *A Metropolitan Art-Museum in the City of New York*, 5; MMA, *Annual Reports . . . 1871–1902*, 24, 35–36; "The Fine Arts Drama," *Tribune*, October 3, 1873, MMA Newspaper Clippings, 1870–1875; "Our Art Museum," *New York Herald*, March 20, 1879.

38. MMA, *Annual Reports . . . 1871–1902*, 195.

39. This discussion is indebted to Rozenzweig and Blackmar, *The Park and the People*, 359–363.

40. James Jackson Jarves, "The Metropolitan Museum: A Curious History of Successful Public Spirit and Impotent Private Spite," *New York World*, June 5, 1882.

41. "Local Miscellany: Reopening the Museum of Art," *New York Tribune*, October 20, 1880, 8.

42. MMA, *Annual Reports . . . 1871–1902*, 324.

43. "The Metropolitan Museum of Art," *New York Evening Post*, February 14, 1879, MMA Newspaper Clippings, 1873–1884, p. 14.

44. See Chapter 6.

45. "Culture and Progress," *Scribner's Monthly*, November 1873, 121; "Fine Arts: Metropolitan Art Museum," *New-York Daily Tribune*, March 28, 1880, 8; "Cesnola's Bogus Antiques," *Police Gazette*, November 24, 1883, MMA Newspaper Clippings, 1873–1884, p. 155.

46. "New York: The Metropolitan Museum," *New York Evening Post*, n.d. [April 1880?], MMA Newspaper Clippings, 1873–1884, p. 36. A writer for the *Herald* also supported the

regulation; see "Fine Arts: The Opening of the Metropolitan Museum," *New York Herald*, April 2, 1880, 8.

47. MMA, *Annual Reports . . . 1871–1902*, 63.

48. *The Metropolitan Museum of Art: Thirty-Fifth Annual Report of the Trustees, 1905* (New York: Metropolitan Museum, n.d.), 29.

49. On the relationship between commercial culture and fine art in the late nineteenth century, see J. M. Mancini, *Pre-Modernism*; and Sarah Burns, *Inventing the Modern Artist: Art and Culture in the Gilded Age* (New Haven, CT: Yale University Press, 1996). See also Neil Harris, *Cultural Excursions: Marketing Appetites and Cultural Taste in Modern America* (Chicago: University of Chicago Press, 1990) 29–95, 174–197. On the post–Civil War urban art scene, see H. Wayne Morgan, *New Muses: Art in American Culture, 1865–1920* (Norman: University of Oklahoma Press, 1978), 3–38. For a discussion of the widespread popular market in cheap paintings, see Saul E. Zalesch, "What the Four Million Bought: Cheap Oil Paintings of the 1880s," *American Quarterly* 48, no. 1 (March 1996): 77–109.

50. "Death List of a Day: William Cowper Prime," *New York Times*, February, 14, 1905, 9; Thomas Bender, *New York Intellect: A History of Intellectual Life in New York City, from 1750 to the Beginnings of Our Own Time* (New York: Knopf, 1987), 176–191; Burrows and Wallace, *Gotham*, 887; Jackson, *Encyclopedia of New York City*, 305–306.

51. See, for example, "List of Editors & Critics Who Should Be Invited to 'Press' Reception," February 1872, unlabeled file, MMA Business Archives. The clippings books are housed in the Watson Library of the Metropolitan Museum.

52. "The Metropolitan Museum of Art," *New York Evening Post*, February 14, 1879.

53. Choate to Cesnola, March 6, 1885, "Admission—Sunday Opening Controversy" folder, MMA Business Archives.

54. Kristin Hoganson, "Cosmopolitan Domesticity: Importing the American Dream, 1865–1920," *American Historical Review* 107, no. 1 (February 2002): 55–83; Martha Crabill McClaugherty, "Household Art: Creating the Artistic Home, 1868–1893," *Winterthur Portfolio* 18, no. 1 (Spring 1983): 1–26; "Ten Lectures on Art," *New York Herald*, August 4, 1879, 2.

55. Doreen Bolger Burke et al., *In Pursuit of Beauty: Americans and the Aesthetic Movement* (New York: Metropolitan Museum of Art, 1986), 23–64; Robert W. Rydell, *All the World's a Fair* (Chicago: University of Chicago Press, 1984), 9–37; William Hosley, *The Japan Idea: Art and Life in Victorian America* (Hartford, CT: Wadsworth Atheneum, 1990); Lionel Lambourne, *The Aesthetic Movement* (London: Phaidon Press, 1996), 27–47. For an exploration of the decorative arts movement and its political implications in France, see Debora L. Silverman, *Art Nouveau in Fin-de-Siècle France: Politics, Psychology, and Style* (Berkeley: University of California Press, 1989).

56. MMA, *Annual Reports . . . 1871–1902*, 121.

57. Ibid., 144, 177; "The Metropolitan Museum of Art," *Harper's New Monthly Magazine* 60 (May 1880): 876.

58. "The Metropolitan Museum," *New York Times*, May 25, 1873, 5.

59. "New Fashions in Jewelry," *Milwaukee Sentinel*, September 17, 1893.

60. "After All, 'The World Moves,'" *Harper's Weekly*, September 19, 1874, 782; "The Metropolitan Museum of Art," *Harper's New Monthly Magazine* 60 (May 1880): 867. See also [untitled article on the Metropolitan Museum of Art], *Harper's Weekly*, October 10, 1874, 842.

61. MMA, *Annual Reports . . . 1871–1902*, 78, 98–99, 104.

62. Ibid., 99; Marilyn G. Karmason with Joan B. Stacke, *Majolica: A Complete History and Illustrated Survey* (New York: Harry N. Abrams, 1989), 11–14; Karen Zukowski, *Creating the Artful Home: The Aesthetic Movement* (Salt Lake City: Gibbs Smith, 2006), 110–111.

63. "The Castellani Collection," *Harper's Weekly*, March 10, 1877, 186.

64. "A Rare Collection of Laces," *New York Times*, November 19, 1877; "Of Interest to the Ladies," *New York World*, November 19, 1877, MMA Newspaper Clippings (1873–1884), p. 9.

65. [Jarves], "Can We Have an Art-Gallery," 212.

66. *The Rise of the Art World in America: Knoedler at 150; An Historical Exhibition Commemorating Knoedler & Company's 150th Anniversary, December 5, 1996–January 12, 1997* (New York: Knoedler & Company, 1996).

67. Jo Ann W. Weiss, "Clarence Cook: His Critical Writings" (Ph.D. diss., Johns Hopkins University, 1976), 69–70.

68. Arnold Lewis et al., *The Opulent Interiors of the Gilded Age* (New York: Dover Publications, 1987), 33–39; Harry E. Resseguie, "Alexander Turney Stewart and the Development of the Department Store, 1823–1876," *Business History Review* 39, no. 3 (Autumn 1965): 301–322.

69. "Notices from the Press," Art Gallery Notes, p. 29, Samuel Putnam Avery Papers, Archives of American Art. For an account of Avery's business, see *The Diaries, 1871–1882, of Samuel P. Avery, Art Dealer*, ed. Madeleine Fidell Beaufort, Herbert L. Kleinfield, and Jeanne K. Welcher (New York: Arno Press, 1979).

70. MMA, *Annual Reports . . . 1871–1902*, 165–166.

71. Metropolitan Museum of Art, *Hand-Book No. 5: Oriental Porcelains in the North Gallery of the Large Hall* (New York: Metropolitan Museum of Art, [1880 or 1881]): 9, 26; "The Metropolitan Museum of Art," *Harper's Weekly*, April 10, 1880, 234.

72. "Something in Which New Yorkers Should Interest Themselves," *New York Evening Post*, May 24, 1879, MMA Newspaper Clippings, 1873–1884, p. 15.

73. *New York Times*, September 25, 1878, 8.

74. Amelia Peck and Carol Irish, *Candace Wheeler: The Art and Enterprise of American Design, 1875–1900* (New York: Metropolitan Museum of Art, 2001), 35–36, 38.

Chapter 5

1. "The Metropolitan Museum of Art," *Harper's Weekly*, April 10, 1880, 234; "A Metropolitan Museum: The Opening of the Institution to Take Place, *New York Times*, March 30, 1880, 10.

2. For discussions of these events, see J. M. Mancini, *Pre-Modernism: Art-World Change and American Culture from the Civil War to the Armory Show* (Princeton, NJ: Princeton University Press, 2005), 125–131; Elizabeth McFadden, *The Glitter and the Gold* (New York: Dial Press, 1971), 183–229; Michael Gross, *Rogues' Gallery: The Secret History of the Moguls and the Money That Made the Metropolitan Museum* (New York: Broadway Books, 2009), 43–58; Calvin Tomkins, *Merchants and Masterpieces: The Story of the Metropolitan Museum of Art*, rev. ed. (New York: Henry Holt, 1989), 60–68. On Cesnola's destructive impact on the cultural legacy of Cyprus, see Anna G. Marangou, *The Consul Luigi Palma Di Cesnola, 1832–1904: Life and Deeds* (Nicosia: Cultural Center of the Popular Bank Group, 2000). For a modern-day

assessment of the Cesnola Collection, see Vassos Karageorghism in collaboration with Joan R. Mertens and Marice E. Rose, *Ancient Art from Cyprus: The Cesnola Collection in the Metropolitan Museum of Art* (New York: Metropolitan Museum of Art, 2000).

3. McFadden, *The Glitter and the Gold*, 209–214; Tomkins, *Merchants and Masterpieces*, 65; Mancini, *Pre-Modernism*, 128–131; "The Metropolitan Museum and Its Director," Topics of the Time, *Century* 24, no. 4 (August 1882): 630; "To Repair and to Restore," *New York Daily Tribune*, November 17, 1883, 3; "Why Mr. Cook Was Silent: Waiting Vainly for the Honest Investigation," *New York Times*, June 4, 1882, 7.

4. On Cesnola's relationships with friends and enemies prior to the 1870s, during his Civil War military service, see McFadden, *The Glitter and the Gold*, 31–80.

5. Tomkins points to the class dimension of the controversy in *Merchants and Masterpieces*, 68.

6. J. M. Mancini locates the Cesnola controversy within a broader effort to professionalize the museum and the art world more generally; see *Pre-Modernism*, 99–131.

7. McFadden, *The Glitter and the Gold*, 1–93. During Cesnola's trial the prosecutor raised questions about his title. See, for example, "Di Cesnola's Examination, His Right to the Title of General," *New-York Daily Tribune*, December 15, 1883, 2; "Gen. Di Cesnola Under Fire," *New-York Daily Tribune*, December 18, 1883, 3.

8. Peter W. Edbury, "Cyprus in the 19th Century: Perceptions and Politics," in *Cyprus in the 19th Century AD: Fact, Fancy and Fiction*, ed. Veronica Tatton-Brown (Oxford: Oxbow Books, 2001), 14; Andrekos Varnava, *British Imperialism in Cyprus, 1878–1915* (Manchester: Manchester University Press, 2009), 1–60; McFadden, *The Glitter and the Gold*, 81–109.

9. Louis Palma di Cesnola, *Cyprus: Its Ancient Cities, Tombs, and Temples; A Narrative of Researches and Excavations During Ten Years' Residence as American Consul in That Island*, 2nd ed. (New York: Harper & Brothers, 1878), 171.

10. McFadden, *The Glitter and the Gold*, 98–139, 146; Cesnola, *Cyprus*, 95–96.

11. Cesnola to Hitchcock, November 5, 1873, Cesnola Papers, Dartmouth College, available in Luigi di Cesnola Selected Papers, 1863–1975, Archives of American Art (AAA), Smithsonian Institution; Cesnola to Charles Eliot Norton, June 6, 1874, Charles Eliot Norton Papers, Houghton Library.

12. Cesnola to Hitchcock, September 12 1875, Cesnola Papers, AAA; McFadden, *The Glitter and the Gold,* 155–156.

13. Cesnola to Mr. Baraeri, January 12, 1875, Cesnola Papers, AAA.

14. Cesnola [to Hitchcock], October 7, 1875, Cesnola Papers, AAA.

15. McFadden, *The Glitter and the Gold*, 154–181.

16. Caroline Winterer, *The Culture of Classicism: Ancient Greece and Rome in American Intellectual Life, 1780–1910* (Baltimore: Johns Hopkins University Press, 2002), 98–151.

17. Cesnola, *Cyprus*, 455. See also H. Guernsey, "Cesnola's Cypriote Antiquities," *National Repository* 3 (June 1878): 481; Luigi Palma di Cesnola, ed., *The Metropolitan Museum of Art*, (New York: D. Appleton, 1882), 13.

18. Cesnola to Hitchcock, "Thursday Morning" [1873, penciled in], Cesnola Papers, AAA.

19. Hiram Hitchcock, "The Explorations of Di Cesnola in Cyprus," *Harper's New Monthly Magazine*, July 1872, 189, 192; McFadden, *The Glitter and the Gold*, 119–123.

20. Henry to Cesnola, January 15, 1878, Cesnola Papers, Rauner Special Collections, Dartmouth College Library.

21. Gaston L. Feuardent, "Tampering with Antiquities: A Serious Charge Against the Director of the Metropolitan Museum of Art," *Art Amateur* 3, no. 3 (August 1880): 48; "The Cypriote Statues," *New York Times*, March 28, 1882, 5.

22. Tomkins, *Merchants and Masterpieces*, 63.

23. Clarence Cook, *Transformations and Migrations of Certain Statues in the Cesnola Collection* (New York: Gaston L. Feuardent, 1882).

24. This discussion of Cook is based on Jo Ann W. Weiss, "Clarence Cook: His Critical Writings" (Ph.D. diss., Johns Hopkins University, 1976). On the *New Path* and Cook's relation to it, see Linda S. Ferber and William H. Gerdts, *The New Path: Ruskin and the American Pre-Raphaelites* (New York: Brooklyn Museum, Schocken Books, 1985), 11–37. See also H. Wayne Morgan, *New Muses: Art in American Culture, 1865–1920* (Norman: University of Oklahoma Press, 1978), 35, 39, 44, 131; John P. Simoni, "Art Critics and Criticism in Nineteenth Century America" (Ph.D. diss., Ohio State University, 1952), 120–138. On Cook's wife, see "Clarence Cook Dead," *New York Times*, June 3, 1900. For a valuable discussion of Cook that differs from mine on some issues, see Mancini, *Pre-Modernism*, 101–109, 125–131.

25. Weiss, "Clarence Cook," 105.

26. Ibid., 104–120, 178.

27. Ibid., 106.

28. Clarence Cook, *The House Beautiful* (1881; repr., New York: Dover Publications, 1995); Cook, *What Shall We Do with Our Walls?* (New York: Warren, Fuller, 1881).

29. Cook, *The House Beautiful*, 48–49. On the articles for the *Art Amateur*, see Simoni, "Art Critics and Criticism," 153, 229. Cook may have authored "How Shall We Furnish Our Houses? Curtains and Carpets," *New Path* 2, no. 8 (August 1865): 121–126.

30. Thomas Bender, *New York Intellect: A History of Intellectual Life in New York City, from 1750 to the Beginning of Our Own Time* (New York: Knopf, 1987), 169–205, quote at 173. On Gilded Age Liberals, including Bryant, see John G. Sproat, *"The Best Men": Liberal Reformers in the Gilded Age* (1968; repr., Chicago: University of Chicago Press, 1982); Nancy Cohen, *The Reconstruction of American Liberalism* (Chapel Hill: University of North Carolina Press, 2002).

31. For examples of Sturgis's publications, see Russell Sturgis, *Homes in City and Country* (New York: C. Scribner's Sons, 1893); Sturgis, *Appreciation of Sculpture: A Handbook* (New York: Baker & Taylor, 1904); Sturgis, *The Appreciation of Pictures: A Handbook* (New York: Baker & Taylor, 1905). On Sturgis's defense of Cook, see Weiss, "Clarence Cook," 64.

32. Cook, *Transformations and Migrations*, 6.

33. "The Metropolitan Museum," *New York Times*, May 25, 1873; Gaston L. Feuardent, "Tampering with Antiquities," *Art Amateur* 3, no. 3 (August 1880): 50.

34. Clarence Cook, "The Metropolitan Museum of Art," *Chautauqun: A Weekly Newsmagazine* 6, no. 1 (October 1885): 21; Cesnola, *Cyprus*, 2. For a discussion of the relationship between biblical studies and the field of Near Eastern studies (including archaeology), see Bruce Kuklick, *Puritans in Babylon: The Ancient Near East and American Intellectual Life, 1880–1930* (Princeton, NJ: Princeton University Press, 1996).

35. Cesnola to Norton, June 6, 1874, Charles Eliot Norton Papers, Houghton Library, Harvard University, Cambridge, MA.

36. Metropolitan Museum of Art, Handbook No. 3, *Sculptures of the Cesnola Collection of Cypriote Antiquities in the East Entrance Hall and North Isle* (New York: Published by the Trustees, 1880), 6.

37. Cesnola, *Cyprus*, 19, 180; Michael Given, "Corrupting Aphrodite: Colonialist Interpre-
tations of the Cyprian Goddess," in *Engendering Aphrodite: Women and Society in Ancient
Cyprus*, ed. Diane Bolger and Nancy Serwint, CAARI Monograph Series, vol. 7 (Boston: American Schools of Oriental Research, 2002), 425–426; Anastasia Serghidou, "Imaginary Cyprus:
Revisiting the Past and Redefining the Ancient Landscape," in Tatton-Brown, *Cyprus in the
19th Century AD*, 24. On the more general tendency of nineteenth-century archaeologists to
see continuities between ancient and indigenous peoples at and around sites of excavation,
see Asher Kaufman, *Reviving Phoenicia: In Search of Identity in Lebanon* (London: I. B. Tauris,
2004), 23–26.

38. Cesnola, *Cyprus*, 7–8.

39. Michael Given points to competing visions of Aphrodite and shows how Cesnola's
account reinforced British colonial assumptions. Given, "Corrupting Aphrodite," 419–429.

40. Cesnola, *Cyprus*, 19–20, 132.

41. Hitchcock, "Explorations of Di Cesnola," 204.

42. Cook, "Metropolitan Museum of Art," 20.

43. Thomas Davidson, review of the Metropolitan Museum of Art, Handbook No. 3,
Sculptures of the Cesnola Collection of Cypriot Antiquities . . . , *American Art Review* 2, no. 7
(May 1881): 34.

44. Kaufman, *Reviving Phoenicia*, 1–54. On the display of Assyrian artifacts at the British
Museum, see Frederick N. Bohrer, "The Times and Spaces of History: Representation, Assyria,
and the British Museum," in *Museum Culture: Histories, Discourses, Spectacles*, ed. Daniel J.
Sherman and Irit Rogoff (Minneapolis: University of Minnesota Press, 1994), 197–222. On the
relationship between racial ideology, immigration, industrialism, and imperialism, see Matthew Frye Jacobson, *Barbarian Virtues: The United States Encounters Foreign Peoples at Home
and Abroad* (New York: Hill and Wang, 2001).

45. Wilhelm Lübke, *Outlines of the History of Art*, ed. Clarence Cook (New York: Dodd,
Mead, 1878), 1:65–66, 80.

46. Arthur Richmond Marsh, review of *A History of Art in Phoenicia*, by Georges Perrot,
American Journal of Archaeology 1, no. 2 (April 1885): 191.

47. "The Metropolitan Museum of Art," *Art Amateur* 2, no. 4 (March 1880): 68.

48. "The Metropolitan Museum and Its Director," *Century* 24, no. 4 (August 1882): 630.

49. Wm. Henry Goodyear, "The Di Cesnola Collection," *Scientific American*, May 20,
1876, 328.

50. R. Stuart Poole, "Cyprus: Its Present and Future," *Contemporary Review* 33 (August
1878): 150.

51. "The Cesnola Statues," *New York Daily Tribune*, April 23, 1882, 2.

52. Metropolitan Museum of Art (MMA), *Annual Reports of the Trustees of the Association, 1871–1902* (New York: Metropolitan Museum of Art, [1903]), 242, 259. On the disciplines
of anthropology, archaeology, and history as they developed in the nineteenth century United
States, with respect to the study of Native Americans in the later nineteenth century, see
Steven Conn, *History's Shadow: Native Americans and Historical Consciousness in the Nineteenth Century* (Chicago: University of Chicago Press, 2004), 116–197.

53. Cook, *The House Beautiful*, 142.

54. On American engagement with Japanese art and culture, see Christopher Bentfey,
The Great Wave: Gilded Age Misfits, Japanese Eccentrics, and the Opening of Old Japan (New

York: Random House, 2003); Warren I. Cohen, *East Asian Art and American Culture* (New York: Columbia University Press, 1992); Neil Harris, *Cultural Excursions: Marketing Appetites and Cultural Tastes in Modern* America (Chicago: University of Chicago Press, 1990), 29–55; William Hosley, *The Japan Idea: Art and Life in Victorian America* (Hartford, CT: Wadsworth Atheneum, 1990).

55. "The Metropolitan Museum," *Century Illustrated Magazine* 43, no. 4 (February 1892): 634. See also Clarence Cook, "Our Mismanaged Museum: Third Article," *Art Amateur* 5, no. 4 (September 1881): 68–69.

56. W. J. Stillman, "Mr. Stillman and the Museum of Art," *Critic*, May 5, 1883, 203.

57. W. J. Stillman, "Boston Museum of Fine Arts," *Nation*, July 24, 1884, 69.

58. "Topics of the Time: The Future of the Metropolitan Museum," *Century* 27, no. 6 (April 1884): 943; "Casts for the Metropolitan Museum," *Art Amateur* 3, no. 4 (September 1880): 68; "Plaster Casts," *Studio: Journal of the Fine Arts*, November 22, 1884, 90; "A Museum of Casts and Photographs," *Studio*, January 3, 1885, 125.

59. Clarence Cook, "Our Mismanaged Museum: Second Article," *Art Amateur* 5, no. 3 (August 1881): 47.

60. Cook, "Metropolitan Museum of Art," 20.

61. "The Metropolitan Museum and Its Director," *Century* 24, no. 4 (August 1882): 630.

62. William C. Prime, "The Golden Treasures of Kurium," *Harper's New Monthly Magazine* 55, no. 327 (August 1877): 338.

63. *The Metropolitan Museum of Art*, ed. L. P. di Cesnola (New York: D. Appleton, 1882), 32 and passim.

64. Ibid., 8, 13.

65. Steven Conn, *Museums and American Intellectual Life, 1876–1926* (Chicago: University of Chicago Press, 1998), 4–9, 22–24; L. P. di Cesnola, *An Address on the Practical Value of the American Museum* (Troy, NY: Stowell Printing House, 1887), 11.

66. Edward Strahan, "The Metropolitan Museum of Art," *Art Amateur* 2, no. 6 (May 1880): 114–116.

67. On Norton, the AIA, and the professionalization of archaeology in the United States, see Winterer, *Culture of Classicism*, 152–163; Stephen L. Dyson, *Ancient Marbles to American Shores: Classical Archaeology in the United States* (Philadelphia: University of Pennsylvania Press, 1998), 33–46.

68. Charles Eliot Norton, Journal, December 11, 1872, in *Letters of Charles Eliot Norton*, ed. Sara Norton and M. A. DeWolfe Howe (Boston: Houghton Mifflin, 1913), 1:440.

69. James Turner, *The Liberal Education of Charles Eliot Norton* (Baltimore: Johns Hopkins University Press, 1999), 250, 274; Cesnola to Norton, June 6, 1874, January 1, 1876, Norton Papers, Houghton Library.

70. Cesnola to Norton, March 27, 1874, Norton Papers, Houghton Library.

71. On Savage, see "The Metropolitan Museum and Its Director," *Century* 24, no. 4 (1882): 634. On Gildersleeve, see Winterer, *The Culture of Classicism*, 112, 154, 160; on Hall, see "Obituary Record: Isaac Hollister Hall," *New York Times*, July 3, 1896; on Pratt, see S. R. Koehler, "American Art Chronicle: Museums and Collections," *American Art Review* 1, no. 8 (June 1880): 359 and Turner, *Liberal Education of Charles Eliot Norton*, 285.

72. On the AIA's contribution to the professionalization of American archaeology, see Dyson, *Ancient Marbles to American Shores*, 31–60, 68–85; Winterer, *Culture of Classicism*, 157–163.

73. Norton to Frederick T. Frelinghuysen, Secretary of State, December 26, 1881, AIA Papers, Box 8, Folder 5, AIA, Boston.

74. "Records of the 'Executive Committee' of the AIA," pp. 19, 21 Box 1, Folder 2; *Rules of the New York Society, Adopted February 19, 1885*, p.7, Box 2, Folder 5, AIA Papers; Dyson, *Ancient Marbles to America Shores*, 61–64.

75. "Records of the General Meetings of the Institute," AIA Papers, Box 1, Folder 1, May 10, 1879, p. 2. On the discipline of classics and tensions within the AIA, see Winterer, *Culture of Classicism*. On archaeology in the United States in the nineteenth century, see Conn, *History's Shadow*, 116–153, By the end of the nineteenth century, Americans were also promoting archaeological expeditions in Mesopotamia, and archaeology was emerging as a subfield of Near Eastern studies; see Kuklick, *Puritans in Babylon*, 3–122, 176–202.

76. Records of the General Meetings of the Institute, pp. 13–16, AIA Papers, Box 1, Folder 1, May 15, 1880. An ally of Norton's within the AIA informed him "about a rumor that certain malcontents were proposing to attack and overthrow the Executive Committee . . . and that they claimed A. Agassiz as their chief ally, as a Traitor within the camp." At issue was the conflict over whether to support excavations in Assos or Central America. W. R. Ware to Norton, May 1, 1882; Ludlow to Norton, April 19, 1882, AIA Papers, President Norton Correspondence: Business, Box 2, Folder 11.

77. On the Assos project, see Winterer, *Culture of Classicism*, 163–170; Dyson, *Ancient Marbles to American Shores*, 68–72.

78. Cesnola to Norton, July 20, 1882, Norton Papers, Houghton Library; T. W. Ludlow to Norton, July 6, 11, 23, and 24, 1882; and Henry Goodyear to Norton, July 8, 1882, AIA Papers, President Norton Correspondence: Business, Box. 2, Folder 11. On the notes of congratulation, see Winifred E. Howe, *A History of the Metropolitan Museum of Art with a Chapter on the Early Institutions of Art in New York* (New York: Metropolitan Museum of Art, 1913), 225.

79. Cesnola to Godkin, May 28, 1881, Edwin Lawrence Godkin Papers, Houghton Library.

80. James Jackson Jarves, "The Metropolitan Museum," *New York World*, June 5, 1882.

81. "The Metropolitan Museum and Its Director," *Century* 24, no. 4 (August 1882): 630. On Gilder's participation in the public investigation, see "To Repair and to Restore," *New York Daily Tribune*, November 17, 1883, 3.

82. "The Metropolitan Museum and Its Director," *Century* 24, no. 4 (August 1882): 625–633. Richard W. Gilder (editor of the *Century*) publicly declared himself "forced to agree with Mr. Savage, late assistant director in charge of the antiquities, that 'there are many restorations; these are serious; they have been concealed; they have been denied'" ("The Cesnola Antiquities," letter to the editor, *New York Tribune*, May 24, 1882, 5).

83. Dyson, *Ancient Marbles to American Shores*, 106.

84. "The Metropolitan Museum and Its Director," *Century* 24, no. 4 (August 1882): 632. On Feuardent's initial charges, see, for example, "The Cesnola Restorations," *New York Herald*, July 31, 1880, 2.

85. "Repairs, Not Restorations," *New York Times*, December 13, 1883, 3. On Sturgis, see "Gen. Di Cesnola Relieved," *New York Daily Tribune*, December 21, 1883, 3; see also "Mr. Di Cesnola on the Stand," *New York Times*, December 12, 1883, 8. Prime also claimed that Sturgis was responsible for work done by Gehlen; see "Mr. Prime Gives His Testimony," *New York Times*, December 28, 1883, 8.

86. "Mr. Braman Cross-Examined," *New York Times*, December 27, 1883, 2.

87. "Repairs, Not Restorations," *New York Times*, December 13, 1883, 3.

88. "To Repair and to Restore: The Difference Pointed Out," *New York Daily Tribune*, November 17, 1883, 3. For Poole's testimony, see "An Expert on Antiquities," *New York Times*, December 2, 1883. The insistence that restorations should be clearly identified was not a late nineteenth-century innovation; see James J. Sheehan, *Museums in the German Art World: From the End of the Old Regime to the Rise of Modernism* (New York: Oxford University Press, 2000), 13.

89. "Mr. Prime's New Art Theories," *New York Times*, January 8, 1884, 5; "Mr. Prime on the Stand," *New York Daily Tribune*, December 28, 1883, 3.

90. "Restoration Number Two," *New York Times,* November 9, 1883, 8.

91. "Mr. Feuardent's Conundrum," *New York Times*, January 16, 1884, 3.

92. "Mr. Bangs Calm and Dignified," *New York Times*, January 31, 1884, 8.

93. "The Cesnola Report," *New York Daily Tribune*, January 28, 1881, 4.

94. "Mr. Choate's Argument: General Di Cesnola a Persecuted Man," *New York Daily Tribune*, January 30, 1884, 3.

95. "The Metropolitan Museum and Its Director," *Century* 24, no. 4 (August 1882): 630; "Cesnola's Bogus Antiques," *Police Gazette* (New York), November 24, 1883, MMA Newspaper Clippings, 1873–1884, p. 155.

96. "The Cesnola Verdict," *New York Times*, February 3, 1884, 6; Tomkins, *Merchants and Masterpieces*, 65–68. On Bangs's "severe cold," see "Mr. Bangs Calm and Dignified," *New York Times*, January 31, 1884, 8.

97. "Correspondence: The Metropolitan Museum," *Studio*, January 17, 1885, 141–143; "Chaos Come Again," *Studio*, May 9, 1885, 240–241; "The Director of the Metropolitan Museum and His Critics," *Studio*, May 1, 1886, 261–262; "Recent Discoveries in Cyprus," *Studio* 2, no. 2 (August 1886): 26.

98. Ohnefalsch-Richter's charge surfaced at the trial but became subject of more widespread conversation later. See "Mr. Feuardent's Criticism," *New York Daily Tribune*, November 29, 1883, 3; "The Museum of Art," *New York Times*, July 7, 1884, 4; "The Cesnola Scandal," *New York Times*, November 24, 1884, 4; "It Does Not Meet the Point," *New York Times*, November 26, 1884, 4; "The Treasure Vault at Curium," *New York World*, October 25, 1885, 8; "The 'Curium Treasures' Again," *New York Times*, October 25, 1885, 8. The French archaeologist Georges Perrot endorsed Ohnefalsch-Richter's critique; see "The Alleged Curium Treasure," *New York Times*, November 24, 1884, 5; and "A French Opinion upon Cesnola," *New York Times*, February 8, 1885, 6.

99. "Thanking Mr. Feuardent," *New York Times*, March 6, 1884, 8; *Report of W. J. Stillman on the Cesnola Collection* (New York: Privately printed, 1885).

100. Thomas Hoving, *Making the Mummies Dance: Inside the Metropolitan Museum of Art* (New York: Touchstone, 1993), 290; MMA, *Annual Reports . . . 1871–1902*, 317; Howe, *History of the Metropolitan Museum of Art*, 212.

101. John L. Myres, *Handbook of the Cesnola Collection of Antiquities from Cyprus* (New York: Metropolitan Museum of Art, 1914), xiv–xvi, xx.

102. Ibid., xx, xxx–xxxii; on the "theory of Mycenaean colonization," see Lone Wriedt Sørensen, "Creating Identity or Identities in Cyprus During the Archaic Period," in *Attitudes Towards the Past in Antiquity: Creating Identities; Proceedings of an International Conference*

Held at Stockholm University, 15–17 May 2009, ed. Brita Alroth and Charlotte Scheffer, Stockholm Studies in Classical Archaeology 14 (Stockholm: Stockholm University, 2013), 33.

103. Myres, *Handbook,* xxii, xxiv.

Chapter 6

1. The most extensive and deeply researched study of the Sunday controversy is Jerri Sherman, "The Classes vs. the Masses: The Struggle to Open the Metropolitan Museum of Art on Sunday, 1870–1891" (master's thesis, Gallatin School of New York University, 2005). See also Roy Rosenzweig and Elizabeth Blackmar, *The Park and the People: A History of Central Park* (Ithaca, NY: Cornell University Press, 1992), 359–363; Calvin Tomkins, *Merchants and Masterpieces: The Story of the Metropolitan Museum of Art,* rev. ed. (New York: Henry Holt, 1989), 75–79.

2. Edwin G. Burrows and Mike Wallace, *Gotham: A History of New York to 1898* (New York: Oxford University Press, 1999), 1111–1112.

3. Edward T. O'Donnell, *Progress and Poverty in the Gilded Age: Henry George and the Crisis of Inequality* (New York: Columbia University Press, 2008), 71.

4. On the exaggerated distinction between German and Eastern European immigrants, see Hasia R. Diner, *The Jews of the United States, 1654–2000* (Berkeley: University of California Press, 2004), 71–111. See also Burrows and Wallace, *Gotham,* 1112–1131; Randa A. Kayyali, *The Arab Americans* (Westport, CT: Greenwood, 2006), 27–29.

5. William D. Howells, *A Hazard of New Fortunes* (New York: Harper & Brothers, 1889), 1:242–243.

6. Rosenzweig and Blackmar, *The Park and the People,* 263–266, 308–309.

7. Peter Conolly-Smith, *Translating America: An Immigrant Press Visualizes American Popular Culture, 1895–1918* (Washington, DC: Smithsonian Books, 2004), 31.

8. Ibid.

9. Sherman, "The Classes vs. the Masses," 48–51; Edward T. James, ed., *Notable American Women, 1607–1950: A Biographical Dictionary* (Cambridge, MA: Belknap Press, 1971), 1:656–657; Conolly-Smith, *Translating America,* 39–40, 57–64.

10. Brewster & Co. to John Taylor Johnston, May 4, 1881, "Admission—Sunday Opening Controversy" folder, Metropolitan Museum of Art (MMA) Business Archives.

11. Horace L. Friess, *Felix Adler and Ethical Culture: Memories and Studies,* ed. Fannia Weingartner (New York: Columbia University Press, 1981), 16–106; Howard B. Radest, *Felix Adler: An Ethical Culture* (New York: Peter Lang, 1998), 7–17, 134–142; Burrows and Wallace, *Gotham,* 1173–1181.

12. "Public Rights in a Public Museum," *Art Amateur* 2 (May 1880): 6.

13. Clarence Cook, "Our Mismanaged Museum: Second Article," *Art Amateur* 5 (August 1881): 46.

14. E. P. Barker to the Trustees of the Metropolitan, April 21, 1881; and Choate to Cesnola, April 11 1880, "Admission—Sunday Opening Controversy" folder, MMA Business Archives.

15. "Mr. Walters and 'Gen.' Cesnola," *New York Times,* March 6, 1889, 4; "Mr. Walters's Offer," *New York Times,* March 22, 1889, 8.

16. Sherman, "The Classes vs. the Masses," 68; Rosenzweig and Blackmar, *The Park and the People,* 309–312.

17. Cesnola to Hitchcock, December 5, 1882, Cesnola Papers, Rauner Special Collections, Dartmouth College.

18. Sherman, "The Classes vs. the Masses," 60–74; Rosenzweig and Blackmar, *The Park and the People*, 309–312; "Like a Laborers' Picnic," *New York Times*, July 7, 1884, 5; "For the People on Sunday," *New York World*, May 8, 1885, 7.

19. [Morris K. Jesup], *The Museums in the Park: Should They Be Opened on Sunday?* (New York: Rufus Adams, 1885), 6.

20. Ibid., 8.

21. Tomkins, *Merchants and Masterpieces*, 75.

22. MMA, *Annual Reports of the Trustees of the Association, 1871–1902* (New York: MMA, [1903]), 324; "We Own the Museum," *New York Herald*, February 9, 1886, 8.

23. James O. Baker and Buster G. Smith, *American Secularism: Cultural Contours of Nonreligious Belief Systems* (New York: New York University Press, 2015), 56–62; "Open the Museums," *New York Herald*, November 22, 1885, 6; "The Museums on Sunday," *New York Times*, December 18, 1885, 8; "Open Museums on Sunday," *New York Times*, March 10, 1886, 8.

24. "Open Museums on Sunday: The Movement Being Pushed Vigorously by Workingmen," *New York Times*, January 17, 1886, 4.

25. On the CLU, see Burrows and Wallace, *Gotham*, 1091–1092.

26. "Open the Museums," *New York Herald*, November 16, 1885, 6.

27. Edward T. O'Donnell, *Henry George and the Crisis of Inequality* (New York: Columbia University Press, 2015), 169–200, Swinton quoted at 197.

28. Ibid., 33–66, 98, 141, 201–238; Radest, *Felix Adler*, 104.

29. On Crimmins, see Rosenzweig and Blackmar, *The Park and the People*, 287, 290, 295, 298–99, 301, 302, 306, 309–310, 312.

30. "Golden Opportunity: Mr. Crimmins Talks Back," *New York Herald*, January 9, 1887, 15.

31. "Mayor Hewitt Says Open the Park Museums for the Public on Sunday," *New York Herald*, March 2, 1887, 6. On Hewitt, see Sven Beckert, *The Monied Metropolis* (Cambridge: Cambridge University Press, 2001), 62–63, 73, 212–213, 215, 316, 275, 328, 330; Rosenzweig and Blackmar, *The Park and the People*, 304.

32. "Keeping Sunday a Day of Rest," *New York Times*, January 25, 1886, 2.

33. Ralph Wells, Rev. Wilber F. Crafts, Rev. James M. King, and Henry C. Robinson to the Park Commissioners [typescript], April 1885, "Admissions—Sunday Opening Controversy" folder, MMA Business Archives. See also "Opening Museums on Sunday . . . Opposition from Baptist Ministers," *New York Tribune*, January 5, 1887, 2.

34. "Pulpit Themes," *New York Herald*, November 23, 1885, 6.

35. "Open the Museums," *New York Herald*, November 22, 1885, 6; "Open Museums on Sunday," *New York Times*, March 10, 1886, 8; "Sunday Opening of Museums," *New York Times*, December 27, 1885, 12; "Sabbath Superstition," *New York Times*, January 25, 1886, 2; Burrows and Wallace, *Gotham*, 1171.

36. "No Compulsory Sacred Day," *New York Times*, February 4, 1889, 3.

37. "In and About the City: The Art Museums," *New York Times*, December 30, 1886, 2.

38. Prime is quoted in Tomkins, *Merchants and Masterpieces*, 77.

39. Prime to Johnston, May 4, 1885, "Admission—Sunday Opening Controversy" folder, MMA Business Archive.

40. Dodge to Cesnola, January 29, 1883, "Admission—Sunday Opening Controversy" folder, MMA Business Archives; "In and About the City: The Art Museums," *New York Times*, December 30, 1886, 2.

41. "What People Think and Say: Museum Privileges on Sunday," *New York Tribune*, February 28, 1887, 5; "Cesnola Boils Over," *New York Herald*, January 2, 1887, 13.

42. Cesnola to Barlow, June 18, 1887, Barlow Papers, Box 180, Huntington Library.

43. "Still Undecided: The Question of Opening on Sunday Troubling Museum Trustees," *New York Times*, April 26, 1884, 4; "Evenings for the People," *New York Times*, December 27, 1888, 8; "Sunday Opening Deferred," *New York Times*, December 28, 1888, 4.

44. "The Museums on Sundays," *New York Times*, November 18, 1885, 8. On concerns about donations from the devout widow of Robert L Stuart, see "Sunday at the Museums," *New York Tribune*, January 3, 1887, 8.

45. "The Trustees Perplexed," *New York Times*, December 29, 1886, 8; "Open the Museums," *New York Herald*, January 3, 1886, 15.

46. "Sunday-Opening of the Metropolitan Museum," *Studio* 4, no. 4 (March 1889): 60.

47. "The Growth of Provinciality," *New York Times*, January 6, 1889, 4.

48. Tomkins, *Merchants and Masterpieces*, 76; "The Trustees Perplexed," *New York Times*, December 29, 1886, 8.

49. "Will the Trustees Yield," *New York Times*, January 1, 1887, 8; "Sunday and the Museums," *New York Tribune*, January 3, 1887, 8.

50. MMA, *Annual Reports . . . 1871–1902*, 349–355.

51. "Sunday Museum Openings," *New York Tribune*, April 3, 1887, 13.

52. "Sunday Opening Deferred," *New York Times*, December 28, 1888, 4; "The Doors Will Be Opened at Night," *New York Tribune*, December 28, 1888, 7; "Money for the Museum," *New York Times*, December 6, 1889, 8.

53. MMA, *Annual Reports . . . 1871–1902*, 416.

54. Sherman, "The Classes and the Masses," 108–111; "W. T. Walters's $10,000 Check," *New York Times*, February 24, 1889, 2; "W. T. Walters's Check," *New York Tribune*, February 26, 1889, 7; "Mr. Walters's Offer: The Liberal Baltimorean Refutes 'Gen.' Di Cesnola's Denial," *New York Times*, March 2, 1889, 8; "Mr. Walters's Offer: Correspondence Setting the Controversy Finally at Rest," *New York Times*, March 5, 1889, 8.

55. "Mr. Walters and 'Gen.' Cesnola," *New York Times*, March 6, 1889, 7.

56. Alvin R. Buechner to Cesnola, January 10, 1882, "Admission—Sunday Opening Controversy" folder, MMA Business Archives.

57. "A Golden Opportunity," *New York Herald*, January 9, 1887, 15; Sherman, "The Classes vs. the Masses," 121.

58. Sherman, "The Classes vs. the Masses," 120–121.

59. "To Open the Museum Sundays: A Petition Started by Women Is in Circulation," *New York Times*, March 20 1891, 4; "Will the Museum Open?," *New York Tribune*, May 18, 1891, 7.

60. Sherman, "The Classes vs. the Masses," 122–123; "Will the Museum Open?," *New York Tribune*, May 18, 1891, 7.

61. "The Masses Will Speak," *New York Times*, May 6, 1891, 8; "A Triumph for the New York Liberals," *Chicago Daily Tribune*, May 22, 1891, 4; James Kirke Paulding, *Charles B. Stover, July 14, 1861–April 24, 1929* (New York: International Press, 1938), 15–21; Allen Freeman Davis, *Spearheads for Reform: The Social Settlements and the Progressive Movement, 1890–1914* (New Brunswick, NJ: Rutgers University Press, 1984).

62. "Benefits from Sunday Opening," *New York World*, May 20, 1891, 4.

63. "Victory Is Won at Last," *New York Times*, May 19, 1891, 1; "To Open the Museum," *New York Tribune*, May 9, 1891, 7.

64. Tomkins, *Merchants and Masterpieces*, 78.

65. "The City and the Museum," *New York World*, May 18, 1891, 4.

66. "Thousands Visit the Museum," *New York Press*, June 1, 1891, MMA Newspaper Clippings, 1891–1894, p. 60; "The C.L.U. Visits the Museum," *New York World*, June 1, 1891:2.

67. "The Museum Thronged," *New York World*, June 8, 1891, 9; "An Auspicious Opening," *New York World*, June 1, 1891; [Untitled], *Washington Post*, July 26, 1891, MMA Newspaper Clippings, 1891–1894, pp. 63–64, 73, 86, Watson Library; "The Art Museum Crowded," *New York Tribune*, June 1, 1891, 7.

68. "The Art Museum Crowded," *New York Tribune*, June 1, 1891, 7; "Sunday at the Museum," *New York Post*, October 3, 1991, MMA Newspaper Clippings, 1891–1894, pp. 64, 91.

69. MMA, *Annual Reports . . . 1871–1902*, 500–501.

70. "The Museum Thronged," *New York World*, June 8, 1891, 9; "An Auspicious Opening," *New York World*, June 1, 1891, MMA Newspaper Clippings, 1891–1894, pp. 63, 73.

71. "It Was a Great Success," *New York Sun*, June 1, 1891, 1; "An Auspicious Opening," *New York World*, June 1, 1891, MMA Newspaper Clippings, 1891–1894, p. 63.

72. "The Museum Thronged," *New York World*, June 8, 1991, 9; "The Public at Last Finds the Metropolitan's Doors Open on Sunday," *New York Continent*, June 1, 1891; [Illegible], *Washington Post*, July 26, 1891; [Illegible], *New York News*, June 1, 1891, MMA Newspaper Clippings, 1891–1894, pp. 60, 62, 73, 86.

73. "The Public at Last Finds the Metropolitan's Doors Open on Sunday," *New York Continent*, June 1, 1891, MMA Newspaper Clippings, p. 60; "It Was a Great Success," *New York Sun*, June 1, 1891, 1.

74. "It Was a Great Success," *New York Sun*, June 1, 1891, 1; "The Public at Last Finds the Metropolitan's Doors Open on Sunday," *New York Continent*, June 1, 1891, MMA Newspaper Clippings, p. 60; "The Art Museum Crowded," *New York Times*, June 1, 1891, 7. Conway was an expatriate reformer, temporarily returned from England, who had participated in England's anti-Sabbatarian campaign. See *Autobiography, Memories and Experiences of Moncure Daniel Conway* (London: Cassell, 1904), 2:294, 406.

75. "The Workingman and Art," *New York Herald*, November 7, 1894, MMA Newspaper Clippings, 1892–1896, p. 145.

76. "Sunday at the Museum," *New York Post*, October 3, 1891, MMA Newspaper Clippings 1891–1894, p. 91.

77. MMA, *Annual Reports . . . 1871–1902*, 500–501, 544, 775; *Annual Report of the Trustees of the Metropolitan Museum of Art*, no. 35 (1905): 23.

78. M. G. Van Rensselaer, "The Metropolitan Museum of Art," *Harper's Weekly*, May 23, 1891, 382–383. See also Judith K. Major, *Mariana Griswold Van Rensselaer: A Landscape Critic in the Gilded Age* (Charlottesville: University of Virginia Press, 2013). Van Rensselaer was identified as a signer of the 1891 petition in "Will the Museum Open!" *New York Tribune*, May 18, 1891, 7.

79. *Annual Report of the Trustees of the Metropolitan Museum*, no. 35 (1905): 13–14.

80. "A Museum Program," *New York Post*, February 20, 1906, MMA Newspaper Clippings (1905–1907), p. 109.

81. *Handbook of the Benjamin Altman Collection* (New York: Metropolitan Museum of Art, 1915).

82. On the Metropolitan Museum in the Progressive Era and the relationship between connoisseurship and education, see Jeffrey Trask, *Things American: Art Museums and Civic Culture in the Progressive Era* (Philadelphia: University of Pennsylvania Press, 2012).

83. On the Hudson-Fulton Exhibition, see ibid.

84. *Annual Report of the Trustees of the Metropolitan Museum of Art*, no. 45 (1914): 34.

Epilogue

1. Edith Wharton, *The Age of Innocence* (1920; repr., New York: Charles Scribner's Sons, 1970), 309.

2. For an analysis of this passage and of Wharton's more general engagement with the issues of authenticity and museum display, see Jennie A. Kassanoff, *Edith Wharton and the Politics of Race* (New York: Cambridge University Press, 2008), 153–161.

3. Wharton, *The Age of Innocence*, 71.

4. Edith Wharton and Ogden Codman Jr., *The Decoration of Houses* (1897; New York: Mount Press, Rizzoli, 2007).

5. Edith Wharton, *The New York Stories of Edith Wharton*, ed. Roxanna Robinson (New York: New York Review Books, 2007), 149–150.

6. Edith Wharton, *The Custom of the Country*, ed. Linda Wagner-Martin (1913; London: Penguin Books, 1990), 110; Wharton to Sara Norton, June 5 [1903], in *The Letters of Edith Wharton*, ed. R. W. B. Lewis and Nancy Lewis (New York: Charles Scribner's Sons, 1988), 84.

INDEX

Page numbers in italics refer to illustrations.

ACKNOWLEDGMENTS

This project began to take shape many years ago when I was at the Huntington Library, browsing somewhat aimlessly through a microfilm reel of the Smithsonian Institution's Archives of American Art in search of a new research topic. I came upon the letters of the artist Lilly Martin Spencer, and they began to open my eyes to a layer of American culture with which I was entirely unfamiliar. The book took far longer to complete than I had hoped or imagined and, in part for that reason, it is a great pleasure to thank the many people who helped along the way.

I am very lucky that *Art Wars* landed at the University of Pennsylvania Press, where my editor, Robert Lockhart, made what might have been an arduous process seem easy. He has all the qualities that authors hope for in an editor, including the ability to be gently pushy when necessary. This book is much better than it would have been without his astute editorial interventions. I am also grateful for the Press's two perceptive readers' reports. One of those readers remains anonymous, but I am delighted to thank the other, Alice Fahs. Any errors that may remain in *Art Wars* have been greatly reduced by the meticulous copyediting of Jennifer Shenk. Erica Ginsburg helped out in the final stages and tolerated my unintentional disobedience to some clear instructions with respect to editing. I am also grateful to Zoe Kovacs for her help with the illustrations. James O'Brien, who created the index, also provided invaluable assistance with the final edit.

This book could not have been completed without the assistance of librarians at numerous institutions. The Geisel Library of the University of California San Diego has been a wonderful resource. I am especially grateful to Elliot Kantor, the now retired U.S. history bibliographer and to Lynda Claassen and Heather Smedberg of Geisel Library's Special Collections, who helped out with illustrations. Thanks are also due to the staff of the Interlibrary Loan Department for their patience and efficiency. Among the joys of working on this book were the many hours spent at the New-York Historical Society and the Watson Library of the Metropolitan Museum of Art, and I am grateful to the librarians who assisted me over the years at those institutions. I also owe a great deal to the staffs at the Archaeological Institute of America, Clements Library of the University of Michigan, the Fales Library of New York University, Houghton Library of Harvard University, the New York Public Library, The American Antiquarian Society, and the Business Archives of the Metropolitan Museum.

Several fellowships helped me bring this book into being. A University of California President's Research Fellowship in the Humanities gave me time to get the project off the ground. Two fellowships at the Huntington Library enabled me to turn bits and pieces of chapters into something that began to resemble a book. I am grateful to Roy Ritchie and Steve Hindle for their help in bringing me to the Huntington and making my time there so enjoyable. The library's Rothenberg Room must be one of the best places in the world for writing. A Huntington Library conference on "Ruins and Antiquities in Nineteenth Century America" was immensely helpful with respect to Chapter 5. I am indebted to all of the participants in that event and especially to Karen Halttunen and Caroline Winterer.

Over many years, the History Department of the University of California San Diego has been my professional home, and I deeply appreciate the support, friendship, conversation, and humor of colleagues there. In some ways, departments are like families, and I am fortunate that mine has been a nurturing one. Several colleagues made direct contributions to this book and require special mention. Rebecca Plant's multiple readings greatly improved the text of *Art Wars*. Our informal two-person writing group was a wonderful gift. Judith Hughes read an early version of the manuscript. From the time of my arrival at UC San Diego, she has been a mentor and friend. Eric Van Young also read the manuscript early on, and his generous assessment gave me a big lift. For their help at critical junctures, I owe special thanks to Frank Biess, Cathy Gere, Denise Demitriou, Thomas Gallant, Deborah Hertz, Hasan Kayali, Ulrike Strasser, and Department Chair Pamela Radcliff whose support in the final stages meant a lot.

Over the years I have learned from my students, undergraduate and graduate alike. For their assistance with this project, I am happy to acknowledge William McGovern, Graeme Mack, Carrie Streetes, and Cameo Lyn West.

I am also grateful for friends and colleagues beyond UC San Diego's History Department. As a result of Julia Smith's friendship and generosity I always had a bed to sleep on, excellent meals, and lots of fun during trips to New York City. To say that Steven Hahn read the manuscript and guided it to the University of Pennsylvania Press does not begin to acknowledge his role in helping me complete this project. From the outset, Debora Silverman provided inspiration and guidance. Casey Blake offered much needed help and encouragement with my first publication on the Art-Union. Many thanks are due as well to Eric Blau, Julie Gollin, Virginia Gordon, Michael Meranze, Marjorie Milstein, Robert Moeller, Lynn Malley, Jeffrey Prager, Lawrence Powell, Julie Saville, Kathryn Shevelow, Fredrika Teute, and Barbara Weinstein. Without even meeting me, Jerri Sherman generously shared her master's thesis, "The Classes vs. the Masses: The Struggle to Open the Metropolitan Museum of Art on Sunday, 1870 to 1891." Thanks are also due to Hasia Diner, for bringing the thesis to my attention.

My greatest debt is to my family. My mother, Bessie Boris, was an artist, and my father, George Klein, a great lover of the arts. Both of them are gone, but in some ways this book is theirs. Aaron Westman brought music into my life and continues to be my partner in the pleasures of aesthetic taste. Jonathan Westman grew up while *Art Wars* was under way and bore the burden of two academic parents with fortitude, wit, and empathy. Seeing him into adulthood has been my most rewarding project by far. Robert Westman's loyalty and support over three decades amazes me. *Art Wars* is dedicated to him, with love.